D0966795

# "We Will Prevail"

# "We Will Prevail"

## President George W. Bush
### on War, Terrorism, and Freedom

Selected and Edited by
National Review

Foreword by
Peggy Noonan

Introduction by
Jay Nordlinger

A National Review Book

**continuum**
NEW YORK • LONDON

2003

The Continuum International Publishing Group Inc
15 East 26 Street, New York, NY 10010

The Continuum International Publishing Group Ltd
The Tower Building, 11 York Road, London SE1 7NX

Printed in the United States of America

Library of Congress Cataloging-in-Publication Data

Bush, George W. (George Walker), 1946–
    We will prevail: President George W. Bush on war, terrorism, and
freedom / selected and edited by National Review; foreword by Peggy
Noonan; introduction by Jay Nordlinger.
    p. cm.
"A National Review book."
ISBN 0-8264-1552-0 (alk. paper)
1. United States—Politics and government—2001—Sources. 2. United
States—Foreign relations—2001—Sources. 3. War on Terrorism,
2001—Sources. 4. Speeches, addresses, etc., American. I. National
Review Books. II. Title.
    E838.5.B875 2003
    973.931—dc22

2003015420

*Yet we're not afraid. Our cause is just, and worthy of sacrifice. Our nation is strong of heart, firm of purpose. Inspired by all the courage that has come before, we will meet our moment and we will prevail.*

President George W. Bush
October 11, 2001


*Steadfast in our purpose, we now press on. We have known freedom's price. We have shown freedom's power. And in this great conflict, my fellow Americans, we will see freedom's victory.*

President George W. Bush
January 29, 2002

# Acknowledgements

I speak for myself only, but I expect many others as well: The words—the very powerful words—of President George W. Bush have been a source of inspiration since that fateful day of September 11, 2001. His persistent urging of all Americans to duty, his swift actions to use the nation's resources to find and to bring to justice the "evil ones" in order to protect the people of the United States from further attacks, and his heartfelt encouragement to all to live not the old "normal" life, but indeed a better life, have given America resolve, purpose, and focus at this critical hour.

I leave it to Jay Nordlinger, my colleague at *National Review*—who played a very important role in organizing this book—to express these sentiments, and more, with greater clarity, as he does in his wonderful Introduction.

As to the book itself: Given the volume and the dignity and the importance and the power of President Bush's words—his speeches to factory workers and federal employees, his addresses to national and international leaders, his commemorative remarks to police officers and firefighters and to the families of fallen soldiers and citizen-heroes—I believe they have, collectively, historical merit, and are worthy of being published.

I broached this idea of collected speeches—related to September 11th and its aftermath—with my friend Evander Lomke, a Vice President and Senior Editor of Continuum International, the distinguished book-publishing house. He agreed, I daresay somewhat enthusiastically. And thus, the project of *"We Will Prevail"* commenced, at breakneck speed.

For the record: The materials herein collected were downloaded directly from the White House website. The materials considered were those—beginning on September 11, 2001, and ending with the President's 2003 Memorial Day speech at Arlington National Cemetery—which, as the subtitle makes clear, address the issues of war, terrorism, and freedom.

Although there are some proclamations, written statements, and executive orders included, the contents of *"We Will Prevail"* are mostly transcripts of the words as spoken—not speeches as prepared to be read—by the President.

Some minor editing has naturally occurred. For example, we chose to remove what I would call repeated words: If the President said, "I did agree," and then immediately corrected himself by saying, "I did not agree," the misspoken first statement is eliminated. In addition to this, misprints of transcriptions were corrected, some punctuation and stylistic changes were made, and, except in rare cases where they clearly are of import, "applause" or other references to any audience reactions were eliminated. Other than that, I can say with complete confidence that *"We Will Prevail"* is true to the words of the President.

Those who merit thanks for their contribution to this book, in addition to Mr. Lomke and Mr. Nordlinger, are Julie Crane, *National Review*'s Associate Editor and very competent proofreader, and Luba Kolomysteva, the magazine's equally fine Art Director, who helped in all production efforts.

The cover photograph was provided by the White House Photo Office, and is used here with permission, for which we thank Dan Bartlett, the President's Director of Communications. The photograph—its formal caption reads "President George W. Bush addresses the nation from Ellis Island on the one-year anniversary of the September 11 terrorist attacks"—was taken by Paul Morse.

Finally, I would also like to thank Edward Capano, *National Review*'s Publisher, who, along with Mr. Lomke, approved and oversaw this project.

While *"We Will Prevail"* has no formal dedication, I will take this opportunity to informally dedicate it to those who died or who were injured on September 11th, to those who risked their lives to save others on that day, and to those men and women in uniform who have gone to foreign lands and risked their lives—often making the supreme sacrifice—to defend our freedoms by working to defeat the network of terrorism and those regimes that support it.

In closing, I will make special note of Thomas E. Burnett Jr., a longtime subscriber to our magazine. On September 11, 2001, Mr. Burnett was a passenger on United Flight 93, which was hijacked by terrorists and targeted toward Washington, D.C. By all accounts, Mr. Burnett was one of the leaders of the passengers who, certain of their fate, but determined to prevent another national tragedy, revolted against the terrorists, and forced the plane to crash in Pennsylvania.

May God grant rest to his soul, and to the souls of all other patriots.

Jack Fowler
Associate Publisher
*National Review*
July, 2003

# TABLE OF CONTENTS

# October 2001

# November 2001

## December 2001

## January 2002

# February 2002

# March 2002

# April 2002

# May 2002

# June 2002

# September 2002

# October 2002

# November 2002

# December 2002

# January 2003

# February 2003

# March 2003

# April 2003

# May 2003

# Foreword

## Peggy Noonan

(Miss Noonan is the author of several best-selling and acclaimed books on politics, history, and culture. Her latest is A Heart, a Cross, and a Flag: America Today. A contributing editor to the Wall Street Journal, Miss Noonan was a special assistant to President Ronald Reagan from 1984 to 1986. In 1988 she was chief speechwriter for Vice President George Bush when he ran for the presidency.)

The theme of this book is "We are going to win this thing." When we do, probably many years from now, much will be owed to the surprising presidency of George W. Bush.

Mr. Bush, the chief executive who went to Harvard Business School, has ever since September 11, 2001, been businesslike in focusing on and checking off the items on his daily international agenda. This has helped him produce obvious and orderly progress in the great challenge of our time. It gets lost sometimes in the day-to-day, but this has been one big and important presidency. Bush has been a *leader*. How has he done it? Many ways, including words.

Bush speaks, by both inclination and experience, the plain language of business, sports, and politics. He sounds like an American man from Texas. His natural speech is not elevated. But the content of his addresses has been. It is now a cliché to say that he found his voice amid the rubble soon after 9/11. This is not untrue, but it may be closer to the truth to say that what he found was the utility of both his natural sound and his natural instincts.

Before the attacks on America, the nation's elites—and I think Bush himself—thought his way of communicating inadequate. But 9/11 came and now it would *have* to be adequate, for it was what he had, and his country was in crisis. And so the famous bullhorn moment—"I can hear you . . ."—which told a wounded nation exactly what it needed to hear. And which encouraged him to be himself some more. And so all of what followed: "Al-Qaeda is to terror what the mafia is to crime," etc.

Bush is unafraid of sounding like what he is, a Christian reborn in faith who sees the world through a prism of belief. Life is not accident; it has meaning and governance. Bush is a pray-er. He has told me he is grateful to be the focus of the prayers of others, and that he feels those prayers. A prayer is among the most direct and succinct of communications. Bush speaks to the nation in a style that suggests he doesn't really think a public proclamation has to be fancier than a prayer.

He has delivered in the past three years a number of memorable speeches, none more so than his January 28, 2003, State of the Union address. It was an important speech; America was on the brink of war and major allies would not back her. The whole world was watching, which was potentially distressing, as a State of the Union address tends to be the result of compromise and the child of bureaucracy. It's an important speech, often the most important of the year, and one always hopes it will be sleek and handsome as an ocean liner cutting through the sea. They sometimes start that way. But then they turn, inevitably, into a greasy old barge weighed down by policy cargo and riding too low in the water.

But Bush's most important State of the Union flipped expectations. It began as a barge and turned into a ship of state. Its early slowness was in fact a stateliness, not a flaw but part of a design.

It was the speech of a practical idealist, practical in that it dealt directly with crucial and immediate challenges, idealistic in that it applied the great American abstractions—freedom, justice, independence—to those challenges. The speech was held together by a theme of *protectiveness*. We must now more than ever, and in spite of the current crisis, continue as a uniquely protective people. We must protect the vulnerable and troubled—the young with parents in prison, workers battered by taxes, victims of late-term abortions, a continent (Africa) dying of AIDS. In foreign policy we must protect ourselves and the world from those who would harm us with massive and evil weapons.

The theme held both halves of the speech together; they cohered and supported each other. The two halves were defined, too, by a change of tone or demeanor on Bush's part that you couldn't quite put your finger on. In the first, domestic part of the speech he was serious and contained, but in the second part of the speech, on Iraq, there was a shift. His voice seemed lower and there seemed a kind of full head-heart engagement in his grave but optimistic message.

The speech was unrelentingly serious, and assumed a seriousness in its audience. It assumed also a high degree of personal compassion and courage on the part of those watching. And so it was subtly rousing without being breast-beating, flag-waving, or cheap.

People talk about "great lines" in speeches. When leaders speak these days, a big problem with their rhetoric is that the great lines—the soundbites—sound like something sprinkled in artificially. They almost jump up and announce themselves—"Main soundbite coming! Runs 14 seconds." This doesn't impress Americans, because Americans are sophisticated. They don't respond saying, "I love what he just said," they nod and say, "That was the big soundbite." Mr. Bush's speech was a departure in this regard. It didn't have "good lines," it had thoughts. The thoughts were pithily, and sometimes memorably, expressed. They didn't seem artificially sprinkled in. They arose from the text, were woven into it, and organic to it. And so they didn't seem showy and insubstantial, they seemed like real thoughts that had a particular weight. This is oratory of the post-soundbite era, and it is a step forward.

A word on the Bush biography. Four years ago I wondered if his life story didn't suggest a reverse Abraham Lincoln. Lincoln was born in low circumstances and rose with superior gifts. Mr. Bush was born in superior circumstances and rose with average gifts. But we all have a sharper sense of him now. A second and third look suggests Bush's gifts are actually not at all average. Backbone is not an average gift, and he has shown it, most spectacularly in prosecuting a war his country's establishments and our allies' establishments opposed, and are opposing, to the end. Guts are not an average gift, and he's shown guts. The willingness to take pain and give pain to make progress in human life is not an average gift. These are amazing qualities in a modern political figure, and in a president.

Another thing. The rap on Bush has always been that it was easy for him, he had everything handed to him. When we all first looked at him, about 1999, we thought, many of us: This is a man who didn't have to struggle. But watching him the past three years, and after interviewing him three times in the Oval Office, I have come to think that Bush has the not-so-polished quality, and the emotional immediacy, of . . . of someone who had to fight for it. The last time I saw him, in an interview for *Ladies' Home Journal* in June 2003, I realized: He spent his adulthood knowing a lot of people thought him not the brightest bulb on the family marquee, certainly no equal to his father the war hero and successful political figure. By the time he was 40, George W. Bush was a good-time boy who'd wasted a lot of whatever potential he had. He knew what it was to try to succeed in business and fail, knew what it was to stop the drinking he'd relied on for joy. He would soon learn what it was to succeed in business, at least in ownership, and try to stay there. And soon he would know what it was to go national in a profession, politics, in which smoothness of expression and verbal ease mean a lot—and he didn't have these things. He made believe all this was funny, and made jokes about it. But maybe it was a bigger struggle than anyone knew, and maybe he had to fight harder than he found it convenient to admit.

When I left him after that interview I thought of an old story about John F. Kennedy. He was a young politician waving from the back of a slow-moving car in a political parade in Boston. The parade route went past the house he'd been a child in. He said, to the politician sitting next to him, "It wasn't easy growing up in that house." The politician cracked, "Yeah, I heard once they didn't bring you breakfast in bed." JFK didn't reply. He just sort of smiled, and started waving again.

We know now it wasn't easy for him. It's never easy for anyone, is it?

This is how I think of George W. Bush now: Little Big Man. A regular guy who's wound up having the most consequential American presidency since Ronald Reagan's changed the map of the world.

*New York City*
*July 2003*

# Introduction

## Jay Nordlinger

*(Mr. Nordlinger is the Managing Editor of* National Review. *He is also a reporter, essayist, and critic. He writes for a variety of publications, on a variety of topics. In 2001, he won the Eric Breindel Award for Excellence in Opinion Journalism.)*

For a man reputed to be "verbally challenged," George W. Bush has given some important speeches—some impressive ones, too. Words matter a great deal to this president. In fact, when all is said and done, his presidency may be known for its rhetoric (among other things). Then George W. Bush, the tongue-tied embarrassment, will have the last laugh—yet another last laugh. "Misunderestimated" once more.

Of course, it "helps" that we are at war. September 11 "changed everything," we are constantly told, and it certainly changed the Bush presidency. A president must find his voice in wartime, as in no other time. Woodrow Wilson and Franklin Roosevelt gave many excellent speeches, on virtually every subject conceivable. But it is their war talk we tend to remember. Abraham Lincoln was sharp and eloquent on agricultural policy, as on everything else. But . . .

George W. Bush is an interesting mixture: He is a Texan and an Easterner; he is Establishment and counter-Establishment; he is fancy and folksy; he is forceful and jocular; he is presidential and everyday. His formal speeches tend to be elegant, polished affairs, crafted by top-notch speechwriters (about whom, more later). But he does well enough on his own: whether winging it before an audience or in responding to reporters. When he is most purely himself, he is blunt, unfussy, a little salty—Trumanesque.

In July 2002, he was asked about the status of Osama bin Laden. "He may be alive," the president said. "If he is, we'll get him. If he's not, we got him." Speechwriters could labor for weeks and not come up with anything better.

This is also a quick and funny president. We all have our favorite examples, but I will cite just one, impressed on me by David Frum (a former Bush speech-writer himself, and the author of the superb memoir *The Right Man: The Surprise Presidency of George W. Bush*—and a contributing editor of *National Review*, to boot). Ozzy Osbourne was a guest at a big Washington dinner. Pointing out his funky tresses, the famous rocker-druggie said, "Mr. President, you should wear your hair like mine!" Bush responded, "Second term, Ozzy, second term."

Yet the book in your hands is a markedly serious one—for it contains various speeches and statements by the president since September 11. It includes very big speeches, like State of the Union addresses; and it includes smaller—though equally resonant—statements, like his message through a bullhorn to the rescue workers of Ground Zero. We have what he said in a defining speech at West Point, and what he said while lighting the national Christmas tree. He speaks to a variety of people—not all of them Americans—in a variety of settings. To military personnel, to world leaders, to the employees of the Dixie Printing Company. You get not only a sense of the time, but a sense of the job of president—and a sense of this country itself.

To read this assemblage of words is to be forced to live through September 11 and its aftermath—once again. It's surprising how much can be forgotten, in such a short space. (The Taliban, anyone?) The president himself recognized this tendency early on. Here he is on October 4, 2001: "I fully understand . . . there will be times when people feel a sense of normalcy—and I hope that happens sooner rather than later—and that September 11th may be a distant memory to some. But not to me, and not to this nation." Some 13 months later, he said, "One of my jobs is to make sure nobody gets complacent. One of my jobs is to remind people of the stark realities that we face. See, every morning I go into that great Oval Office and read threats to our country—every morning. . . . Some of them are blowhards [!], but we take every one of them seriously. It's the new reality."

Indeed.

As has often been noted, the president, on September 11, 2001, was reading to schoolchildren—a common event in that more luxurious age. Then we suffered that shock. Quick as a flash—that very day—Bush said, "We will make no distinction between the terrorists who committed these acts and those who harbor them." Many times later, he would refer to this policy as his "doctrine." He would state it and re-state it in assorted ways, giving the impression that he was ever more committed to it. He also said on September 11, "America has stood down enemies before, and we will do so this time. None of us will ever forget this day. Yet we go forward to defend freedom and all that is good and just in our world."

That may sound like the language of a comic book—but it was, to most of us, suitable language, and it reflected Bush's conviction that the current and ongoing conflict is one of good versus evil. You will see, in these pages, that he speaks frequently of "evildoers," "the evil ones," "the forces of evil," and the like. And he has endured some mockery for this.

But he addressed such criticism head-on in that speech at West Point: "Some worry that it is somehow undiplomatic or impolite to speak the language of right and wrong. I disagree. Different circumstances require different methods, but not different moralities." And then he went into a flight of universalism worthy of Wilson: "Moral truth is the same in every culture, in every time, and in every place. Targeting innocent civilians for murder is always and everywhere wrong. Brutality against women is always and everywhere wrong. There can be no neutrality between justice and cruelty, between the innocent and the guilty. We are in a conflict between good and evil, and America will call evil by its name. By confronting evil and lawless regimes, we do not create a problem, we reveal a problem. And we will lead the world in opposing it."

Well, then.

In the days and months after September 11, the president did many things: He comforted the grieving; he exalted the dead; he assuaged fears; he encouraged alertness; he pledged victory. He stepped into—and up to—any number of roles. He was mourner-in-chief, explainer-in-chief, inspirer-in-chief—and, of course, as the Constitution dictates, commander-in-chief. We see, in perusing this volume, that he combined what you might call the soft and the hard. He said, "I'm encouraging schoolchildren to write letters of friendship to Muslim children in different countries." He also said—just to take one example of thousands—"I'm going to talk about homeland security, but the best way to secure our homeland is to hunt the killers down one by one and bring them to justice, and that is what we're going to do."

We see Bush in the full range of his moods. He is purposeful and defiant; humble and prayerful; cocky and sarcastic; angry and slashing; sentimental and weepy; playful and twitting. He has his favorite words, as we all do. One of his is "fabulous." ("What a fabulous land we have, and the reason why is because we've got such fabulous citizens." Bush says "fabulous" at least as much as any interior decorator.) He has a knack for speaking directly to people, without talking down to them: "I want to explain to you about Saddam Hussein, just quickly, if I might." On October 17, 2001, he said one of the most Bushian things I've ever heard. See if you agree: "Now, there's the long version, and there's a short version. So I'm going to start with the short version: Our people are united; our government is determined; our cause is right; and justice will be done."

End of story, pretty much.

Sometimes Bush is archly funny. Speaking to high-school students, he said,

"You've been learning this by studying your history—at least some of you by studying your history." Often he is funny-serious: "You know, when the enemy hit us, they must have not known what they were doing. I like to tell people, they must have been watching too much TV, because they didn't understand America" (thinking that we were soft, materialistic, and cringing). On another occasion, Bush said, "See, they thought we'd probably just file a lawsuit or two! . . . They don't have any idea about what makes the people here tick."

Get a load of Bush in what I dub his full Texas-sheriff mode. Before a political audience in October 2002, he said, "We still got this coalition of freedom-loving nations we're working with. And we're hunting 'em down. The other day, one of 'em popped up—popped his head up—named al-Shibh. He's no longer a problem."

This is the kind of talk that thrills Bush's fans, and exasperates his critics.

I have been thinking about this president and words for some time now. In the fall of 2000, I took a leave of absence from *National Review* to assist the speechwriting staff on the Bush campaign (ah, the flexibility of the opinion journalist). At that time, the speechwriters were Michael Gerson (the chief), John McConnell, and Matthew Scully. They are still with George W. Bush, doing an extraordinary job (a *fabulous* job). And most would agree that Bush has grown in his ability to communicate, both in his prepared, professionalized speeches and in his unscripted remarks.

The proof is in this compilation: which begins on September 11 and concludes with the Iraq phase of the War on Terror. There is much repetition in this book, no doubt—it is inevitable. But these utterances, as a whole, are strangely compelling. As the war unfolds, Bush gives you new wrinkles, new information, new thrusts. Once or twice, I got a shiver, reminded of something I'd forgotten: "I'm told that one of the pilots here, a fellow named Randy, was asked if anyone at Travis [Air Force Base] had personal connections to any of the victims of the attacks of September the 11th. And here's what he said: 'I think we all do; they're all Americans. When you strike one American, you strike us all.'"

My suspicion is that "history," if it is fair, will recall that Bush did a splendid job rhetorically, as well as in other, more concrete respects, in a most difficult time. When it mattered terribly, his words came true. Like Reagan, he speaks as though he believes what he is saying—because he actually does. (You can tell—very easily—when Bush's heart isn't really in it.) Shortly before the Iraq war, Bush observed that "this call of history has come to the right country." Many of us contend that—to borrow from David Frum's title—it came to the right man, too.

*New York City*
*July 2003*

# September 2001

### Remarks by the President After Two Planes Crash
### Into the World Trade Center
Emma Booker Elementary School, Sarasota, Florida
September 11, 2001

Ladies and gentlemen, this is a difficult moment for America. I, unfortunately, will be going back to Washington after my remarks. Secretary Rod Paige and the Lt. Governor will take the podium and discuss education. I do want to thank the folks here at Booker Elementary School for their hospitality.

Today we've had a national tragedy. Two airplanes have crashed into the World Trade Center in an apparent terrorist attack on our country. I have spoken to the Vice President, to the Governor of New York, to the Director of the FBI, and have ordered that the full resources of the federal government go to help the victims and their families, and to conduct a full-scale investigation to hunt down and to find those folks who committed this act.

Terrorism against our nation will not stand.

And now, if you would join me in a moment of silence. May God bless the victims, their families, and America. Thank you very much.

### Remarks by the President upon Arrival at
### Barksdale Air Force Base
Barksdale Air Force Base, Louisiana
September 11, 2001

I want to reassure the American people that the full resources of the federal government are working to assist local authorities to save lives and to help the victims of these attacks. Make no mistake: The United States will hunt down and punish those responsible for these cowardly acts.

I've been in regular contact with the Vice President, the Secretary of Defense, the national security team, and my Cabinet. We have taken all appropriate security precautions to protect the American people. Our military at home and around the world is on high-alert status, and we have taken the necessary security precautions to continue the functions of your government.

We have been in touch with the leaders of Congress and with world leaders to assure them that we will do whatever is necessary to protect America and Americans.

I ask the American people to join me in saying a thanks for all the folks who have been fighting hard to rescue our fellow citizens and to join me in saying a prayer for the victims and their families.

The resolve of our great nation is being tested. But make no mistake: We will show the world that we will pass this test. God bless.


## Presidential Address to the Nation
September 11, 2001

Good evening. Today, our fellow citizens, our way of life, our very freedom came under attack in a series of deliberate and deadly terrorist acts. The victims were in airplanes, or in their offices: secretaries, businessmen and women, military and federal workers, moms and dads, friends and neighbors. Thousands of lives were suddenly ended by evil, despicable acts of terror.

The pictures of airplanes flying into buildings, fires burning, huge structures collapsing, have filled us with disbelief, terrible sadness, and a quiet, unyielding anger. These acts of mass murder were intended to frighten our nation into chaos and retreat. But they have failed; our country is strong.

A great people has been moved to defend a great nation. Terrorist attacks can shake the foundations of our biggest buildings, but they cannot touch the foundation of America. These acts shattered steel, but they cannot dent the steel of American resolve.

America was targeted for attack because we're the brightest beacon for freedom and opportunity in the world. And no one will keep that light from shining.

Today, our nation saw evil, the very worst of human nature. And we responded with the best of America—with the daring of our rescue workers, with the caring for strangers and neighbors who came to give blood and help in any way they could.

Immediately following the first attack, I implemented our government's emergency-response plans. Our military is powerful, and it's prepared. Our emergency teams are working in New York City and Washington, D.C., to help with local rescue efforts.

Our first priority is to get help to those who have been injured, and to take every precaution to protect our citizens at home and around the world from further attacks.

The functions of our government continue without interruption. Federal agencies in Washington, which had to be evacuated today, are reopening for essential personnel tonight, and will be open for business tomorrow. Our financial institutions remain strong, and the American economy will be open for business as well.

The search is underway for those who are behind these evil acts. I've directed the full resources of our intelligence and law-enforcement communities to find those responsible and to bring them to justice. We will make no distinction between the terrorists who committed these acts and those who harbor them.

I appreciate so very much the members of Congress who have joined me in strongly condemning these attacks. And on behalf of the American people, I thank the many world leaders who have called to offer their condolences and assistance.

America and our friends and allies join with all those who want peace and security in the world, and we stand together to win the war against terrorism. Tonight, I ask for your prayers for all those who grieve, for the children whose worlds have been shattered, for all whose sense of safety and security has been threatened. And I pray they will be comforted by a power greater than any of us, spoken [of] through the ages in Psalm 23: "Even though I walk through the valley of the shadow of death, I fear no evil, for You are with me."

This is a day when all Americans from every walk of life unite in our resolve for justice and peace. America has stood down enemies before, and we will do so this time. None of us will ever forget this day. Yet, we go forward to defend freedom and all that is good and just in our world.

Thank you. Good night, and God bless America.

## Presidential Proclamation Declaring National Day of Prayer and Remembrance for the Victims of the Terrorist Attacks
September 13, 2001

By the President of the United States of America
A Proclamation

On Tuesday morning, September 11, 2001, terrorists attacked America in a series of despicable acts of war. They hijacked four passenger jets, crashed two of them into the World Trade Center's twin towers and a third into the Headquarters of the U.S. Department of Defense at the Pentagon, causing great loss of life and tremendous damage. The fourth plane crashed in the Pennsylvania countryside, killing all on board but falling well short of its intended target apparently because of the heroic efforts of passengers on board. This carnage, which caused the collapse of both Trade Center towers and the destruction of part of the Pentagon, killed more than 250 airplane passengers and thousands more on the ground.

Civilized people around the world denounce the evildoers who devised and executed these terrible attacks. Justice demands that those who helped or harbored the terrorists be punished—and punished severely. The enormity of their evil demands it. We will use all the resources of the United States and our cooperating friends and allies to pursue those responsible for this evil, until justice is done.

We mourn with those who have suffered great and disastrous loss. All our hearts have been seared by the sudden and senseless taking of innocent lives. We pray for healing and for the strength to serve and encourage one another in hope and faith.

Scripture says: "Blessed are those who mourn for they shall be comforted." I call on every American family and the family of America to observe a National Day of Prayer and Remembrance, honoring the memory of the thousands of victims of these brutal attacks and comforting those who lost loved ones. We will persevere through this national tragedy and personal loss. In time, we will find healing and recovery; and, in the face of all this evil, we remain strong and united, "one Nation under God."

NOW THEREFORE I, GEORGE W. BUSH, President of the United States of America, by virtue of the authority vested in me by the Constitution and laws of the United States, do hereby proclaim Friday, September 14, 2001, as a National Day of Prayer and Remembrance for the Victims of the Terrorist

Attacks on September 11, 2001. I ask that the people of the United States and places of worship mark this National Day of Prayer and Remembrance with noontime memorial services, the ringing of bells at that hour, and evening candlelight remembrance vigils. I encourage employers to permit their workers time off during the lunch hour to attend the noontime services to pray for our land. I invite the people of the world who share our grief to join us in these solemn observances.

IN WITNESS WHEREOF, I have hereunto set my hand this thirteenth day of September, in the year of our Lord two thousand one, and of the Independence of the United States of America the two hundred and twenty-sixth.

GEORGE W. BUSH

### Remarks by the President from Speech at National Day of Prayer and Remembrance Ceremony
The National Cathedral, Washington, D.C.
September 14, 2001

We are here in the middle hour of our grief. So many have suffered so great a loss, and today we express our nation's sorrow. We come before God to pray for the missing and the dead, and for those who love them.

On Tuesday, our country was attacked with deliberate and massive cruelty. We have seen the images of fire and ashes, and bent steel.

Now come the names, the list of casualties we are only beginning to read. They are the names of men and women who began their day at a desk or in an airport, busy with life. They are the names of people who faced death, and in their last moments called home to say, be brave, and I love you.

They are the names of passengers who defied their murderers, and prevented the murder of others on the ground. They are the names of men and women who wore the uniform of the United States, and died at their posts.

They are the names of rescuers, the ones whom death found running up the stairs and into the fires to help others. We will read all these names. We will linger over them, and learn their stories, and many Americans will weep.

To the children and parents and spouses and families and friends of the lost, we offer the deepest sympathy of the nation. And I assure you, you are not alone.

Just three days removed from these events, Americans do not yet have the distance of history. But our responsibility to history is already clear: To answer these attacks and rid the world of evil.

War has been waged against us by stealth and deceit and murder. This nation is peaceful, but fierce when stirred to anger. This conflict was begun on the timing and terms of others. It will end in a way, and at an hour, of our choosing.

Our purpose as a nation is firm. Yet our wounds as a people are recent and unhealed, and lead us to pray. In many of our prayers this week, there is a searching, and an honesty. At St. Patrick's Cathedral in New York on Tuesday, a woman said, "I prayed to God to give us a sign that He is still here." Others have prayed for the same, searching hospital to hospital, carrying pictures of those still missing.

God's signs are not always the ones we look for. We learn in tragedy that his purposes are not always our own. Yet the prayers of private suffering, whether in our homes or in this great cathedral, are known and heard, and understood.

There are prayers that help us last through the day, or endure the night. There are prayers of friends and strangers, that give us strength for the journey. And there are prayers that yield our will to a will greater than our own.

This world He created is of moral design. Grief and tragedy and hatred are only for a time. Goodness, remembrance, and love have no end. And the Lord of life holds all who die, and all who mourn.

It is said that adversity introduces us to ourselves. This is true of a nation as well. In this trial, we have been reminded, and the world has seen, that our fellow Americans are generous and kind, resourceful and brave. We see our national character in rescuers working past exhaustion; in long lines of blood donors; in thousands of citizens who have asked to work and serve in any way possible.

And we have seen our national character in eloquent acts of sacrifice. Inside the World Trade Center, one man who could have saved himself stayed until the end at the side of his quadriplegic friend. A beloved priest died giving the last rites to a firefighter. Two office workers, finding a disabled stranger, carried her down sixty-eight floors to safety. A group of men drove through the night from Dallas to Washington to bring skin grafts for burn victims.

In these acts, and in many others, Americans showed a deep commitment to one another, and an abiding love for our country. Today, we feel what Franklin Roosevelt called the warm courage of national unity. This is a unity of every faith, and every background.

It has joined together political parties in both houses of Congress. It is evident in services of prayer and candlelight vigils, and American flags, which are displayed in pride, and wave in defiance.

Our unity is a kinship of grief, and a steadfast resolve to prevail against our enemies. And this unity against terror is now extending across the world.

America is a nation full of good fortune, with so much to be grateful for. But we are not spared from suffering. In every generation, the world has produced enemies of human freedom. They have attacked America, because we are freedom's home and defender. And the commitment of our fathers is now the calling of our time.

On this National Day of Prayer and Remembrance, we ask almighty God to watch over our nation, and grant us patience and resolve in all that is to come. We pray that He will comfort and console those who now walk in sorrow. We thank Him for each life we now must mourn, and the promise of a life to come.

As we have been assured, neither death nor life, nor angels nor principalities nor powers, nor things present nor things to come, nor height nor depth, can separate us from God's love. May He bless the souls of the departed. May He comfort our own. And may He always guide our country.

God bless America.


## Remarks by the President to Police Officers, Firefighters, and Rescue Workers at Ground Zero
New York City
September 14, 2001

CROWD: USA! USA!

THE PRESIDENT: Thank you all. I want you all to know—

CROWD: Can't hear you.

THE PRESIDENT: I can't talk any louder. (Laughter)

I want you all to know that America today—that America today is on bended knee in prayer for the people whose lives were lost here, for the workers who work here, for the families who mourn. This nation stands with the good people of New York City, and New Jersey and Connecticut, as we mourn the loss of thousands of our citizens.

CROWD: Can't hear you.

THE PRESIDENT: I can hear you. (Applause) I can hear you. The rest of the world hears you. (Applause) And the people who knocked these buildings down will hear all of us soon. (Applause)

CROWD: USA! USA!

THE PRESIDENT: The nation sends its love and compassion to everybody who is here. Thank you for your hard work. Thank you for making the nation proud. And may God bless America. (Applause)

CROWD: USA! USA!


## Presidential Radio Address to the Nation
September 15, 2001

Good morning. This weekend I am engaged in extensive sessions with members of my National Security Council, as we plan a comprehensive assault on terrorism. This will be a different kind of conflict against a different kind of enemy.

This is a conflict without battlefields or beachheads, a conflict with opponents who believe they are invisible. Yet, they are mistaken. They will be exposed, and they will discover what others in the past have learned: Those who make war against the United States have chosen their own destruction. Victory against terrorism will not take place in a single battle, but in a series of decisive actions against terrorist organizations and those who harbor and support them.

We are planning a broad and sustained campaign to secure our country and eradicate the evil of terrorism. And we are determined to see this conflict through. Americans of every faith and background are committed to this goal.

Yesterday I visited the site of the destruction in New York City and saw an amazing spirit of sacrifice and patriotism and defiance. I met with rescuers who have worked past exhaustion, who cheered for our country and the great cause we have entered.

In Washington, D.C., the political parties and both Houses of Congress have shown a remarkable unity, and I'm deeply grateful. A terrorist attack designed to tear us apart has instead bound us together as a nation. Over the past few days, we have learned much about American courage—the courage of firefighters and police officers who suffered so great a loss, the courage of passengers aboard United 93 who may well have fought with the hijackers and saved many lives on the ground.

Now we honor those who died, and prepare to respond to these attacks on our nation. I will not settle for a token act. Our response must be sweeping, sustained, and effective. We have much do to, and much to ask of the American people.

You will be asked for your patience, for the conflict will not be short. You will be asked for resolve, for the conflict will not be easy. You will be asked for your strength, because the course to victory may be long.

In the past week, we have seen the American people at their very best everywhere in America. Citizens have come together to pray, to give blood, to fly our country's flag. Americans are coming together to share their grief and gain strength from one another.

Great tragedy has come to us, and we are meeting it with the best that is in our country, with courage and concern for others. Because this is America. This is who we are. This is what our enemies hate and have attacked. And this is why we will prevail.

### Remarks by the President from Speech at the Islamic Center of Washington, D.C.
September 17, 2001

Thank you all very much for your hospitality. We've just had wide-ranging discussions on the matter at hand. Like the good folks standing with me, the American people were appalled and outraged at last Tuesday's attacks. And so were Muslims all across the world. Both Americans and Muslim friends and citizens, tax-paying citizens, and Muslims in [all] nations were just appalled and could not believe what we saw on our TV screens.

These acts of violence against innocents violate the fundamental tenets of the Islamic faith. And it's important for my fellow Americans to understand that.

The English translation is not as eloquent as the original Arabic, but let me quote from the Koran itself: "In the long run, evil in the extreme will be the end of those who do evil. For that they rejected the signs of Allah and held them up to ridicule."

The face of terror is not the true faith of Islam. That's not what Islam is all about. Islam is peace. These terrorists don't represent peace. They represent evil and war.

When we think of Islam we think of a faith that brings comfort to a billion people around the world. Billions of people find comfort and solace and peace. And that's made brothers and sisters out of every race—out of every race.

America counts millions of Muslims amongst our citizens, and Muslims make an incredibly valuable contribution to our country. Muslims are doctors, lawyers, law professors, members of the military, entrepreneurs, shopkeepers, moms and dads. And they need to be treated with respect. In our anger and emotion . . . Americans must treat each other with respect.

Women who cover their heads in this country must feel comfortable going outside their homes. Moms who wear [coverings] must be not intimidated in America. That's not the America I know. That's not the America I value.

I've been told that some fear to leave [their homes]; some don't want to go shopping for their families; some don't want to go about their ordinary daily routines because, by wearing [coverings], they're afraid they'll be intimidated. That should not and that will not stand in America.

Those who feel like they can intimidate our fellow citizens to take out their anger don't represent the best of America, they represent the worst of humankind, and they should be ashamed of that kind of behavior.

This is a great country. It's a great country because we share the same values of respect and dignity and human worth. And it is my honor to be meeting with leaders who feel just the same way I do. They're outraged, they're sad. They love America just as much as I do.

I want to thank you all for giving me a chance to come by. And may God bless us all.


### Statement by the President upon Signing the Authorization for Use of Military Force Bill
September 18, 2001

Today I am signing Senate Joint Resolution 23, the "Authorization for Use of Military Force."

On September 11, 2001, terrorists committed treacherous and horrific acts of violence against innocent Americans and individuals from other countries. Civilized nations and people around the world have expressed outrage at, and have unequivocally condemned, these attacks. Those who plan, authorize, commit, or aid terrorist attacks against the United States and its interests—including those who harbor terrorists—threaten the national security of the United States. It is, therefore, necessary and appropriate that the United States exercise its rights to defend itself and protect United States citizens both at home and abroad.

In adopting this resolution in response to the latest terrorist acts committed against the United States and the continuing threat to the United States and its citizens from terrorist activities, both Houses of Congress have acted wisely, decisively, and in the finest traditions of our country. I thank the leadership of both Houses for their role in expeditiously passing this historic joint resolution. I have had the benefit of meaningful consultations with members of the Congress since the attacks of September 11, 2001, and I will continue to consult closely with them as our Nation responds to this threat to our peace and security.

Senate Joint Resolution 23 recognizes the seriousness of the terrorist threat to our Nation and the authority of the President under the Constitution to take action to deter and prevent acts of terrorism against the United States. In signing this resolution, I maintain the longstanding position of the executive branch regarding the President's constitutional authority to use force, including the Armed Forces of the United States, and regarding the constitutionality of the War Powers Resolution.

Our whole Nation is unalterably committed to a direct, forceful, and comprehensive response to these terrorist attacks and the scourge of terrorism directed against the United States and its interests.

### Presidential Address to a Joint Session of Congress
September 23, 2001

Mr. Speaker, Mr. President Pro Tempore, members of Congress, and fellow Americans:

In the normal course of events, Presidents come to this chamber to report on the state of the Union. Tonight, no such report is needed. It has already been delivered by the American people.

We have seen it in the courage of passengers, who rushed terrorists to save others on the ground—passengers like an exceptional man named Todd Beamer. And would you please help me to welcome his wife, Lisa Beamer, here tonight.

We have seen the state of our Union in the endurance of rescuers, working past exhaustion. We have seen the unfurling of flags, the lighting of candles, the giving of blood, the saying of prayers—in English, Hebrew, and Arabic. We have seen the decency of a loving and giving people who have made the grief of strangers their own.

My fellow citizens, for the last nine days, the entire world has seen for itself the state of our Union—and it is strong.

Tonight we are a country awakened to danger and called to defend freedom. Our grief has turned to anger, and anger to resolution. Whether we bring our enemies to justice, or bring justice to our enemies, justice will be done.

I thank the Congress for its leadership at such an important time. All of America was touched on the evening of the tragedy to see Republicans and Democrats joined together on the steps of this Capitol, singing "God Bless America." And you did more than sing; you acted, by delivering $40 billion to rebuild our communities and meet the needs of our military.

Speaker Hastert, Minority Leader Gephardt, Majority Leader Daschle, and Senator Lott, I thank you for your friendship, for your leadership and for your service to our country.

And on behalf of the American people, I thank the world for its outpouring of support. America will never forget the sounds of our National Anthem playing at Buckingham Palace, on the streets of Paris, and at Berlin's Brandenburg Gate.

We will not forget South Korean children gathering to pray outside our embassy in Seoul, or the prayers of sympathy offered at a mosque in Cairo. We will not forget moments of silence and days of mourning in Australia and Africa and Latin America.

Nor will we forget the citizens of eighty other nations who died with our own: Dozens of Pakistanis; more than 130 Israelis; more than 250 citizens of India; men and women from El Salvador, Iran, Mexico, and Japan; and hundreds of British citizens. America has no truer friend than Great Britain. Once again, we are joined together in a great cause—[and] so honored the British Prime Minister has crossed an ocean to show his unity of purpose with America. Thank you for coming, friend.

On September the 11th, enemies of freedom committed an act of war against our country. Americans have known wars—but for the past 136 years, they have been wars on foreign soil, except for one Sunday in 1941. Americans have known the casualties of war—but not at the center of a great city on a peaceful morning. Americans have known surprise attacks—but never before on thousands of civilians. All of this was brought upon us in a single day—and night fell on a different world, a world where freedom itself is under attack.

Americans have many questions tonight. Americans are asking: Who attacked our country? The evidence we have gathered all points to a collection of loosely affiliated terrorist organizations known as al Qaeda. They are the same murderers indicted for bombing American embassies in Tanzania and Kenya, and responsible for bombing the *USS Cole.*

Al Qaeda is to terror what the mafia is to crime. But its goal is not making money; its goal is remaking the world—and imposing its radical beliefs on people everywhere.

The terrorists practice a fringe form of Islamic extremism that has been rejected by Muslim scholars and the vast majority of Muslim clerics—a fringe movement that perverts the peaceful teachings of Islam. The terrorists' directive commands them to kill Christians and Jews, to kill all Americans, and make no distinction among military and civilians, including women and children.

This group and its leader—a person named Osama bin Laden—are linked to many other organizations in different countries, including the Egyptian Islamic Jihad and the Islamic Movement of Uzbekistan. There are thousands of these terrorists in more than sixty countries. They are recruited from their own nations and neighborhoods and brought to camps in places like Afghanistan, where they are trained in the tactics of terror. They are sent back to their homes or sent to hide in countries around the world to plot evil and destruction.

The leadership of al Qaeda has great influence in Afghanistan and supports the Taliban regime in controlling most of that country. In Afghanistan, we see al Qaeda's vision for the world.

Afghanistan's people have been brutalized—many are starving and many have fled. Women are not allowed to attend school. You can be jailed for owning a television. Religion can be practiced only as their leaders dictate. A man can be jailed in Afghanistan if his beard is not long enough.

The United States respects the people of Afghanistan—after all, we are currently its largest source of humanitarian aid—but we condemn the Taliban regime. It is not only repressing its own people, it is threatening people everywhere by sponsoring and sheltering and supplying terrorists. By aiding and abetting murder, the Taliban regime is committing murder.

And tonight, the United States of America makes the following demands on the Taliban: Deliver to United States authorities all the leaders of al Qaeda who hide in your land. Release all foreign nationals, including American citizens, you have unjustly imprisoned. Protect foreign journalists, diplomats, and aid workers in your country. Close immediately and permanently every terrorist training camp in Afghanistan, and hand over every terrorist, and every person in their support structure, to appropriate authorities. Give the United States full access to terrorist training camps, so we can make sure they are no longer operating.

These demands are not open to negotiation or discussion. The Taliban must act, and act immediately. They will hand over the terrorists, or they will share in their fate.

I also want to speak tonight directly to Muslims throughout the world. We respect your faith. It's practiced freely by many millions of Americans, and by millions more in countries that America counts as friends. Its teachings are good and peaceful, and those who commit evil in the name of Allah blaspheme the name of Allah. The terrorists are traitors to their own faith, trying, in effect, to hijack Islam itself. The enemy of America is not our many Muslim friends; it is not our many Arab friends. Our enemy is a radical network of terrorists, and every government that supports them.

Our war on terror begins with al Qaeda, but it does not end there. It will not end until every terrorist group of global reach has been found, stopped, and defeated.

Americans are asking: Why do they hate us? They hate what we see right here in this chamber—a democratically elected government. Their leaders are self-appointed. They hate our freedoms—our freedom of religion, our freedom of speech, our freedom to vote and assemble and disagree with each other.

They want to overthrow existing governments in many Muslim countries, such as Egypt, Saudi Arabia, and Jordan. They want to drive Israel out of the Middle East. They want to drive Christians and Jews out of vast regions of Asia and Africa.

These terrorists kill not merely to end lives, but to disrupt and end a way of life. With every atrocity, they hope that America grows fearful, retreating from the world, and forsaking our friends. They stand against us, because we stand in their way.

We are not deceived by their pretenses to piety. We have seen their kind before. They are the heirs of all the murderous ideologies of the 20th century. By sacrificing human life to serve their radical visions—by abandoning every value except the will to power—they follow in the path of fascism, and Nazism, and totalitarianism. And they will follow that path all the way, to where it ends: In history's unmarked grave of discarded lies.

Americans are asking: How will we fight and win this war? We will direct every resource at our command—every means of diplomacy, every tool of intelligence, every instrument of law enforcement, every financial influence, and every necessary weapon of war—to the disruption and to the defeat of the global terror network.

This war will not be like the war against Iraq a decade ago, with a decisive liberation of territory and a swift conclusion. It will not look like the air war above Kosovo two years ago, where no ground troops were used and not a single American was lost in combat.

Our response involves far more than instant retaliation and isolated strikes. Americans should not expect one battle, but a lengthy campaign, unlike any other we have ever seen. It may include dramatic strikes, visible on TV, and covert operations, secret even in success. We will starve terrorists of funding, turn them one against another, drive them from place to place, until there is no refuge or no rest. And we will pursue nations that provide aid or safe haven to terrorism. Every nation, in every region, now has a decision to make. Either you are with us, or you are with the terrorists. From this day forward, any nation that continues to harbor or support terrorism will be regarded by the United States as a hostile regime.

Our nation has been put on notice: We are not immune from attack. We will take defensive measures against terrorism to protect Americans. Today, dozens of federal departments and agencies, as well as state and local governments, have responsibilities affecting homeland security. These efforts must be coordinated at the highest level. So tonight I announce the creation of a Cabinet-level position reporting directly to me—the Office of Homeland Security.

And tonight I also announce a distinguished American to lead this effort, to strengthen American security: A military veteran, an effective governor, a true patriot, a trusted friend—Pennsylvania's Tom Ridge. He will lead, oversee, and coordinate a comprehensive national strategy to safeguard our country against terrorism, and respond to any attacks that may come.

These measures are essential. But the only way to defeat terrorism as a threat to our way of life is to stop it, eliminate it, and destroy it where it grows.

Many will be involved in this effort, from FBI agents to intelligence operatives to the reservists we have called to active duty. All deserve our thanks, and all have our prayers. And tonight, a few miles from the damaged Pentagon, I have a message for our military: Be ready. I've called the Armed Forces to alert, and there is a reason. The hour is coming when America will act, and you will make us proud.

This is not, however, just America's fight. And what is at stake is not just America's freedom. This is the world's fight. This is civilization's fight. This is the fight of all who believe in progress and pluralism, tolerance and freedom.

We ask every nation to join us. We will ask, and we will need, the help of police forces, intelligence services, and banking systems around the world. The United States is grateful that many nations and many international organizations have already responded—with sympathy and with support: Nations from Latin America, to Asia, to Africa, to Europe, to the Islamic world.

Perhaps the NATO Charter reflects best the attitude of the world: An attack on one is an attack on all.

The civilized world is rallying to America's side. They understand that if this terror goes unpunished, their own cities, their own citizens may be next. Terror, unanswered, can not only bring down buildings, it can threaten the stability of legitimate governments. And you know what?—we're not going to allow it.

Americans are asking: What is expected of us? I ask you to live your lives, and hug your children. I know many citizens have fears tonight, and I ask you to be calm and resolute, even in the face of a continuing threat.

I ask you to uphold the values of America, and remember why so many have come here. We are in a fight for our principles, and our first responsibility is to live by them. No one should be singled out for unfair treatment or unkind words because of their ethnic background or religious faith.

I ask you to continue to support the victims of this tragedy with your contributions. . . .

The thousands of FBI agents who are now at work in this investigation may need your cooperation, and I ask you to give it.

I ask for your patience, with the delays and inconveniences that may accompany tighter security; and for your patience in what will be a long struggle.

I ask your continued participation and confidence in the American economy. Terrorists attacked a symbol of American prosperity. They did not touch its source. America is successful because of the hard work, and creativity, and enterprise of our people. These were the true strengths of our economy before September 11th, and they are our strengths today.

And, finally, please continue praying for the victims of terror and their families, for those in uniform, and for our great country. Prayer has comforted us in sorrow, and will help strengthen us for the journey ahead.

Tonight I thank my fellow Americans for what you have already done and for what you will do. And ladies and gentlemen of the Congress, I thank you, their representatives, for what you have already done and for what we will do together.

Tonight, we face new and sudden national challenges. We will come together to improve air safety, to dramatically expand the number of air marshals on domestic flights, and [to] take new measures to prevent hijacking. We will come together to promote stability and keep our airlines flying, with direct assistance during this emergency.

We will come together to give law enforcement the additional tools it needs to track down terror here at home. We will come together to strengthen our intelligence capabilities to know the plans of terrorists before they act, and find them before they strike.

We will come together to take active steps that strengthen America's economy, and put our people back to work.

Tonight we welcome two leaders who embody the extraordinary spirit of all New Yorkers: Governor George Pataki and Mayor Rudolph Giuliani. As a symbol of America's resolve, my administration will work with Congress, and these two leaders, to show the world that we will rebuild New York City.

After all that has just passed—all the lives taken, and all the possibilities and hopes that died with them—it is natural to wonder if America's future is one of fear. Some speak of an age of terror. I know there are struggles ahead, and dangers to face. But this country will define our times, not be defined by them. As long as the United States of America is determined and strong, this will not be an age of terror; this will be an age of liberty, here and across the world.

Great harm has been done to us. We have suffered great loss. And in our grief and anger we have found our mission and our moment. Freedom and fear are at war. The advance of human freedom—the great achievement of our time, and the great hope of every time—now depends on us. Our nation—this generation—will lift a dark threat of violence from our people and our future. We will rally the world to this cause by our efforts, by our courage. We will not tire, we will not falter, and we will not fail. It is my hope that in the months and years ahead, life will return almost to normal. We'll go back to our lives and routines, and that is good. Even grief recedes with time and grace. But our resolve must not pass. Each of us will remember what happened that day, and to whom it happened. We'll remember the moment the news came—where we were and what we were doing. Some will remember an image of a fire, or a story of rescue. Some will carry memories of a face and a voice gone forever.

And I will carry this: It is the police shield of a man named George Howard, who died at the World Trade Center trying to save others. It was given to me by his mom, Arlene, as a proud memorial to her son. This is my reminder of lives that ended, and a task that does not end.

I will not forget this wound to our country or those who inflicted it. I will not yield; I will not rest; I will not relent in waging this struggle for freedom and security for the American people.

The course of this conflict is not known, yet its outcome is certain. Freedom and fear, justice and cruelty, have always been at war, and we know that God is not neutral between them.

Fellow citizens, we'll meet violence with patient justice—assured of the rightness of our cause, and confident of the victories to come. In all that lies before us, may God grant us wisdom, and may He watch over the United States of America.

## Letter to Congress Transmitting a Presidential Executive Order Declaring a National Emergency
### September 23, 2001

Pursuant to section 204(b) of the International Emergency Economic Powers Act, 50 U.S.C. 1703(b) (IEEPA), and section 301 of the National Emergencies Act, 50 U.S.C. 1631, I hereby report that I have exercised my statutory authority to declare a national emergency in response to the unusual and extraordinary threat posed to the national security, foreign policy, and economy of the United States by grave acts of terrorism and threats of terrorism committed by foreign terrorists, including the September 11, 2001, terrorist attacks at the World Trade Center, New York, at the Pentagon, and in Pennsylvania. I have also issued an Executive Order to help deal with this threat by giving the United States more powerful tools to reach the means by which terrorists and terrorist networks finance themselves and to encourage greater cooperation by foreign financial institutions and other entities that may have access to foreign property belonging to terrorists or terrorist organizations.

The attacks of September 11, 2001, highlighted in the most tragic way the threat posed to the security and national interests of the United States by terrorists who have abandoned any regard for humanity, decency, morality, or honor. Terrorists and terrorist networks operate across international borders and derive their financing from sources in many nations. Often, terrorist property and financial assets lie outside the jurisdiction of the United States. Our effort to combat and destroy the financial underpinnings of global terrorism must therefore be broad, and not only provide powerful sanctions against the U.S. property of terrorists and their supporters, but also encourage multilateral cooperation in identifying and freezing property and assets located elsewhere.

This Executive Order is part of our national commitment to lead the international effort to bring a halt to the evil of terrorist activity. In general terms, it provides additional means by which to disrupt the financial-support network for terrorist organizations by blocking the U.S. assets not only of foreign persons or entities who commit or pose a significant risk of committing acts of terrorism, but also by blocking the assets of their subsidiaries, front organizations, agents, and associates, and any other entities that provide services or assistance to them. Although the blocking powers enumerated in the order are broad, my Administration is committed to exercising them responsibly, with due regard for the culpability of the persons and entities potentially covered by the order, and in consultation with other countries.

The specific terms of the Executive Order provide for the blocking of the property and interests in property, including bank deposits, of foreign persons designated in the order or pursuant thereto, when such property is within the United States or in the possession or control of United States persons. In addition, the Executive Order prohibits any transaction or dealing by United States persons in such property or interests in property, including the making or receiving of any contribution of funds, goods, or services to or for the benefit of such designated persons.

I have identified in an Annex to this order eleven terrorist organizations, twelve individual terrorist leaders, three charitable or humanitarian organizations that operate as fronts for terrorist financing and support, and one business entity that operates as a front for terrorist financing and support. I have determined that each of these organizations and individuals have committed, supported, or threatened acts of terrorism that imperil the security of U.S. nationals or the national security, foreign policy, or economy of the United States. I have also authorized the Secretary of State to determine and designate additional foreign persons who have committed or pose a significant risk of committing acts of terrorism that threaten the security of U.S. nationals or the national security, foreign policy, or economy of the United States. Such designations are to be made in consultation with the Secretary of the Treasury and the Attorney General.

The Executive Order further authorizes the Secretary of the Treasury to identify, in consultation with the Secretary of State and the Attorney General, additional persons or entities that:

● are owned or controlled by, or that act for or on behalf of, those persons designated in or pursuant to the order;

● assist in, sponsor, or provide financial, material, or technological support for, or financial or other services to or in support of acts of terrorism or those persons designated in or pursuant to the order; or

● are otherwise associated with those persons designated in or pursuant to the order.

Prior to designating persons that fall within the latter two categories, the Secretary of the Treasury is authorized to consult with any foreign authorities the Secretary of State deems appropriate, in consultation with the Secretary of the Treasury and the Attorney General. Such consultation is intended to avoid the need for additional designations by securing bilateral or multilateral cooperation from foreign governments and foreign financial and other institutions. Such consultation may include requests to foreign governments to seek, in accordance with international law and their domestic laws, information from financial institutions regarding terrorist property and to take action to deny terrorists the use of such property. The order also provides broad authority, with respect to the latter two categories, for the Secretary of the Treasury, in his discretion, and in consultation with the Secretary of State and the Attorney General, to take lesser action than the complete blocking of property or interests in property if such lesser action is deemed consistent with the national interests of the United States. Some of the factors that may be considered in deciding whether a lesser action against a foreign person is consistent with the national interests of the United States include:

- the impact of blocking on the U.S. or international financial system;
- the extent to which the foreign person has cooperated with U.S. authorities;
- the degree of knowledge the foreign person had of the terrorist-related activities of the designated person;
- the extent of the relationship between the foreign person and the designated person; and
- the impact of blocking or other measures on the foreign person.

The Executive Order also directs the Secretary of State, the Secretary of the Treasury, and other agencies to make all relevant efforts to cooperate and coordinate with other countries, including through existing and future multilateral and bilateral agreements and arrangements, to achieve the objectives of this order, including the prevention and suppression of acts of terrorism, the denial of the financing of and financial services to terrorists and terrorist organizations, and the sharing of intelligence about funding activities in support of terrorism.

In the Executive Order, I also have made determinations to suspend otherwise applicable exemptions for certain humanitarian, medical, or agricultural transfers or donations. Regrettably, international terrorist networks make frequent use of charitable or humanitarian organizations to obtain clandestine financial and other support for their activities. If these exemptions were not suspended, the provision of humanitarian materials could be used as a loophole through which support could be provided to individuals or groups involved with terrorism and whose activities endanger the safety of United States nationals, both here and abroad.

The Secretary of the Treasury, in consultation with the Secretary of State and the Attorney General, is authorized to issue regulations in exercise of my authorities under IEEPA to implement the prohibitions set forth in the Executive Order. All federal agencies are also directed to take actions within their authority to carry out the provisions of the order, and, where applicable, to advise the Secretary of the Treasury in a timely manner of the measures taken.

The measures taken here will immediately demonstrate our resolve to bring new strength to bear in our multifaceted struggle to eradicate international terrorism. It is my hope that they will point the way for other civilized nations to adopt similar measures to attack the financial roots of global terrorist networks.

In that regard, this Executive Order is an integral part of our larger effort to form a coalition in the global war against terrorism. We have already worked with nations around the globe and groups such as the G-8, the European Union, and the Rio Group, all of which have issued strong statements of their intention to take measures to limit the ability of terrorist groups to operate. In the next several weeks the 33rd Session of the International Civil Aviation Organization (ICAO) General Assembly and other [forums] will focus on terrorism worldwide. It is our intention to work within the G-7/G-8, the ICAO, and other [forums] to reach agreement on strong concrete steps that will limit the ability of terrorists to operate. In the G-7/G-8, the United States will work with its partners, drawing on the G-8 Lyon Group on Transnational Crime, the G-8 Group on Counterterrorism, the G-7 Financial Action Task Force, and the existing G-8 commitments to build momentum and practical cooperation in the fight to stop the flow of resources to support terrorism. In addition, both the Convention for the Suppression of the Financing of Terrorism and the Convention for the Suppression of Terrorist Bombings have been forwarded to the Senate, and I will be forwarding shortly to the Congress implementing legislation for both Conventions.

I am enclosing a copy of the Executive Order I have issued. This order is effective at 12:01 A.M. eastern daylight time on September 24, 2001.

GEORGE W. BUSH

## Excerpted Remarks by the President from Speech
## to Employees at the Federal Bureau of Investigation
September 25, 2001

First, as I mentioned to many of your colleagues, we're facing a different kind of war than our country is used to . . . two weeks ago there was an act of war declared on America. No one could have possibly dreamed that it would come in the way it did. And it shocked our nation, of course.

And we've had time to think about it here in the country, and we're angry. But we're also clear—we've got clear vision about what the country needs to do. This is a nation that has come together to defend our freedom and our way of life.

I see things this way: The people who did this act on America, and who may be planning further acts, are evil people. They don't represent an ideology, they don't represent a legitimate political group of people. They're flat evil. That's all they can think about, is evil. And as a nation of good folks, we're going to hunt them down, and we're going to find them, and we will bring them to justice.

Ours is a nation that does not seek revenge, but we do seek justice. And I don't care how long it takes to root out terrorism, we're going to do it. We will take the time and effort and spend the resources necessary to not only find these evildoers who did what they did to America on September the 11th, this is a larger campaign against anybody who hates freedom, anybody who can't stand what America and our allies and friends stand for.

And so I'm here at the FBI to thank you for your work. Most of your job is to help us win the war here at home. Most of your job is to prevent something else from happening. And I know that hundreds of FBI agents and other employees of the Agency are working long, long hours to do that. I was able to see the war rooms where information is being collected and analyzed and dispersed.

I was able to see the consoles, where people have been sitting at long hours, detailing every piece of information that is being gathered across the country. I know there are over 4,000 employees of the FBI working on not only gathering evidence for the particular actions that took place on September the 11th, but running down every scrap of information that is being found all across our land, and analyzing the information, and preparing our great nation to disrupt any action that may be being planned.

There are some other things we can do in the country, and our Congress needs to work with us. And I believe—I had breakfast this morning with

Republican and Democrat leaders—and I will tell you, the spirit on Capitol Hill is good for America. It's a united spirit.

I want to thank the leaders from both parties, and both Houses for their willingness to listen to anybody who has got a good idea about how to fight terrorist activity in the country. And I believe the Attorney General has taken some good ideas to Capitol Hill, and I'd like to share some of them with you.

First, what we've seen is these terrorists are very sophisticated, and so are their communications. Their calls must be penetrated when we feel there's a threat to America. We've got to know what's on their mind. And so, therefore, we must give the FBI the ability to track calls when they make calls from different phones, for example.

Now, this is what we do for drug dealers and members of organized crime, and it seems . . . to make sense to me, if it's good enough for the FBI to use these techniques for facing down those threats to America, that now that we're at war, we ought to give the FBI the tools necessary to track down terrorists. And so I hope Congress will listen to the wisdom of the proposals that the Attorney General brought up, to give the tools necessary to our agents in the field to find those who may think they want to disrupt America again.

We're asking Congress for the authority to hold suspected terrorists who are in the process of being deported, until they're deported. That seems to make sense—that if a suspected terrorist is detained, and our nation has decided to deport the person, then they ought to be held in custody until the action actually takes place. We believe it's a necessary tool to make America a safe place.

Now, this would of course be closely supervised by an immigration judge. . . . The only alternative is to let suspected terrorists loose in our country. I don't think anybody wants to do that. I certainly hope not. And we're asking for the authority to share information between intelligence operations and law enforcement, so we can direct the best of both in the critical effort. That, too, is a reasonable request to make of Congress.

I want you to know that every one of the proposals we've made on Capitol Hill, carried by the Attorney General, has been carefully reviewed. They are measured requests, they are responsible requests, they are constitutional requests. Ours is a land that values the constitutional rights of every citizen. And we will honor those rights, of course.

But we're at war, a war we're going to win. And in order to win the war, we must make sure that the law enforcement men and women have got the tools necessary, within the Constitution, to defeat the enemy.

And there's going to be one other thing that's required to defeat the enemy, and that's the will and determination of the American people. I believe the evildoers miscalculated when they struck America. They thought we would shy away. They thought their threats could hold this nation hostage. They must have felt like they could diminish our soul. But quite the opposite has taken place. They've strengthened the spirit of America. They have united the country. They have awoken a mighty nation that understands that freedom is under assault; a mighty nation that will not rest until those who think they can take freedom away from any citizen in the world are brought to justice.

They've got a problem on their hands. We're going to find them. And if they're hiding, we're going to smoke them out. And we'll bring them to justice. And not only will we bring them to justice, we will bring those who harbor them, who hide them, who feed them, who encourage them, to justice.

America is a nation built upon freedom, and the principles of freedom, the values of freedom. And this is a nation that will not—will not—blink from the fight. This is a nation that will stand strong for the great values that have made us unique.

I'm proud of the work of the FBI. I want to thank you all for your dedication. Stay at it. The nation is counting on you. You're making a great, great contribution for the country.

May God bless you all and your families, and may God continue to bless the United States of America.

## Excerpted Remarks by the President from Speech to Employees of the Central Intelligence Agency
### September 26, 2001

We are on a mission to make sure that freedom is enduring. We're on a mission to say to the rest of the world, come with us—come with us, stand by our side to defeat the evil-doers who would like to rid the world of freedom as we know it. There is no better institute to be working with than the Central Intelligence Agency, which serves as our ears and our eyes all around the world.

This is a war that is unlike any other war that our nation is used to. It's a war of a series of battles [where] sometimes we'll see the fruits of our labors, and sometimes we won't. It's a war that's going to require cooperation with our friends. It is a war that requires the best of intelligence. You see, the enemy is sometimes hard to find; they like to hide. They think they can hide—but we know better.

This is a war [against] those who believe they can disrupt American lives—or, for that matter, any society that believes in freedom. . . . It's also a war that [issues] a new declaration, that says if you harbor a terrorist you're just as guilty as the terrorist; if you provide safe haven to a terrorist, you're just as guilty as the terrorist; if you fund a terrorist, you're just as guilty as a terrorist.

And in order to make sure that we're able to conduct a winning [war], we've got to have the best intelligence we can possibly have. And my report to the nation is, we've got the best intelligence we can possibly have thanks to the men and women of the CIA.

The cooperation with Capitol Hill is unique and, I hope, lasting. I can't tell you how much I appreciate the work of Senator Daschle and Senator Lott, Speaker Hastert and Leader Gephardt. There's deep concern amongst Republicans and Democrats on Capitol Hill to do what's right for America . . .to come together to provide the necessary support for an effective war.

And that includes making sure that the CIA is well-funded, well-staffed, has . . . the latest in technology. I believe we can work together to make sure that that's the case. After all, as America is learning, the CIA is on the front line of making sure our victory will be secure.

I intend to continue to work with Congress to make sure that our law enforcement officials at home have . . . the tools necessary—obviously, within the confines of our Constitution—to make sure the homeland is secure; to make sure America can live as peacefully as possible; to make sure that we run down every threat, take [seriously] every incident. And we've got to make sure, as well, that those who work for the nation overseas have got the best available technologies and the best tools and the best funding possible.

There is a good spirit on Capitol Hill because Americans want to win. They want to win the first war of the 21st century. And win we must—we have no choice, we can't relent. Now, there's going to be a time, hopefully in the near future, where people say, gosh, my life is almost normal; September 11th is a sad memory, but it's a memory.

But those of us on the front lines of this war must never forget September 11th. And that includes the men and women of the CIA. We must never forget that this is a long struggle, that there are evil people in the world who hate America. And we won't relent. The folks who [attacked] our country on September 11th made a big mistake. They underestimated America. They underestimated our resolve, our determination, our love for freedom. . . .

I know how hard you're working. And I hope all the Americans who are listening to this TV broadcast understand how hard you're working, too. You're giving your best shot, long hours, all your brain power, to [wage] a war that we're going to win. And I can't thank you enough on behalf of the American people.

Keep doing it. America relies upon your intelligence and your judgment. America relies upon our capacity to work together as a nation to do what the American people expect. They expect a 100 percent effort, a full-time, non-stop effort on not only securing our homeland, but [on] bringing to justice terrorists, no matter where they live, no matter where they hide. And that's exactly what we're going to do.

Thank you very much. May God bless your work, and may God bless America.

# October 2001

**Excerpted Remarks by the President from Speech to the
Employees of the Federal Emergency Management Agency**
October 1, 2001

I . . . want to talk about the battle we face, the campaign to protect freedom; the willingness of the American people to not only repair the damage done, but the willingness of our nation to stand united, to say loud and clear that freedom will stand; that you can tear down our buildings, but you can't tear down our spirit; that we're strong and united in the cause of freedom not only here in America, but all around the world.

This will be a different kind of campaign than Americans are used to. It's a campaign that must be fought on many fronts. And I'm proud to report that we're making progress on many fronts. . . .

As you may remember, I made it clear that part of winning the war against terror would be to cut off these evil people's money; it would be to trace their assets and freeze them, cut off their cash flows, hold people accountable who fund them, who allow the funds to go through their institutions; and not only do that at home, but to convince others around the world to join us in doing so.

Thus far, we've frozen $6 million in bank accounts linked to terrorist activity. We've frozen thirty al Qaeda accounts in the United States and twenty overseas. And we're just beginning.

As I said, this is a different kind of war. It's hard to fight a guerrilla war with [conventional] forces. But our military is ready. And as I said to the Congress, they will make us proud.

In this new kind of war, one that requires a coalition, we're making good progress on the diplomatic front. At our request, the United Nations unanimously enacted a binding resolution requiring all its members to deny [financial] support or safe harbor to terrorists. We've had forty-six declarations of support from organizations, including NATO, the Association of Southeast Asian Nations, the Organization of Islamic Conference, and the Organization of American States.

You see, the evildoers like to hit and then they try to hide. And slowly, but surely, we're going to make sure they have no place to hide. Slowly, but surely, we're going to move them out of their holes and what they think is safe havens, and get them on the move.

We're a patient nation. We're a nation who has got a long-term view; a nation that's come to realize that in order to make freedom prevail, the evildoers will be forced to run, and will eventually be brought to justice.

Now, along those lines, we're taking any threat seriously here at home. The FBI has conducted hundreds of interviews and searches, issued hundreds of subpoenas, and arrested or detained more than four hundred people as it investigates the attacks. About one hundred fifty terrorists and their supporters, as well, have been arrested or detained in twenty five different countries.

In my speech to the Congress, I said, sometimes the American people aren't going to see exactly what's taking place on their TV screens. But slowly, but surely, the results are coming in. You see, we've said to people around the world, this could have happened to you, this could have easily have taken place on your soil, so you need to take threats seriously, as well.

We're beginning to share intelligence amongst our nations. We're finding out members of the al Qaeda organization, who they are, where they think they can hide. And we're slowly, but surely, bringing them to justice. We're slowly, but surely, calling their hand and reining them in.

We've just begun. There's one hundred fifty detained, and more to come. And along these lines, this weekend, through the collaborative efforts of intelligence and law enforcement, we've arrested a known terrorist who was responsible for the deaths of two U.S. citizens during a hijacking in 1986. This terrorist, by the name of Zayd Hassin Safarini, is not affiliated with al Qaeda. Yet he's an example of the wider war on terrorism and what we intend to do.

Here's a man who killed two of our own citizens when he hijacked a plane in Pakistan. . . . [H]e was convicted and sentenced to death. Yet he only served fourteen years. Well, we arrested him; we got him; we brought him into Alaska. And today the United States of America will charge him with murder.

Sometimes we'll have success in the near-term; sometimes we have to be patient. Sometimes we'll be able to round somebody up who threatens us today; sometimes it may take us a while to catch him. But the lesson of this case, and every case, is that this mighty nation won't rest until we protect our-selves, our citizens, and freedom-loving people around the world.

The evildoers struck, and when they did, they aroused a mighty land, a land of compassionate people, a land [that] wants to help a neighbor in need, but a land [that] stands solidly on principles—the principles of freedom—freedom to worship, freedom to govern, freedom to speak, freedom to assemble.

We sent a loud message to the world: We will not be cowed by a few. We sent another message to the world: Together we're going to bring these peo-ple to justice. And that's exactly what we're going to do.

Thank you for your hard work. I want to thank you all so very much for your hard work and for your love for America. May God bless you all. May God continue to bless America. Thank you very much.

## Excerpted Remarks by the President from Speech to the Employees of the Department of Labor
October 4, 2001

The evildoers struck: . . . they may have hurt our buildings, and they are obvi-ously affecting some family lives in such a profound and sad way. But they will not touch the soul of America. They cannot dim our spirit.

We've got a job to do, all of us. And I'm here to thank you in the Department of Labor for your hard work, your concern for your fellow Americans. All of us, from the President all the way throughout our govern-ment, must be diligent and strong and unwavering in our determination and our dedication to win the war on terrorism.

I've got a job to do, and that's to explain to the American people the truth. And the truth is that we're now facing a new threat [to] freedom; that on September 11th, war was declared on the United States, not by a religious group, not by one country versus another, but by people motivated by evil. And I'm going to make it clear to the world what I made clear to America, that this great country will not let evil stand.

The attack on our land roused a mighty nation. We've never been united as we are today. And we're examining a lot of things. We're examining, as moms and dads, what it means to be a parent. There are many Americans on bended knee, from all different religions, praying to an almighty God. We're a nation united in our conviction that we must find those evildoers and bring them to jus-tice. We seek not revenge; in America, we seek justice.

Americans understand that this is a different type of campaign; it's a different type of struggle to defeat an enemy that's sometimes hard to see, and sometimes hard to find. But what the enemy has found out is we're a determined people, and we're patient, and we will do what it takes to bring them to justice.

We built a vast coalition of nations from all around the world to join us—nations which understand that what happened in New York and Washington could happen to them, as well. They understand it's now time to unite to defeat evil. Each nation comes with a different set of capabilities and a different willingness to help. America says, we don't care how you help, just help. Either you're for us, or you're against us.

And the progress to date has been positive, really positive. We've got nations around the world willing to join us in cutting off the money of the evil ones. Our attitude is, if they can't fund evil deeds, they're not going to be able to affect freedom. And so we're talking to countries and banks and financial institutions, and saying either you're with us, or against us: Cut off their money.

We're applying diplomatic pressure . . . around the world. I promise you this: I will enforce the doctrine that says that if you house a terrorist, you're just as guilty as the terrorists themselves. This is our calling. This is our nation's time to lead the world, and we're going to do that. And we must do so in a bold and strong and determined fashion. We will not waver.

I fully understand, as I said to Congress, there will be times when people feel a sense of normalcy—and I hope that happens sooner rather than later—and that September 11th may be a distant memory to some. But not to me, and not to this nation. Now is the time—now is the time to root out evil so that our children and grandchildren can live with freedom as the beacon all around the world.

The evildoers cost America a lot of lives. And for the two here in the Labor Department, I say, we will get justice, and we grieve with you—two good folks who suffer as a result of September the 11th. I can't tell you how many people are praying for you and praying for the victims all across America; people you can't even imagine, will never know, are on bended knee.

And they've also changed a lot of lives, these evil actions. It's clear, as a result of today's new unemployment claims, that the attack of September the 11th sent a shock wave throughout our economy. And we need to do something about it. And I'm going to lead the Congress in a way that provides the help and stimulus necessary for there to be economic growth.

It is not time to worry about partisan politics here in America. It is time for our government to continue to work together—to say, we hear the cries of those who have been laid off; we worry about the shock waves throughout our economy, and instead of talking, we're going to do something about it. . . .

We know what we need to do. And I look forward to working with both Republicans and Democrats to get it done. It's the right thing for the American people. And there is no question that not only should our government act to encourage economic growth, our government [should] act to take care of people whose lives were affected on September the 11th. . . .

Congress [must] work together to help the American people, stimulate growth, and at the same time, take care of the workers whose lives have been impacted by the September 11th attack.

And that's what we must do. Because, you see, the terrorists hope to change our way of life. On the one hand, they hope that America would become timid and cower in the face of their barbaric acts. They were wrong. On the other hand, they [hoped] that we'd become paralyzed and unable to act at home in order to do what's right for the American people. They were wrong again.

Instead, they have provided interesting opportunities for America. I told some world leaders, through our tears we see opportunity; that we're sad and angry, but we've got a clear vision of the world; that this is a remarkable moment in history, which our nation will seize. We'll act boldly at home to encourage economic growth. We'll take care of people who hurt. We will comfort those who lost [loved ones]. We'll be compassionate as to how we deal with Afghan citizens, for example, by making sure there's humanitarian aid.

And we'll be tough and resolute as we unite, to make sure freedom stands, to rout out evil, to say to our children and grandchildren, we were bold enough to act, without tiring, so that you can live in a great land and in a peaceful world.

And there's no doubt in my mind, not one doubt in my mind, that we will fail. Failure is not a part of our vocabulary. This great nation will lead the world and we will be successful.

Thank you for working for the government. Thank you for caring about our fellow Americans. May God bless you all and your families, and may God bless America.

## Presidential Radio Address to the Nation
### October 6, 2001

Good morning. Today I want to update Americans on our global campaign against terror. The United States is presenting a clear choice to every nation:

Stand with the civilized world, or stand with the terrorists. And for those nations that stand with the terrorists, there will be a heavy price.

America is determined to oppose the state sponsors of terror. Yet we are equally determined to respect and help the men and women those regimes oppress. Our enemy is not the Arab world. Many friendly Arab governments are, themselves, the targets of extremist terror. Our enemy is not Islam, a good and peace-loving faith, that brings direction and comfort to over one billion people, including millions of Americans. And our enemy is not the people of any nation, even when their leaders harbor terrorists. Our enemy is the terrorists themselves, and the regimes that shelter and sustain them.

Afghanistan is a case in point. Its Taliban regime has made that nation into a sanctuary and training ground for international terrorists—terrorists who have killed innocent citizens of many nations, including our own. The Taliban promotes terror abroad, and practices terror against its people, oppressing women and persecuting all who dissent.

The Taliban has been given the opportunity to surrender all the terrorists in Afghanistan and to close down their camps and operations. Full warning has been given, and time is running out.

The Afghan people, however, are the victims of oppression, famine, and misrule. Many refugees from that unfortunate nation are on the move, and sadly, many Afghans are on the verge of starvation.

America respects the Afghan people, their long tradition and their proud independence. And we will help them in this time of confusion and crisis in their country.

America has long been the largest source of food and humanitarian assistance to Afghanistan. This week I announced an additional $320 million in aid to the Afghan people, to those within Afghanistan and those who have fled across borders. Despite efforts by the Taliban to disrupt these critical aid shipments, we will deliver food and seeds, vaccines and medicines by truck, and even by draft animals. Conditions permitting, we will bring help directly to the people of Afghanistan by air drops.

This aid will help Afghans make it through the upcoming winter. For the longer term, I urge Congress to make funds available so that one day the United States can contribute, along with other friends of Afghanistan, to the reconstruction and development of that troubled nation.

Helping people in great need is a central part of the Jewish, Christian, and Islamic traditions, as well as many other faiths. It is also a central part of the American tradition. Even as we fight evil regimes, we are generous to the people they oppress. Following World War II, America fed and rebuilt Japan and

Germany, and their people became some of our closest friends in the world.

In the struggle ahead, we will act in accordance with American ideals. We're offering help and friendship to the Afghan people. It is their Taliban rulers, and the terrorists they harbor, who have much to fear.

## Presidential Address to the Nation
October 7, 2001

Good afternoon. On my orders, the United States military has begun strikes against al Qaeda terrorist training camps and military installations of the Taliban regime in Afghanistan. These carefully targeted actions are designed to disrupt the use of Afghanistan as a terrorist base of operations, and to attack the military capability of the Taliban regime.

We are joined in this operation by our staunch friend, Great Britain. Other close friends, including Canada, Australia, Germany, and France, have pledged forces as the operation unfolds. More than 40 countries in the Middle East, Africa, Europe, and across Asia have granted air-transit or landing rights. Many more have shared intelligence. We are supported by the collective will of the world.

More than two weeks ago, I gave Taliban leaders a series of clear and specific demands: Close terrorist training camps; hand over leaders of the al Qaeda network; and return all foreign nationals, including American citizens, unjustly detained in your country. None of these demands were met. And now the Taliban will pay a price. By destroying camps and disrupting communications, we will make it more difficult for the terror network to train new recruits and coordinate their evil plans.

Initially, the terrorists may burrow deeper into caves and other entrenched hiding places. Our military action is also designed to clear the way for sustained, comprehensive, and relentless operations to drive them out and bring them to justice.

At the same time, the oppressed people of Afghanistan will know the generosity of America and our allies. As we strike military targets, we'll also drop food, medicine, and supplies to the starving and suffering men and women and children of Afghanistan.

The United States of America is a friend to the Afghan people, and we are the friends of almost a billion worldwide who practice the Islamic faith. The United States of America is an enemy of those who aid terrorists and of the barbaric criminals who profane a great religion by committing murder in its name.

This military action is a part of our campaign against terrorism, another front in a war that has already been joined through diplomacy, intelligence, the freezing of financial assets, and the arrests of known terrorists by law-enforcement agents in 38 countries. Given the nature and reach of our enemies, we will win this conflict by the patient accumulation of successes, by meeting a series of challenges with determination and will and purpose.

Today we focus on Afghanistan, but the battle is broader. Every nation has a choice to make. In this conflict, there is no neutral ground. If any government sponsors the outlaws and killers of innocents, they have become outlaws and murderers, themselves. And they will take that lonely path at their own peril.

I'm speaking to you today from the Treaty Room of the White House, a place where American Presidents have worked for peace. We're a peaceful nation. Yet, as we have learned, so suddenly and so tragically, there can be no peace in a world of sudden terror. In the face of today's new threat, the only way to pursue peace is to pursue those who threaten it.

We did not ask for this mission, but we will fulfill it. The name of today's military operation is Enduring Freedom. We defend not only our precious freedoms, but also the freedom of people everywhere to live and raise their children free from fear.

I know many Americans feel fear today. And our government is taking strong precautions. All law-enforcement and intelligence agencies are working aggressively around America, around the world, and around the clock. At my request, many governors have activated the National Guard to strengthen airport security. We have called up Reserves to reinforce our military capability and strengthen the protection of our homeland.

In the months ahead, our patience will be one of our strengths—patience with the long waits that will result from tighter security; patience and understanding that it will take time to achieve our goals; patience in all the sacrifices that may come.

Today, those sacrifices are being made by members of our Armed Forces who now defend us so far from home, and by their proud and worried families. A Commander-in-Chief sends America's sons and daughters into a battle in a foreign land only after the greatest care and a lot of prayer. We ask a lot of those who wear our uniform. We ask them to leave their loved ones, to travel great distances, to risk injury, even to be prepared to make the ultimate sacrifice of their lives. They are dedicated, they are honorable; they represent the best of our country. And we are grateful.

To all the men and women in our military—every sailor, every soldier, every airman, every coastguardsman, every Marine—I say this: Your mission is defined; your objectives are clear; your goal is just. You have my full confidence, and you will have every tool you need to carry out your duty.

I recently received a touching letter that says a lot about the state of America in these difficult times—a letter from a 4th-grade girl, with a father in the military: "As much as I don't want my Dad to fight," she wrote, "I'm willing to give him to you."

This is a precious gift, the greatest she could give. This young girl knows what America is all about. Since September 11, an entire generation of young Americans has gained new understanding of the value of freedom, and its cost in duty and in sacrifice.

The battle is now joined on many fronts. We will not waver; we will not tire; we will not falter; and we will not fail. Peace and freedom will prevail.

Thank you. May God continue to bless America.


## Excerpted Remarks by the President from Speech at the National Fallen Firefighters Memorial Tribute
Emmitsburg, Maryland
October 7, 2001

I want to thank the local officials who are here. I want to thank the firefighters from all around America who have come to comfort the families of the fallen.

I want to say hello to moms and dads and husbands and wives and sons and daughters of the fallen. Laura and I are honored to be here with you today, as we remember the lives and sacrifices of your brave relatives.

Two years ago this weekend, I attended a memorial ceremony in New York City honoring fallen firefighters. And standing nearby were Chief Peter Ganci and many others who are now gone. None of us on that day could have imagined what was to come, the scale of the emergency, the enormity of the danger, the magnitude of the evil. Yet, each one of those firefighters felt a strong calling and knew its risks.

On September 11th, that calling led them into burning towers on a mission of rescue. Within a single hour, more than 300 firefighters were lost. And our nation still mourns. They did not live to know who had caused the destruction, or why. They only knew their duty. And that was to go in, to follow the faintest cry, to search for the trapped and helpless, and to save those who could be saved.

A few days ago, one New Yorker described firefighters as "the kind of guys you look up to." Every one of you here [know] exactly what he meant. The courage and loss we saw in New York is found in every community that has laid a firefighter to rest. Hardly a week passes in America when a career or a volunteer firefighter does not fall in the line of duty.

Fire-fighting is a hard and demanding job. And it may at any moment send a person to the high heat or thick smoke. It's been said that a firefighter's first act of bravery is taking the oath to serve. And all of them serve, knowing that one day they may not come home.

Today we honor 101 who did not come home. They were all people who accepted the dangers of fire-fighting, and were last seen on duty. We add their names to this national monument. We do so with pride, and with deep gratitude.

The nation pays respect to them for their service and their sacrifice. And we respect you, their families, for your sacrifice—for the heavy burden you carry to this day. The McCormicks of Arkansas; the Hendricks of Kentucky; the Pascatores of Pennsylvania—each lost a son who was not yet twenty years old. The families of Bo Rathbun of Wyoming; Jim Reavis of Missouri; Fred Brain and Pete Scannell of New York; Kenneth Jesse of Pennslyvania, lost loved ones who were willing to serve, even in the latter years of life.

Many were taken during the fullest days of life, that time when we are needed most by the people we love. Kimberly Smith of Texas was engaged to be married. Robert Crump of Colorado was home after honorable service in the Marine Corps. Marvin Bartholemew of Florida had paid his way through college and was working his way up the ranks of the department.

Roger Bookout was 34 years old when he died, and he was a loving dad. He had a great outlook, and it was summed up on a sign he kept on his locker— "Love your wife; love your life." All these firefighters loved life. And Scripture teaches, there is no greater love than to lay down one's life for another.

Sometimes a person cannot know for sure what mark he or she has left on the world. That will never be said of the people we remember today, or of their kind. They were strong and caring people, brave and upright. You could always count on them. You could always look up to them.

This firefighters monument belongs to the nation, and represents a national loss. The firefighters belong to you. And I know that loss can never be recovered.

A fireman's widow recently said that her husband was her hero, "and there's nothing I wouldn't do to have my hero here." That same feeling is shared by many here today, and time won't ever take it away. But the years can bring comfort—and they can bring hope. You'll always know that your hero died in the service of others. You can give one another the strength to go on. You can find the comfort of God, who is with us, especially in sorrow. And you can know today that your loved ones are not forgotten. They hold an honored, cherished place in the memories of their comrades, and an honored place in the memory of our country. God bless you all.

### Excerpted Remarks by the President from Speech at the Swearing-in Ceremony for Governor Thomas Ridge
October 8, 2001

Together, we will confront the threat of terrorism. We will take strong precautions aimed at preventing terrorist attacks and prepare to respond effectively if they . . . come again. We will defend our country; and while we do so, we will not sacrifice the freedoms that make our land unique. . . .

We face a united, determined enemy. We must have a united and determined response. The Homeland Security Office has a series of specific goals and will have my authority to meet them. One, take the strongest possible precautions against terrorism by bringing together the best information and intelligence. In the war on terror, knowledge is power.

Strengthen and help protect our transportation systems, our food and water systems, and our critical infrastructure by making them less vulnerable to attack. Respond effectively to terrorist actions if they come. The Office will coordinate federal assistance with state and local efforts. America is going to be prepared.

The Office will work in conjunction with the new Homeland Security Council, chaired by me and made up of my Cabinet and other senior officials; the Office mission will have the full attention and complete support of the very highest levels of our government.

I know that many Americans at this time have fears. We've learned that America is not immune from attack. We've seen that evil is real. It's hard for us to comprehend the mentality of people that will destroy innocent folks the way they have. Yet, America is equal to this challenge, make no mistake about it. They've roused a mighty giant. A compassionate land will rise united . . . not only [to] protect ourselves, not only [to] make our homeland as secure as possible—but to bring the evildoers to justice so that our children might live in freedom.

## Excerpted Remarks by the President from Speech Unveiling "Most Wanted" Terrorist List
FBI Headquarters, Washington, D.C.
October 10, 2001

I'm pleased to be back at the FBI to unveil a new line of attack on our war against terrorism: The Most Wanted Terrorist list.

Terrorists try to operate in the shadows. They try to hide. But we're going to shine the light of justice on them. We list their names, we publicize their pictures, we rob them of their secrecy. Terrorism has a face, and today we expose it for the world to see.

The men on the wall here have put themselves on the list because of great acts of evil. They plan, promote, and commit murder. They fill the minds of others with hate and lies. And by their cruelty and violence, they betray whatever faith they espouse.

These 22 individuals do not account for all the terrorist activity in the world, but they're among the most dangerous: The leaders and key supporters, the planners and strategists. They must be found; they will be stopped; and they will be punished

This effort is part of a worldwide assault on terror. All our allies and friends will now be familiar with these evildoers and their associates. For those who join our coalition, we expect results. And a good place to start—help us bring these folks to justice.

Eventually, no corner of the world will be dark enough to hide in. I want to thank all the State Department employees for helping to build an unprecedented—I mean *unprecedented*—coalition to stand with us for freedom. I want to thank the American people for understanding that we are engaged in a new war, a war that will require a new way of thinking.

There is a fascination about the conventional aspects of the military operations that are taking place now, and I can understand that. But the American people must understand that we're making great progress [on] other fronts: That we're halting their money, that we've got allies around the world helping us close the net. And today, by shining the spotlight on the first 22, it's going to make it more likely they will be brought to justice.

I say "the first 22" because our war is not just against 22 individuals. Our war is against networks and groups, people who coddle them, people who try to hide them, people who fund them. This is our calling. This is the calling of the United States of America, the [freest] nation in the world. A nation built on fundamental values that rejects hate, rejects violence, rejects murderers, rejects evil. And we will not tire. We will not relent. It is not only important for the homeland security of America that we succeed, it is equally as important for generations of Americans who have yet to be born.

Now is the time to draw the line in the sand against the evil ones. And this government is committed to doing just that.

I also want to remind my fellow Americans as we round up the evildoers, as we look for those who might harm our fellow Americans, we must remember not to violate the rights of the innocent.

Our war is not against a religion. Our war is against evil. There are thousands of Muslim Americans who love America just as much as I do. And we will respect their rights. We will not let the terrorists cause decay of the fundamental rights that make our nation unique. As a matter of fact, what they'll find out is that our nation has responded in a way they never envisioned. We're united. People of all faiths, all religions, all areas of our country are united in the common effort to stamp out evil where we find it. It is the right thing to do. It is the right course of action for our nation and the world, and I want to thank you all for helping.

## Excerpted Remarks by the President from Speech at the Department of Defense Service of Remembrance
October 11, 2001

We have come here to pay our respects to 125 men and women who died in the service of America. We also remember 64 passengers on a hijacked plane; those men and women, boys and girls who fell into the hands of evildoers, and also died here exactly one month ago.

On September 11th, great sorrow came to our country. And from that sorrow has come great resolve. Today, we are a nation awakened to the evil of terrorism, and determined to destroy it. That work began the moment we were attacked; and it will continue until justice is delivered.

Americans are returning, as we must, to the normal pursuits of life. But we know that if you lost a son or daughter here, or a husband, or a wife, or a mom or dad, life will never again be as it was. The loss was sudden, and hard, and permanent. So difficult to explain. So difficult to accept.

Three schoolchildren traveling with their teacher. An Army general. A budget analyst who reported to work here for thirty years. A lieutenant commander in the Naval Reserve who left behind a wife, a four-year-old son, and another child on the way.

One life touches so many others. One death can leave sorrow that seems almost unbearable. But to all of you who lost someone here, I want to say: You are not alone. The American people will never forget the cruelty that was done here and in New York, and in the sky over Pennsylvania.

We will never forget all the innocent people killed by the hatred of a few. We know the loneliness you feel in your loss. The entire nation shares in your sadness. And we pray for you and your loved ones. And we will always honor their memory.

The hijackers were instruments of evil who died in vain. Behind them is a cult of evil which seeks to harm the innocent and thrives on human suffering. Theirs is the worst kind of cruelty, the cruelty that is fed, not weakened, by tears. Theirs is the worst kind of violence, pure malice, while daring to claim the authority of God. We cannot fully understand the designs and power of evil. It is enough to know that evil, like goodness, exists. And in the terrorists, evil has found a willing servant.

In New York, the terrorists chose as their target a symbol of America's freedom and confidence. Here, they struck a symbol of our strength in the world. And the attack on the Pentagon, on that day, was more symbolic than they knew. It was on another September 11th—September 11th, 1941—that construction on this building first began. America was just then awakening to another menace: The Nazi terror in Europe.

And on that very night, President Franklin Roosevelt spoke to the nation. The danger, he warned, has long ceased to be a mere possibility. The danger is here now. Not only from a military enemy, but from an enemy of all law, all liberty, all morality, all religion.

For us too, in the year 2001, an enemy has emerged that rejects every limit of law, morality, and religion. The terrorists have no true home in any country, or culture, or faith. They dwell in dark corners of earth. And there, we will find them.

This week, I have called the Armed Forces into action. One by one, we are eliminating power centers of a regime that harbors al Qaeda terrorists. We gave that regime a choice: Turn over the terrorists, or face your ruin. They chose unwisely.

The Taliban regime has brought nothing but fear and misery to the people of Afghanistan. These rulers call themselves holy men, even with their record of drawing money from heroin trafficking. They consider themselves pious and devout, while subjecting women to fierce brutality.

The Taliban has allied itself with murderers and [given] them shelter. But today, for al Qaeda and the Taliban, there is no shelter. As Americans did 60 years ago, we have entered a struggle of uncertain duration. But now, as then, we can be certain of the outcome, because we have a number of decisive assets.

We have a unified country. We have the patience to fight and win on many fronts: Blocking terrorist plans, seizing their funds, arresting their networks, disrupting their communications, opposing their sponsors. And we have one more great asset in this cause: The brave men and women of the United States military.

From my first days in this office, I have felt and seen the strong spirit of the Armed Forces. I saw it at Fort Stewart, Georgia, when I first reviewed our troops as Commander-in-Chief, and looked into the faces of proud and determined soldiers. I saw it in Annapolis on a graduation day, at Camp Pendleton in California, Camp Bondsteel in Kosovo. And I have seen this spirit at the Pentagon, before and after the attack on this building.

You've responded to a great emergency with calm and courage. And for that, your country honors you. A Commander-in-Chief must know that he can count on the skill and readiness of servicemen and women at every point in the chain of command. You have given me that confidence.

And I give you these commitments. The wound to this building will not be forgotten, but it will be repaired. Brick by brick, we will quickly rebuild the Pentagon. In the missions ahead for the military, you will have everything you need, every resource, every weapon, every means to assure full victory for the United States and the cause of freedom.

And I pledge to you that America will never relent [in] this war against terror. There will be times of swift, dramatic action. There will be times of steady, quiet progress. Over time, with patience, and precision, the terrorists will be pursued. They will be isolated, surrounded, cornered, until there is no place to run, or hide, or rest.

As military and civilian personnel in the Pentagon, you are an important part of the struggle we have entered. You know the risks of your calling, and you have willingly accepted them. You believe in our country, and our country believes in you.

Within sight of this building is Arlington Cemetery, the final resting place of many thousands who died for our country over the generations. Enemies of America have now added to these graves, and they wish to add more. Unlike our enemies, we value every life, and we mourn every loss.

Yet we're not afraid. Our cause is just, and worthy of sacrifice. Our nation is strong of heart, firm of purpose. Inspired by all the courage that has come before, we will meet our moment and we will prevail.

May God bless you all, and may God bless America.

### Excerpted Remarks by the President from
### Speech to the California Business Association
Sacramento, California
October 17, 2001

Now, there's the long version, and there's a short version. So I'm going to start with the short version: Our people are united; our government is determined; our cause is right; and justice will be done.

This great state is known for its diversity—people of all races, all religions, and all nationalities. They've come here to live a better life, to find freedom, to live in peace and security, with tolerance and with justice. When the terrorists attacked America, this is what they attacked. And when we defend America, this is what we defend.

We are fighting for the security of our people, for the success of our ideals, and for stability in large parts of the world. We fight evil people who are distorting and betraying a great religion to justify . . . murder. Our cause is just. We will not tire. We will not falter. And, my fellow Americans, we will not fail.

New York City and Washington, D.C., are 2,500 miles from here. Yet, for all of us, an American is an American, no matter where we live, no matter what our race, no matter how we pray. The people of New York and Washington are our neighbors, and when terrorists attack them, they attack us all. And the terrorists are hearing from us all.

They are hearing from a compassionate nation—a nation that sends food and medicine to starving people of Afghanistan; a nation whose children—and I know we've got some here who have raised money at the elementary school—whose children are sending their dollars to save the children of Afghanistan.

They are hearing from a tolerant nation, a nation that respects Islam and values our many Muslim citizens. They are hearing from a prayerful nation, a nation that prays to an almighty God for protection and for peace. And they are hearing from a patient and determined nation, a nation that will continue this war for as long as it takes to win.

Ours will be a broad campaign, fought on many fronts. It's a campaign that will be waged by day and by night, in the light and in the shadow, in battles you will see and battles you won't see. It's a campaign waged by soldiers and sailors, Marines and airmen; and also by FBI agents and law-enforcement officials and diplomats and intelligence officers. It's a campaign that is being waged in distant lands, and a campaign being waged by our new Office of Homeland Security.

To keep us safe, we're working around the clock. We're on the lookout. We have questioned and detained more than 750 terror suspects and material witnesses in our country. And the broad coalition we put together has detained hundreds of suspected members of the al Qaeda organization. Our world coalition is working. We are taking apart the terrorist network, piece by piece. We're taking away their money by freezing their assets and choking off their incomes.

Our campaign will be difficult, and it's going to take time. But I can promise you this: It will be waged with determination, and it will be waged until we win. We will do whatever it takes to protect our country, protect . . . good American families. And we will do whatever it takes to punish those who have attacked us.

We'll do whatever it takes to defeat terror abroad, wherever it grows or wherever it hides. In Afghanistan, our Armed Forces are performing their duty with skill and success. We've destroyed many terrorist camps. We've damaged the Taliban's air defenses. We've seriously weakened all those in Afghanistan who wish to inflict harm on people anywhere in the world.

We're paving the way for friendly troops to defeat the Taliban and root out the al Qaeda parasites that the Taliban hosts and protects. We're enforcing the doctrine that says this: If you harbor the terrorists, you are guilty of terror. And like the terrorists, you will be held responsible.

We are not alone in this struggle. The war against terrorism is an international war, and we're fighting with a broad, broad coalition. Many nations around the world have joined with us in this cause, including nations from the Islamic world.

Some countries contribute intelligence. Some help with law enforcement. Some join with military power, like our friend Great Britain. We are supported by the conscience of the world. And we are surrounding terrorists and their sponsors in a tightening net of justice.

The terrorists want us to stop our lives—that's what they want. They want us to stop flying, and they want us to stop buying. But this great nation will not be intimidated by the evildoers.

America will do whatever it takes to get our economy moving again. These are difficult times. Too many Americans are hurting. Too many are worried about their jobs and their businesses. And I know that California has been hit especially hard. America has got great resources, though. We've got the most skilled workers in the world, the best work force. Taxpayers have just received their rebates. Interest rates have been cut to the lowest level in years. Energy prices are declining. The entrepreneurial spirit has never been stronger in America. The basics of our economy are ripe for growth.

Yet recent events have been a shock, no question about it, have shocked our economy. And people need help. And the government in Washington is actively responding. We've already announced additional spending to rebuild New York and the Pentagon, to stabilize our airline industry, and to make sure we have enough money to defend our country. And I'll work with Congress to help workers who have lost their jobs because of the sudden economic slowdown.

I've outlined [an] additional economic-stimulus package. I've listened carefully to members from both political parties. It's a package that will provide a needed lift for our economy. I urge Congress to act now to accelerate the tax relief we've already planned for the years ahead, so consumers will have more money to spend. I urge Congress to have more tax relief for lower- and moderate-income families in America who are especially hard hit. And I urge Congress to reform the corporate income tax, and as well, [to] allow businesses to deduct more of the costs of new investments immediately, so as to create jobs for American people.

And I ask Congress to now act on an energy bill that the House of Representatives passed back in August. This is an issue of special importance to California. Too much of our energy comes from the Middle East. The plan I sent up to Congress promotes conservation, expands energy supplies, and improves the efficiency of our energy network. Our country needs greater energy independence. This issue is a matter of national security, and I hope the Senate acts quickly.

On all these great issues, there's a spirit of respect and cooperation in Washington—I'm pleased to report. (Laughter and applause) This morning, I had breakfast with the four leaders of the Congress. And, while we have our differences, I do want you to know there is a strong determination to do what's right for the American people.

I have butted heads in the past—(laughter)—with the leadership. But I want you to know, I applaud their love for America and their determination—their determination—to get the people's business done in a way that will make you proud. We're making good progress about changing the tone. The terrorists thought they affected us, but they've only made this nation stronger.

Not only do I applaud the leadership, I applaud the American people for your courage in a time of trial. We're living through a unique moment in American history. This is a time of rediscovery, of heroism and sacrifice and duty and patriotism. These are core values of our country, and they're being renewed. We found them waiting for us just when we needed them.

Our forefathers would be proud, really proud of what they see in America today. They would be proud of the selfless duty of the fire-fighters and police officers of New York, fire-fighters and police officers all around our country, and the men and women who wear the uniform of the United States of America.

Our forefathers would salute the modern-day sacrifice of the brave passengers on Flight 93, who, after reciting the Lord's Prayer, said, "Let's roll," and stormed the hijackers, taking the plane down and probably saving thousands of lives on the ground.

Our forefathers would know and recognize the spirit of unity and patriotism everywhere in our country, and they would say, well done, America.

No, the true character of this great land has been revealed in adversity. Americans are generous to our neighbors in need. Americans are tolerant toward our fellow citizens of every background. Americans are alert to danger, but calm and determined in the work ahead. And Americans are reaching out across the world to say: We wage a war on the guilty, not the innocent. We're friends to people of all faiths and enemies only to those who choose to make enemies of us. . . .

Americans know we must act now. We must be strong and we must be decisive. We must stop the evil ones, so our children and grandchildren can know peace and security and freedom in the greatest nation on the face of the Earth.

Our nation has felt great sorrow. Yet this can be a time of great achievement. A great evil can be turned to greater good. The terrorists did not intend to create a new American spirit of unity and resolve, but they are powerless to stop it.

At my inaugural, I said that some Americans feel as if they share a continent, but not a country. We don't feel that any longer. We know we're one people; we know we're one country. We're united from coast to coast by a determination and a firm resolve to see that right prevails.

I will take that determination with me to meet leaders of the world in Shanghai. And America will take that determination all the way to victory.

Thank you for having me. God bless. Thank you all.

### Excerpted Remarks by the President from Speech to Military Personnel at Travis Air Force Base
October 17, 2001

The planes to the left and right of where we stand here represent the unmatched air power of the United States. But that's not our real strength. Our real strength are the people who fly them, and who maintain them, the people who make the military go. The real strength of this proud nation are the men and women who wear the uniform. That's the real strength of this country.

You're among the first to be deployed in America's new war against terror and against evil, and I want you to know, America is proud—proud of your deeds, proud of your talents, proud of your service to our country.

I'm told that one of the pilots here, a fellow named Randy, was asked if anyone at Travis had personal connections to any of the victims of the attacks on September the 11th. And here's what he said: I think we all do; they're all Americans. When you strike one American, you strike us all.

The victims of September 11th were innocent, and this nation will never forget them. The men and women who murdered them were instruments of evil, and they have died in vain. This nation is strong. This nation is united. This nation is resolved. This nation will defeat terror wherever we find it across the globe.

And not only will we find the terrorists, we will enforce the doctrine that says if you harbor a terrorist, you're a terrorist. If you feed a terrorist, if you fund a terrorist, you're a terrorist. And this great, proud nation of free men and women will hold you just as responsible for the actions that take place on American soil. And that's what's happening in Afghanistan. I gave the people in Afghanistan a choice. I said to the Taliban, turn them over, destroy the camps, free people you're unjustly holding. I said, you've got time to do it. But they didn't listen. They didn't respond, and now they're paying a price. They are learning that anyone who strikes America will hear from our military, and they're not going to like what they hear. In choosing their enemy, the evildoers and those who harbor them have chosen their fate.

We don't quarrel with the innocent folks of Afghanistan; they're not our enemy. Nor is any religion the enemy of the United States of America. The evil ones have tried to hijack a religion to justify their murder. But I want to assure the people of the world that our military fights not against Muslims or . . . the Islam religion; we fight against evil people. We fight against people who believe that they can harm the United States of America. We fight against people who have no country, no ideology; they're motivated by hate.

And make no mistake about it; this great nation will do what it takes to win. We are determined. We are patient. We are steadfast. We are resolved. We will not tire and we will not fail. . . .

And you must have confidence in this, my commitment: That for the mission that lies ahead, our military, the men and women who wear our uniform, will have everything [they] need to win—every resource, every weapon, every means to assure full victory for the United States and our allies and our friends in the cause of freedom.

There is no question that we're inflicting pain upon the Taliban government. There is also no question that we're a compassionate nation; at the same time we do so, we're dropping airlifts of food and medicine, so the innocent citizens of that country can survive the brutal winter.

As I walked up, I saw some of the schoolchildren here holding dollar bills. We've got schoolchildren all across the country out raising a dollar to send to the children of Afghanistan. We've got boys and girls from all religions and all walks of life who have heard the call to love a neighbor just as they'd like to be loved themselves.

The evildoers have struck our nation, but out of evil comes good. We are a good, kindhearted, decent people, and we're showing the world just that in our compassion and our resolve.

And one thing I fully understand is that when American forces answer the call of duty, they count on their families for support and encouragement. Every deployment brings uncertainty and, I know, every deployment brings worry and concern. Our military is made up of brave men and women, and brave families, as well.

Recently, a four-year-old son of a cargo specialist said good-bye to his dad here at Travis. And according to his mom, the boy has been telling the neighbors that "Daddy is saving the world."

The boy is right. The boy is right. The future of the world is at stake. Freedom is at stake. But I want to tell that boy his daddy has got plenty of help. There are a lot of people like his daddy fighting this war. We fight it overseas and we fight it at home, as well.

We must be steadfast. We must be resolved. We must not let the terrorists cause our nation to stop traveling, to stop buying, to stop living ordinary lives. We can be alert and we will be alert, but we must show them that they cannot terrorize the greatest nation on the face of the earth. . . . We will not be terrorized, we will not be cowed.

We've got a homeland security that's strong. I want to tell the moms and dads here that we're doing everything we can to find [terrorists] and disrupt them and stop them, if they happen to try to strike on American soil. We're strong at home. We're active at home. But make no mistake about it; the best homeland defense is to find them and bring them to justice—and that's exactly what our nation will do.

Now that [they've] got the plane fueled up, I'm heading over to China. Of course, we'll talk about economics and trade. But the main thing that will be on my mind is to continue to rally the world against terrorists; is to remind people that it happened to us, sure, but it could happen to them, as well; is to remind them that evil knows no borders, no boundaries, and to remind them that we must take a stand; that those of us who have been given the responsibility of high office must not shirk from our duty; that now is the time to claim freedom for future generations. . . .

People have struck us. They've tested our mettle and tested our character. But they are going to find that this nation understands we've reached a pivotal moment in history, where we will plant our flag on the ground—a flag that stands for freedom—and say to anybody who wants to harm us or our friends or allies, you will pay a serious price, because we're a nation that is strong and resolved and united.

You all are here to serve your country, and your country is grateful. You have confidence in America. But make no mistake about it: America has confidence in you.

Thank you all for such a warm greeting. May God bless the men and women who wear our uniform. May God protect this great land. And may God bless America. Thank you all very much.

### Excerpted Remarks by the President from Speech to Employees of the Dixie Printing Company
Glen Burnie, Maryland
October 24, 2001

Some might ask why, in the midst of war, I would come to Dixie Printing. They say, here you are conducting a campaign against terrorists, and you take time to come to a small business. And the answer is, because we fight the war on two fronts. We fight a war at home; and part of the war we fight is to make sure that our economy continues to grow.

When the terrorists struck our homeland, they thought we would fold. They thought our economy would crater. That's what they wanted. But they don't understand America. They don't understand the entrepreneurial spirit of our country. They don't understand the spirit of the working men and women of America. They don't understand that small business owners all across our country are saying, we're not going to allow you to terrorize us. . . .

I am here to report that we're doing well on both fronts. Overseas, our diplomatic efforts are strong. Nations all across the globe have bound with the United States to send a clear message that we'll fight terrorism wherever it may exist.

Recently I was in China. I had an interesting meeting, as you can imagine, with the President of Russia, the heads of China, Mexico, Chile—all were represented. And to a leader, from all kinds of nations—some Muslim, some not—the people said, we stand with America. We stand with America in [the] noble goal of finding the evildoers and bringing them to justice.

As you know, I have asked our military to take an active role in the campaign. I set out a doctrine to America that said the following: Not only will we hold terrorists accountable for their activities, we will also hold those nations accountable that harbor them, that hide them, that try to feed them. And that's exactly what we're doing in Afghanistan.

I gave the Afghan government, the Taliban government, plenty of time to respond to the demands of the United States. I said, you must hand over the al Qaeda leadership which hides in your country. I said, you must free those who you illegally detain in your country. And I said, you must destroy the camps that have been used to train the terrorists. And they had time to respond, and they didn't respond positively, and, therefore, they're paying a price.

Our military is conducting a campaign to bring the terrorists to justice, not to harm the Afghan people. While we are holding the Taliban government accountable, we're also feeding Afghan people. You need to be proud of the United States military. It's doing its job. It is slowly, but surely, encircling the terrorists so that we'll bring them to justice. We're patient. We're firm. We have . . . a strategy that is going to work. And make no mistake about it, justice will be done.

But there is another front in this war, and the front is here at home. It's something that, obviously, we're not used to in America. We've had oceans which have protected us over our history. Except for Pearl Harbor, we've never really been hit before. And yet, on September 11th, this great land came under attack. And it's still under attack as we speak. Anybody who puts poison in mail is a terrorist. Anybody who tries to affect the lives of our good citizens is evil.

I'm oftentimes asked by our friends in the press, do I know if there's a direct connection between what took place on September the 11th and what's happening today. I have no direct evidence, but there are some links. Both series of actions are motivated by evil and hate. Both series of actions are meant to disrupt Americans' way of life. Both series of actions are an attack on our homeland. And both series of actions will not stand.

It's important for the American people to know our government is doing everything we can on both fronts of this war. On the home front, we've got an Office of Homeland Security, the job of which is to organize and coordinate our functions of government in such a way as to disrupt and find those who would harm our citizens. We've got thousands of FBI agents scouring the information, asking questions, following up leads, all aimed to raise the risk [to] someone who would harm our citizens.

And, as well, we've responded to every incident that has occurred. Our nation has responded with bravery and courage. I'm proud of our health officials who responded so quickly to the incidents that took place. And, unfortunately, we lost life, and our prayers are with anybody who lose life in America. But I firmly believe their quick actions saved many lives, as well.

We're learning about terror and evil, and our country is responding forcefully. The American people have got remarkable spirit and remarkable resolve. We are strong, we are united, and we are determined to prevail.

One of the effects of the attacks has been on our economy. Make no mistake about it: September 11th affected economic growth, and our government must respond in an effective way. And so I'm here to talk about an important part of . . . homefront security, and that is our economy.

First of all, the bases for economic growth are very strong. The entrepreneurial spirit is really strong in America. We're the haven for small business opportunity in our country. I mean, more jobs are created through small business owners and the entrepreneurs of America than they are through large corporate America.

And so, as we think through how to encourage economic growth, we've got to always keep in mind the small . . . and the medium-sized businesses of America.

Secondly, our tax structure has been improved. In other words, we're giving people more of their own money back. And that's an important part of economic growth. . . .

And we've acted confidently and quickly to spend money necessary to help the country recover from the attacks. We spent money on helping rebuild New York City and the Pentagon. We have spent money to stabilize our airline industry, which was the industry most directly affected by the attacks of September the 11th. We've spent money to take care of workers who have lost jobs, and that's necessary and that's important.

And we're spending money to make sure we defend our country and accomplish our mission overseas. That spending has amounted to about $60 billion, above and beyond our budget. That money will help with job creation and will help our economy grow. It's necessary to spend that kind of money in a time of emergency, and we're in times of emergency.

But I strongly believe it's time to balance this amount of spending with additional tax relief. [In] my judgment, we've provided a lot of money in the short run, and in order to encourage and stimulate our economy, we ought to offset that money with additional tax relief—and I want to describe some of what that means.

First, we need to accelerate the tax relief that is already going to happen. In other words, instead of waiting for next year's tax relief to happen, let's put it into this year, to bolster consumer spending. We want you to have more money to spend, particularly as we head into the Christmas season. We want our consumers feeling confident.

One way to feel confident is for the people to know there's a strong homeland security initiative and strategy, that our country is doing everything we can to succeed. And there's nothing [for] boosting confidence [like] a little extra money in the pocket, too.

I also believe we ought to have rebates for low- and moderate-income workers, people who might have filed an income tax return, but didn't get any rebate last time. Those good folks have been particularly hard-hit as a result of September the 11th. And that ought to be a part of our consumer confidence package.

And then there's the business side, and I want you to know that we've thought very carefully about how to stimulate economic vitality and growth. And it's a package that will help small business America. It's a package that will do two things: One, encourage more investment, immediate investment in plant and equipment, and, therefore, one that will help small businesses not only retain their work force, but, hopefully, expand their work forces.

And, therefore, we need to reform the corporate income tax to get rid of the alternative minimum tax, which so severely affects small businesses like Dixie. As well, we need to allow businesses to deduct more of the cost of new investments immediately. We need to say to the Dixie Printings of America, if you invest in equipment now, you're rewarded for that investment. . . . It's a good way to make sure that we enhance the employment opportunities of America.

The terrorists wanted our economy to stop. It hasn't. They wanted to diminish the spirit of America. It didn't. They thought the government wouldn't be able to react. The government is going to react—with an economic-stimulus package that is good for workers. The House is getting ready to vote on that package. I urge them to pass it. And then I urge the Senate to act quickly to make sure that the American people understand that at this part of our homeland defense, our country and the Congress [are] united.

You know, I said early on that through my tears I see opportunity. And I believe my faith teaches that out of evil can come good. And there's been a lot of good that has come out of this terrible situation. By the way, there's a spirit of cooperation in Washington that is very positive. We've got Republicans and Democrats talking to each other. That's good. It's very important during this time in our history that we in Washington, D.C., show that we can work together.

I don't know if you know this or not, but I'm now having a weekly breakfast with the leaders of the House and the Senate, both Republicans and Democrats. And I can report that there is no party that has got a lock on patriotism. The Democrats, just like Republicans, want to win this war. And we're talking about how to best solve the problems with which we're confronted.

But there's also a lot of other good, too. We've got moms and dads reassessing values, recognizing there are things that are so precious in life, like their children and their marriage and their family, and their church and their synagogue and their mosque. Values are strong in America. Those who struck our country didn't realize—didn't realize because they're so evil and so dark and so negative, they couldn't realize that there's going to be such good that comes out of what took place in America.

We're resolved. We are strong. We're determined. We're patient. And this nation is going to do whatever it takes. You see, my attitude is . . . how the Dixie Printings behave, and how the workers behave here, and how the citizens of Maryland behave are incredibly important. How you respond to these attacks are incredibly important, not only to help win the war today, but to set the example for future generations of Americans.

It's important that we win today, place that flag of freedom squarely in the world. Because this is the first battle of the 21st century, and it's a battle we must win—we have no choice—for our children and our grandchildren. And it means that the country is going to have to do what it takes.

And I'm here to report, we are. We are going to do it.

So I want to thank you for giving me a chance to drop in to say hello. I am so honored to be the President of this great nation—and I mean great. What a fabulous land we have. And the reason why is because we've got such fabulous citizens.

## Excerpted Remarks by the President from Speech
## at the Patriot Act Signing Ceremony
October 26, 2001

Today, we take an essential step in defeating terrorism, while protecting the constitutional rights of all Americans. With my signature, this law will give intelligence and law-enforcement officials important new tools to fight a present danger.

I commend the House and Senate for the hard work they put into this legislation. Members of Congress and their staffs spent long nights and weekends to get this important bill to my desk. I appreciate their efforts, and bipartisanship, in passing this new law. . . .

The changes, effective today, will help counter a threat like no other our nation has ever faced. We've seen the enemy, and the murder of thousands of innocent, unsuspecting people. They recognize no barrier of morality. They have no conscience. The terrorists cannot be reasoned with. Witness the recent anthrax attacks through our Postal Service. . . .

But one thing is for certain: These terrorists must be pursued, they must be defeated, and they must be brought to justice. And that is the purpose of this legislation. Since the 11th of September, the men and women of our intelligence and law-enforcement agencies have been relentless in their response to new and sudden challenges.

We have seen the horrors terrorists can inflict. We may never know what horrors our country was spared by the diligent and determined work of our police forces, the FBI, ATF agents, federal marshals, Customs officers, Secret Service, intelligence professionals, and local law-enforcement officials, under the most trying conditions. They are serving this country with excellence, and often with bravery.

They deserve our full support and every means of help that we can provide. We're dealing with terrorists who operate by highly sophisticated methods and technologies, some of which were not even available when our existing laws were written. The bill before me takes account of the new realities and dangers posed by modern terrorists. It will help law enforcement to identify, to dismantle, to disrupt, and to punish terrorists before they strike.

For example, this legislation gives law-enforcement officials better tools to put an end to financial counterfeiting, smuggling, and money-laundering. Second, it gives intelligence operations and criminal operations the chance to operate not on separate tracks, but to share vital information so necessary to disrupt a terrorist attack before it occurs.

As of today, we're changing the laws governing information-sharing. And as [important], we're changing the culture of our various agencies that fight terrorism. Countering and investigating terrorist activity is the number one priority for both law enforcement and intelligence agencies.

Surveillance of communications is another essential tool to pursue and stop terrorists. The existing law was written in the era of rotary telephones. This new law that I sign today will allow surveillance of all communications used by terrorists, including e-mails, the Internet, and cell phones.

As of today, we'll be able to better meet the technological challenges posed by this proliferation of communications technology. Investigations are often slowed by limits on the reach of federal search warrants.

Law-enforcement agencies have to get a new warrant for each new district they investigate, even when they're after the same suspect. Under this new law, warrants are valid across all districts and across all states. And, finally, the new legislation greatly enhances the penalties that will fall on terrorists or anyone who helps them.

Current statutes deal more severely with drug-traffickers than with terrorists. That changes today. We are enacting new and harsh penalties for possession of biological weapons. We're making it easier to seize the assets of groups and individuals involved in terrorism. The government will have wider latitude in deporting known terrorists and their supporters. The statute of limitations on terrorist acts will be lengthened, as will prison sentences for terrorists.

This bill was carefully drafted and considered. Led by the members of Congress on this stage, and those seated in the audience, it was crafted with skill and care, determination and a spirit of bipartisanship for which the entire nation is grateful. This bill met with overwhelming—overwhelming—agreement in Congress, because it upholds and respects the civil liberties guaranteed by our Constitution.

This legislation is essential not only to pursuing and punishing terrorists, but also preventing more atrocities [at] the hands of the evil ones. This government will enforce this law with all the urgency of a nation at war. The elected branches of our government, and both political parties, are united in our resolve to fight and stop and punish those who would do harm to the American people.

### Excerpted Remarks by the President from Speech on the "Lessons of Liberty" Initiative
Thomas Wootton High School, Rockville, Maryland
October 30, 2001

I'm honored to be here to announce a national effort to bring together veterans and students all across America during the week of Veterans Day, to give our young examples of duty and courage at a time when both are sorely needed.

I also want to thank the students, and the veterans, and my fellow Americans. I can assure you it makes some of us old guys feel warm in our hearts when we see the enthusiasm you have for your school and the love you have for your country. I am proud to be standing with the Patriots.

We're a nation of patriots. The attacks of September 11th, and the attacks that have followed, were designed to break our spirit. But instead, they've created a new spirit in America. We have a renewed spirit of patriotism. We see it in the countless flags that are flying everywhere in America. We hear it in familiar phrases that move us more deeply than ever before. We all know that this is one nation, under God. And we pray that God will bless America, the land that we all love, regardless of our race, regardless of our religion, regardless of where we live.

We have a renewed appreciation of the character of America. We are a generous people, a thoughtful people who hurt, and share the sadness when people lose their [lives] or when people are hurt. We've helped each other in every way we know, in donations, in acts of kindness, in public memorials, in private prayer. We have shown in difficult times that we're not just a world power, that we're a good and kind and courageous people.

As we pursue the enemy in Afghanistan, we feed the innocents. As we try to bring justice to those who have harmed us, we find those who need help. The events of these seven weeks have shown something else. They have shown a new generation, your generation, that America and the cause of freedom have determined enemies; that there are people in this world who hate what America stands for. They hate our success, they hate our liberty. We have learned all too suddenly that there are evil people who have no regard for human life, and will do whatever it takes to try to bring this mighty nation to its knees.

On the Korean War Memorial in Washington are these words: "Freedom is not free." Our commitment to freedom has always made us a target of tyranny and intolerance. Anyone who sets out to destroy freedom must eventually attack America, because we're freedom's home. And we must always be freedom's home and freedom's defender. We must never flinch in the face of adversity, and we won't.

You've been learning this by studying your history—at least some of you by studying your history. (Laughter) Now you're learning the price of freedom by following the news. You're learning that to be an American citizen in a time of war is to have duties. You're learning how a strong country responds to a crisis, by being alert and calm, resolute and patient.

And you're the first students who have had to learn the reality that we're having to fight a war on our own land. You're the first generation of students who has ever witnessed a war fought in America. This is a two-front war we fight. [One] front is the home front. Our government is doing everything we possibly can to disrupt and deny and destroy anyone who would harm America again. And the truth of the matter is, the best way to fight for the homeland is to find the terrorists, wherever they hide, wherever they run, and to bring them to justice.

I also want to make it clear that the doctrine I laid out to the United States Congress is a doctrine this nation will enforce. It says clearly that if you harbor a terrorist, if you feed a terrorist, if you provide sanctuary to a terrorist, if you fund a terrorist, you are just as guilty as the terrorist that inflicted the harm on the American people.

Our nation gave those who harbor the al Qaeda organization ample opportunity to respond to reasonable demands. Our demands were just, and they were fair. We said very simply: Turn over al Qaeda. Send the terrorists out of your land. Release the innocent Americans and other foreigners you hold hostage in Afghanistan, and destroy al Qaeda terrorist camps and training activity camps. And we gave them ample opportunity to respond. And they chose the wrong course. And then—they will now pay a price for choosing the wrong course.

This is a nation that is resolved to win. And win we must, not only for your generation, but for generations to come.

This country has always been able to count on men and women of great courage. From the day America was founded, 48 million have worn the uniform of the United States. More than 25 million veterans are living today, some of whom are with us at Wootton High. And you may know some of them in your families. I know one such veteran. He fought in World War II, like Senator Dole—my dad.

We must remember that many who served in our military never lived to be called veterans. We must remember many had their lives changed forever by experiences or the injuries of combat. All veterans are examples of service and citizenship for every American to remember and to follow. . . .

[On] Veterans Day, we will honor them. We will remember the Bob Doles of the world. We will remember a generation that liberated Europe and Asia, and put an end to concentration camps. We will remember generations that fought in the cold mountains of Korea, and manned the outposts of the Cold War. We will remember those who served in the jungles of Vietnam, and on the sands of the Persian Gulf. In each of these conflicts, Americans answered danger with incredible courage. We were equal to every challenge. And now, a great mission has been given a new generation—our generation—and we vow not to let America down.

Today I have a special mission for our veterans, and a special request of our schools. I ask all public, private, and home schools to join our Lessons for Liberty Initiative, by inviting a veteran to speak to your students during the week of Veterans Day. I'm particularly pleased to announce that Wootton High has already put out the call, and Ron Ten Eyck has answered. Ron's a veteran of World War II. You need to listen to what he has to say.

Lessons of Liberty is supported by veterans groups all across America: American Legion, VFW, Military Order of the World Wars, as well as education groups all across our country. . . .

In addition to launching Lessons of Liberty, I will sign a proclamation in a minute, asking all Americans to observe the week of November 11th as National Veterans Awareness Week. In these difficult days here in America, I ask all of us, children and adults, to remember the valor and sacrifice of our veterans. American veterans have extraordinary stories. We should listen to them. American veterans preserved our world and freedom, and we should honor them. American veterans show us the meaning of sacrifice and citizenship, and we should learn from them.

Americans should always honor our veterans. At this moment, we especially need the example of their character. And we need a new generation to set examples of its own, examples in service and sacrifice and courage. These veterans have shaped our history, and with their values, your generation will help guide our future.

God bless, and may God bless America.

# November 2001

**Excerpted Remarks by the President from**
**Speech to the Warsaw Conference**
Warsaw, Poland
November 6, 2001

I thank all the nations of Central and Eastern Europe at this conference. You are our partners in the fight against terrorism, and we share an important moment in history.

For more than fifty years, the peoples of your region suffered under repressive ideologies that tried to trample human dignity. Today, our freedom is threatened once again. Like the fascists and totalitarians before them, these terrorists—al Qaeda, the Taliban regime that supports them, and other terror groups across our world—try to impose their radical views through threats and violence. We see the same intolerance of dissent; the same mad, global ambitions; the same brutal determination to control every life and all of life.

We have seen the true nature of these terrorists in the nature of their attacks—they kill thousands of innocent people and then rejoice about it. They kill fellow Muslims, many of whom died in the World Trade Center that terrible morning—and then they gloat. They condone murder and claim to be doing so in the name of a peaceful religion.

We have also seen the true nature of these terrorists in the nature of the regime they support in Afghanistan—and it's terrifying. Women are imprisoned in their homes, and are denied access to basic health care and education. Food sent to help starving people is stolen by their leaders. The religious monuments of other faiths are destroyed. Children are forbidden to fly kites, or sing songs, or build snowmen. A girl of seven is beaten for wearing white shoes. Our enemies have brought only misery and terror to the people of Afghanistan—and now they are trying to export that terror throughout the world.

Al Qaeda operates in more than sixty nations, including some in Central and Eastern Europe. These terrorist groups seek to destabilize entire nations and regions. They are seeking chemical, biological, and nuclear weapons. Given the means, our enemies would be a threat to every nation and, eventually, to civilization itself.

So we're determined to fight this evil, and fight until we're rid of it. We will not wait for the authors of mass murder to gain the weapons of mass destruction. We act now, because we must lift this dark threat from our age and save generations to come. . . .

The defeat of terror requires an international coalition of unprecedented scope and cooperation. It demands the sincere, sustained actions of many nations against the network of terrorist cells and bases and funding. Later this week, at the United Nations, I will set out my vision of our common responsibilities in the war on terror. I will put every nation on notice that these duties involve more than sympathy or words. No nation can be neutral in this conflict, because no civilized nation can be secure in a world threatened by terror.

I thank the many nations of Europe, including our NATO allies, who have offered military help. I also thank the nations who are sharing intelligence and working to cut off terrorist financing. And I thank all of you for the important, practical work you are doing at this conference. The war against terrorism will be won only when we combine our strengths.

We have a vast coalition that is uniting the world and increasingly isolating the terrorists—a coalition that includes many Arab and Muslim countries. I am encouraged by what their leaders are saying. The head of the twenty-two nation Arab League rejected the claims of the terrorist leader and said he— Osama bin Laden—"doesn't speak in the name of Arabs and Muslims." Increasingly, it is clear that this is not just a matter between the United States and the terror network. As the Egyptian Foreign Minister said, "There is a war between bin Laden and the whole world."

All of us here today understand this: We do not fight Islam, we fight against evil.

I thank all of our coalition partners, and all of you, for your steadfast support. The last time I was in Warsaw, I talked of our shared vision of a Europe that is whole and free and at peace. I said we are building a House of Freedom, whose doors are open to all of Europe's people, and whose windows look out to global opportunities beyond. Now that vision has been challenged, but it will not change. With your help, our vision of peace and freedom will be realized. And with your help, we will defend the values we hold in common.

### Excerpted Remarks by the President from Speech to the Financial Crime Enforcement Network
Vienna, Virginia
November 7, 2001

The United States is pressing the war against terror on every front, from the mountains of Afghanistan to the bank accounts of terrorist organizations. The first strike in the war against terror targeted the terrorists' financial support. We put the world's financial institutions on notice: If you do business with terrorists, if you support them or sponsor them, you will not do business with the United States of America.

Today, we are taking another step in our fight against evil. We are setting down two major elements of the terrorists' international financial network, both at home and abroad. Ours is not a war just of soldiers and aircraft. It's a war fought with diplomacy, by the investigations of law enforcement, by gathering intelligence, and by cutting off the terrorists' money. . . .

Acting on solid and credible evidence, the Treasury Department of the United States today blocked the U.S. assets of sixty-two individuals and organizations connected with two terror-supporting financial networks—the al Taqua and the al Barakaat. Their offices have been shut down in four U.S. states. And our G8 partners and other friends, including the United Arab Emirates, have joined us in blocking assets and coordinating enforcement action.

Al Taqua is an association of offshore banks and financial-management firms that have helped al Qaeda shift money around the world. Al Barakaat is a group of money-wiring and communication companies owned by a friend and supporter of Osama bin Laden. Al Taqua and al Barakaat raise funds for al Qaeda; they manage, invest, and distribute those funds. They provide terrorist supporters with Internet service, secure telephone communications, and other ways of sending messages and sharing information. They even arrange for the shipment of weapons.

They present themselves as legitimate businesses. But they skim money from every transaction, for the benefit of terrorist organizations. They enable the proceeds of crime in one country to be transferred to pay for terrorist acts in another.

The entry point for these networks may be a small storefront operation—but follow the network to its center and you discover wealthy banks and sophisticated technology, all at the service of mass murderers. By shutting these networks down, we disrupt the murderers' work. Today's action interrupts al Qaeda's communications; it blocks an important source of funds. It provides us with valuable information and sends a clear message to global financial institutions: You are with us or you are with the terrorists. And if you're with the terrorists, you will face the consequences.

We fight an enemy who hides in caves in Afghanistan, and in the shadows within in our own society. It's an enemy who can only survive in darkness. Today, we've taken another important action to expose the enemy to the light and to disrupt its ability to threaten America and innocent life.

I'm proud of the actions of our agencies. We're making a difference. We're slowly but surely tightening the noose, and we will be victorious.

### Excerpted Remarks from Presidential
### Address to the Nation
Atlanta, Georgia
November 8, 2001

We meet tonight after two of the most difficult—and most inspiring—months in our nation's history. We have endured the shock of watching so many innocent lives ended in acts of unimaginable horror. We have endured the sadness of so many funerals. We have faced unprecedented bioterrorist [attacks] delivered in our mail.

Tonight, many thousands of children are tragically learning to live without one of their parents. And the rest of us are learning to live in a world that seems very different than it was on September the 10th.

The moment the second plane hit the second building—when we knew it was a terrorist attack—many felt that our lives would never be the same. What we couldn't be sure of then—and what the terrorists never expected—was that America would emerge stronger, with a renewed spirit of pride and patriotism.

I said in my speech to a Joint Session of Congress that we are a nation awakened to danger. We're also a nation awakened to service, and citizenship, and compassion. None of us would ever wish the evil that has been done to our country, yet we have learned that out of evil can come great good. . . .

We are a different country than we were on September the 10th—sadder and less innocent; stronger and more united; and in the face of ongoing threats, determined and courageous.

Our nation faces a threat to our freedoms, and the stakes could not be higher. We are the target of enemies who boast they want to kill—kill all Americans, kill all Jews, and kill all Christians. We've seen that type of hate before—and the only possible response is to confront it, and to defeat it.

This new enemy seeks to destroy our freedom and impose its views. We value life; the terrorists ruthlessly destroy it. We value education; the terrorists do not believe women should be educated or should have health care, or should leave their homes. We value the right to speak our minds; for the terrorists, free expression can be grounds for execution. We respect people of all faiths and welcome the free practice of religion; our enemy wants to dictate how to think and how to worship even to their fellow Muslims.

This enemy tries to hide behind a peaceful faith. But those who celebrate the murder of innocent men, women, and children have no religion, have no conscience, and have no mercy.

We wage a war to save civilization itself. We did not seek it, but we must fight it—and we will prevail.

This is a different war from any our nation has ever faced, a war on many fronts, against terrorists who operate in more than 60 different countries. And this is a war that must be fought not only overseas, but also here at home. I recently spoke to high-school students in Maryland, and realized that for the first time ever, these seniors will graduate in the midst of a war in our own country. We've [entered] a new era, and this new era requires new responsibilities, both for the government and for our people.

The government has a responsibility to protect our citizens—and that starts with homeland security. The first attack against America came by plane, and we are now making our airports and airplanes safer. We have posted the National Guard in America's airports and placed undercover air marshals on many flights. I call on Congress to quickly send me legislation that makes cockpits more secure, baggage screening more thorough, and puts the federal government in charge of all airport screening and security. . . .

To coordinate our efforts, we've created the new Office of Homeland Security. Its director, my good friend and former governor, Tom Ridge, reports directly to me—and works with all our federal agencies, state and local governments, and the private sector on a national strategy to strengthen our homeland protections. For example, the Coast Guard has taken on expanded duties to protect our shores and our ports. The National Guard has an increased role in surveillance at our border. We're imposing new licensing requirements for safer transportation of hazardous material.

We've passed a new antiterrorism law which gives our law-enforcement officers the necessary tools to track terrorists before they harm Americans. A new terrorism task force is tightening immigration controls to make sure no one enters or stays in our country who would harm us. We are a welcoming country, we will always value freedom—yet we will not allow those who plot against our country to abuse our freedoms and our protections.

Our enemies have threatened other acts of terror. We take each threat seriously. And when we have evidence of credible threats, we will issue appropriate alerts.

A terrorism alert is not a signal to stop your life. It is a call to be vigilant—to know that your government is on high alert, and to add your eyes and ears to our efforts to find and stop those who want to do us harm.

A lot of people are working really hard to protect America. But in the long run, the best way to defend our homeland—the best way to make sure our children can live in peace—is to take the battle to the enemy and to stop them.

I have called our military into action to hunt down the members of the al Qaeda organization who murdered innocent Americans. I gave fair warning to the government that harbors them in Afghanistan. The Taliban made a choice to continue hiding terrorists, and now they are paying a price.

I'm so proud of our military. Our military is pursuing its mission. We are destroying training camps, disrupting communications, and dismantling air defenses. We are now bombing Taliban front lines. We are deliberately and systematically hunting down these murderers, and we will bring them to justice.

Throughout this battle, we adhere to our values. Unlike our enemy, we respect life. We do not target innocent civilians. We care for the innocent people of Afghanistan, so we continue to provide humanitarian aid, even while their government tries to steal the food we send. When the terrorists and their supporters are gone, the people of Afghanistan will say with the rest of the world: Good riddance.

We are at the beginning of our efforts in Afghanistan, and Afghanistan is only the beginning of our efforts in the world. No group or nation should mistake Americans' intentions: Where a terrorist group exists of global reach, the United States and our friends and allies will seek it out and we will destroy it.

After September the 11th, our government assumed new responsibilities to strengthen security at home and track down our enemies abroad. And the American people are accepting new responsibilities, as well.

I recently received a letter from a fourth-grade girl that seemed to say it all: "I don't know how to feel," she said, "sad, mad, angry. It has been different lately. I know the people in New York are scared because of the World Trade Center and all, but if we're scared, we are giving the terrorists all the power." In the face of this great tragedy, Americans are refusing to give terrorists the power. Our people have responded with courage and compassion, calm and reason, resolve and fierce determination. We have refused to live in a state of panic—or a state of denial. There is a difference between being alert and being intimidated—and this great nation will never be intimidated.

People are going about their daily lives, working and shopping and playing, worshiping at churches and synagogues and mosques, going to movies and to baseball games. Life in America is going forward—and as the fourth-grader who wrote me knew, that is the ultimate repudiation of terrorism.

And something even more profound is happening across our country. The enormity of this tragedy has caused many Americans to focus on the things that have not changed—the things that matter most in life: Our faith, our love for family and friends, our commitment to our country and to our freedoms and to our principles. . . .

Flags are flying everywhere—on houses, in store windows, on cars and lapels. Financial donations to the victims' families have reached more than a billion dollars. Countless Americans gave blood in the aftermath of the attacks. New Yorkers opened their homes to evacuated neighbors. We are waiting patiently in long security lines. Children across America have organized lemonade and cookie sales for children in Afghanistan.

And we can do more. Since September the 11th, many Americans, especially young Americans, are rethinking their career choices. They're being drawn to careers of service, as police or firemen, emergency health workers, teachers, counselors, or in the military. And this is good for America.

Many ask, what can I do to help in our fight? The answer is simple. All of us can become a September the 11th volunteer by making a commitment to service in our own communities. So you can serve your country by tutoring or mentoring a child, comforting the afflicted, housing those in need of shelter and a home. You can participate in your Neighborhood Watch or Crime Stoppers. You can become a volunteer in a hospital, emergency medical, fire or rescue unit. You can support our troops in the field and, just as [important], support their families here at home, by becoming active in the USO or groups and communities near our military installations.

We also will encourage service to country by creating new opportunities within the AmeriCorps and Senior Corps programs for public safety and public-health efforts. We'll ask state and local officials to create a new, modern civil-defense service similar to local volunteer fire departments, to respond to local emergencies when the manpower of governments is stretched thin. We will find ways to train and mobilize more volunteers to help when rescue and health emergencies arise.

Americans have a lot to offer, so I've created a task force to develop additional ways people can get directly involved in this war effort, by making our homes and neighborhoods and schools and workplaces safer. And I call on all Americans to serve by bettering our communities and, thereby, defy and defeat the terrorists.

Our great national challenge is to hunt down the terrorists and strengthen our protection against future attacks. Our great national opportunity is to preserve forever the good that has resulted. Through this tragedy, we are renewing and reclaiming our strong American values.

Both Laura and I were touched by a recent newspaper article that quoted a little four-year-old girl, who asked a telling and innocent question. Wondering how terrorists could hate a whole nation of people they don't even know, she asked, "Why don't we just tell them our names?" (Laughter) Well, we can't tell them all our names—but together we can show them our values.

Too many have the wrong idea of Americans as shallow, materialistic consumers who care only about getting rich or getting ahead. But this isn't the America I know. Ours is a wonderful nation, full of kind and loving people; people of faith who want freedom and opportunity for people everywhere. One way to defeat terrorism is to show the world the true values of America through the gathering momentum of a million acts of responsibility and decency and service.

I'm encouraging schoolchildren to write letters of friendship to Muslim children in different countries. Our college students and those who travel abroad for business or vacation can all be ambassadors of American values. Ours is a great story, and we must tell it—through our words and through our deeds.

I came to Atlanta today to talk about an all-important question: How should we live in the light of what has happened? We all have new responsibilities. Our government has a responsibility to hunt down our enemies—and we will. Our government has a responsibility to put needless partisanship behind us and meet new challenges—better security for our people, and help for those who have lost jobs and livelihoods in the attacks that claimed so many lives. I made some proposals to stimulate economic growth which will create new jobs, and make America less dependent on foreign oil. And I ask Congress to work hard and put a stimulus plan into law to help the American people.

Our citizens have new responsibilities. We must be vigilant. Obviously, we must inspect our mail, and stay informed on public-health matters. We will not give in to exaggerated fears or passing rumors. We will rely on good judgment and good old common sense. We will care for those who have lost loved ones, and comfort those who might at times feel afraid.

We will not judge fellow Americans by appearance, ethnic background, or religious faith. We will defend the values of our country, and we will live by them. We will persevere in this struggle, no matter how long it takes to prevail.

Above all, we will live in a spirit of courage and optimism. Our nation was born in that spirit, as immigrants yearning for freedom courageously risked their lives in search of greater opportunity. That spirit of optimism and courage still beckons people across the world who want to come here. And that spirit of optimism and courage must guide those of us fortunate enough to live here.

Courage and optimism led the passengers on Flight 93 to rush their murderers to save lives on the ground, led by a young man whose last known words were the Lord's Prayer and "Let's roll." He didn't know he had signed on for heroism when he boarded the plane that day. Some of our greatest moments have been acts of courage for which no one could have ever prepared.

We will always remember the words of that brave man, expressing the spirit of a great country. We will never forget all we have lost, and all we are fighting for. Ours is the cause of freedom. We've defeated freedom's enemies before, and we will defeat them again.

We cannot know every turn this battle will take. Yet we know our cause is just and our ultimate victory is assured. We will, no doubt, face new challenges. But we have our marching orders: My fellow Americans, let's roll.

### Remarks by the President from Speech to the United Nations General Assembly
New York, New York
November 10, 2001

Thank you. Mr. Secretary General, Mr. President, distinguished delegates, and ladies and gentlemen. We meet in a hall devoted to peace, in a city scarred by violence, in a nation awakened to danger, in a world uniting for a long struggle. Every civilized nation here today is resolved to keep the most basic commitment of civilization: We will defend ourselves and our future against terror and lawless violence.

The United Nations was founded in this cause. In a Second World War, we learned there is no isolation from evil. We affirmed that some crimes are so terrible they offend humanity itself. And we resolved that the aggressions and ambitions of the wicked must be opposed early, decisively, and collectively, before they threaten us all. That evil has returned, and that cause is renewed.

A few miles from here, many thousands still lie in a tomb of rubble. Tomorrow, the Secretary General, the President of the General Assembly, and I will visit that site, where the names of every nation and region that lost citizens will be read aloud. If we were to read the names of every person who died, it would take more than three hours.

Those names include a citizen of Gambia, whose wife spent their fourth wedding anniversary, September the 12th, searching in vain for her husband. Those names include a man who supported his wife in Mexico, sending home money every week. Those names include a young Pakistani who prayed toward Mecca five times a day, and died that day trying to save others.

The suffering of September the 11th was inflicted on people of many faiths and many nations. All of the victims, including Muslims, were killed with equal indifference and equal satisfaction by the terrorist leaders. The terrorists are violating the tenets of every religion, including the one they invoke.

Last week, the Sheikh of Al-Azhar University, the world's oldest Islamic institution of higher learning, declared that terrorism is a disease, and that Islam prohibits killing innocent civilians. The terrorists call their cause holy, yet they fund it with drug dealing; they encourage murder and suicide in the name of a great faith that forbids both. They dare to ask God's blessing as they set out to kill innocent men, women, and children. But the God of Isaac and Ishmael would never answer such a prayer. And a murderer is not a martyr; he is just a murderer.

Time is passing. Yet, for the United States of America, there will be no forgetting September the 11th. We will remember every rescuer who died in honor. We will remember every family that lives in grief. We will remember the fire and ash, the last phone calls, the funerals of the children.

And the people of my country will remember those who have plotted against us. We are learning their names. We are coming to know their faces. There is no corner of the earth distant or dark enough to protect them. However long it takes, their hour of justice will come.

Every nation has a stake in this cause. As we meet, the terrorists are planning more murder—perhaps in my country, or perhaps in yours. They kill because they aspire to dominate. They seek to overthrow governments and destabilize entire regions.

Last week, anticipating this meeting of the General Assembly, they denounced the United Nations. They called our Secretary General a criminal and condemned all Arab nations here as traitors to Islam.

Few countries meet their exacting standards of brutality and oppression. Every other country is a potential target. And all the world faces the most horrifying prospect of all: These same terrorists are searching for weapons of mass destruction, the tools to turn their hatred into holocaust. They can be expected to use chemical, biological, and nuclear weapons the moment they are capable of doing so. No hint of conscience would prevent it.

This threat cannot be ignored. This threat cannot be appeased. Civilization itself, the civilization we share, is threatened. History will record our response, and judge or justify every nation in this hall.

The civilized world is now responding. We act to defend ourselves and deliver our children from a future of fear. We choose the dignity of life over a culture of death. We choose lawful change and civil disagreement over coercion, subversion, and chaos. These commitments—hope and order, law and life—unite people across cultures and continents. Upon these commitments depend all peace and progress. For these commitments, we are determined to fight.

The United Nations has risen to this responsibility. On the 12th of September, these buildings opened for emergency meetings of the General Assembly and the Security Council. Before the sun had set, these attacks on the world stood condemned by the world. And I want to thank you for this strong and principled stand.

I also thank the Arab Islamic countries that have condemned terrorist murder. Many of you have seen the destruction of terror in your own lands. The terrorists are increasingly isolated by their own hatred and extremism. They cannot hide behind Islam. The authors of mass murder and their allies have no place in any culture, and no home in any faith.

The conspiracies of terror are being answered by an expanding global coalition. Not every nation will be a part of every action against the enemy. But every nation in our coalition has duties. These duties can be demanding, as we in America are learning. We have already made adjustments in our laws and in our daily lives. We're taking new measures to investigate terror and to protect against threats.

The leaders of all nations must now carefully consider their responsibilities and their future. Terrorist groups like al Qaeda depend upon the aid or indifference of governments. They need the support of a financial infrastructure, and safe havens to train and plan and hide.

Some nations want to play their part in the fight against terror, but tell us they lack the means to enforce their laws and control their borders. We stand ready to help. Some governments still turn a blind eye to the terrorists, hoping the threat will pass them by. They are mistaken. And some governments, while pledging to uphold the principles of the U.N., have cast their lot with the terrorists. They support them and harbor them, and they will find that their welcome guests are parasites that will weaken them, and eventually consume them.

For every regime that sponsors terror, there is a price to be paid. And it will be paid. The allies of terror are equally guilty of murder and equally accountable to justice.

The Taliban are now learning this lesson—that regime and the terrorists who support it are now virtually indistinguishable. Together they promote terror abroad and impose a reign of terror on the Afghan people. Women are executed in Kabul's soccer stadium. They can be beaten for wearing socks that are too thin. Men are jailed for missing prayer meetings.

The United States, supported by many nations, is bringing justice to the terrorists in Afghanistan. We're making progress against military targets, and that is our objective. Unlike the enemy, we seek to minimize, not maximize, the loss of innocent life.

I'm proud of the honorable conduct of the American military. And my country grieves for all the suffering the Taliban [has] brought upon Afghanistan, including the terrible burden of war. The Afghan people do not deserve their present rulers. Years of Taliban misrule have brought nothing but misery and starvation. Even before this current crisis, four million Afghans depended on food from the United States and other nations, and millions of Afghans were refugees from Taliban oppression.

I make this promise to all the victims of that regime: The Taliban's days of harboring terrorists and dealing in heroin and brutalizing women are drawing to a close. And when that regime is gone, the people of Afghanistan will say with the rest of the world: Good riddance.

I can promise, too, that America will join the world in helping the people of Afghanistan rebuild their country. Many nations, including mine, are sending food and medicine to help Afghans through the winter. America has airdropped over 1.3 million packages of rations into Afghanistan. Just this week, we air-lifted twenty thousand blankets and over two hundred tons of provisions into the region. We continue to provide humanitarian aid, even while the Taliban [tries] to steal the food we send.

More help eventually will be needed. The United States will work closely with the United Nations and development banks to reconstruct Afghanistan after hostilities there have ceased and the Taliban are no longer in control. And the United States will work with the UN to support a post-Taliban government that represents all of the Afghan people.

In this war of terror, each of us must answer for what we have done or what we have left undone. After tragedy, there is a time for sympathy and condolence. And my country has been very grateful for both. The memorials and vigils around the world will not be forgotten. But the time for sympathy has now passed; the time for action has now arrived.

The most basic obligations in this new conflict have already been defined by the United Nations. On September the 28th, the Security Council adopted Resolution 1373. Its requirements are clear: Every United Nations member has a responsibility to crack down on terrorist financing. We must pass all necessary laws in our own countries to allow the confiscation of terrorist assets. We must apply those laws to every financial institution in every nation.

We have a responsibility to share intelligence and coordinate the efforts of law enforcement. If you know something, tell us. If we know something, we'll tell you. And when we find the terrorists, we must work together to bring them to justice. We have a responsibility to deny any sanctuary, safe haven, or transit to terrorists. Every known terrorist camp must be shut down, its operators apprehended, and evidence of their arrest presented to the United Nations. We have a responsibility to deny weapons to terrorists and to actively prevent private citizens from providing them.

These obligations are urgent and they are binding on every nation with a place in this chamber. Many governments are taking these obligations seriously, and my country appreciates it. Yet, even beyond Resolution 1373, more is required, and more is expected of our coalition against terror.

We're asking for a comprehensive commitment to this fight. We must unite in opposing all terrorists, not just some of them. In this world there are good causes and bad causes, and we may disagree on where the line is drawn. Yet, there is no such thing as a good terrorist. No national aspiration, no remembered wrong can ever justify the deliberate murder of the innocent. Any government that rejects this principle, trying to pick and choose its terrorist friends, will know the consequences.

We must speak the truth about terror. Let us never tolerate outrageous conspiracy theories concerning the attacks of September the 11th; malicious lies that attempt to shift the blame away from the terrorists themselves, away from the guilty. To inflame ethnic hatred is to advance the cause of terror.

The war against terror must not serve as an excuse to persecute ethnic and religious minorities in any country. Innocent people must be allowed to live their own lives, by their own customs, under their own religion. And every nation must have avenues for the peaceful expression of opinion and dissent. When these avenues are closed, the temptation to speak through violence grows.

We must press on with our agenda for peace and prosperity in every land. My country is pledged to encouraging development and expanding trade. My country is pledged to investing in education and combatting AIDS and other infectious diseases around the world. Following September 11th, these pledges are even more important. In our struggle against hateful groups that exploit poverty and despair, we must offer an alternative of opportunity and hope.

The American government also stands by its commitment to a just peace in the Middle East. We are working toward a day when two states, Israel and Palestine, live peacefully together within secure and recognized borders as called for by the Security Council resolutions. We will do all in our power to bring both parties back into negotiations. But peace will only come when all have sworn off, forever, incitement, violence, and terror.

And, finally, this struggle is a defining moment for the United Nations, itself. And the world needs its principled leadership. It undermines the credibility of this great institution, for example, when the Commission on Human Rights offers seats to the world's most persistent violators of human rights. The United Nations depends, above all, on its moral authority—and that authority must be preserved.

The steps I described will not be easy. For all nations, they will require effort. For some nations, they will require great courage. Yet the cost of inaction is far greater. The only alternative to victory is a nightmare world where every city is a potential killing field.

As I've told the American people, freedom and fear are at war. We face enemies that hate not our policies, but our existence; the tolerance of openness and creative culture that defines us. But the outcome of this conflict is certain: There is a current in history and it runs toward freedom. Our enemies resent it and dismiss it, but the dreams of mankind are defined by liberty—the natural right to create and build and worship and live in dignity.

When men and women are released from oppression and isolation, they find fulfillment and hope, and they leave poverty by the millions.

These aspirations are lifting up the peoples of Europe, Asia, Africa, and the Americas, and they can lift up all of the Islamic world.

We stand for the permanent hopes of humanity, and those hopes will not be denied. We're confident, too, that history has an Author who fills time and eternity with His purpose. We know that evil is real, but good will prevail against it. This is the teaching of many faiths, and in that assurance we gain strength for a long journey.

It is our task—the task of this generation—to provide the response to aggression and terror. We have no other choice, because there is no other peace.

We did not ask for this mission, yet there is honor in history's call. We have a chance to write the story of our times, a story of courage defeating cruelty and light overcoming darkness. This calling is worthy of any life, and worthy of every nation. So let us go forward, confident, determined, and unafraid.

### Excerpted Remarks by the President from Speech to the Veterans Day Prayer Breakfast
New York City
November 11, 2001

Thank you very much. At ease.

AUDIENCE MEMBER: Let's roll!

THE PRESIDENT: Let's roll. (Applause)

Thank you so much, Commissioner. I'm so pleased to be back in New York City to pay honor to our veterans, those from the New York State and New York City area, and those all around America. It's such an honor to say on behalf of the American people, thanks for your service. . . .

I also want to recognize a person who I became friends with in a very difficult moment, and that's Ms. Arlene Howard. Arlene, would you stand up for a second, please? Good to see you, Arlene. Arlene is a veteran. She served in the United States Navy, as did her late husband, Robert. And she's a veteran of September the 11th in a sad way. Her son George was at the World Trade Center. She gave me something that I showed the nation a while ago, the badge of George. It's a reminder of the wrong done to our country. Arlene, thank you for that reminder. It is also a reminder of the great purpose of our great land, and that is to rid this world of evil and terror.

The evil ones have roused a mighty nation, a mighty land. And for however long it takes, I am determined that we will prevail. And prevail we must, because we fight for one thing, and that is the freedom of our people, and the freedom of people everywhere.

And I want to thank the Commissioner, who is a veteran as well—a veteran in the military, and a veteran of a new kind of war, one fought here on the home front. He represents the fabulous men and women who wear the uniform of the police and fire and rescue units, the Port Authority here in New York City, people who serve with such distinction and such courage that whenever an American hears the word police or fire we think differently. We think differently about the job. We think differently about the character of those who serve on a daily basis. We think differently about those who go to work every single day to protect us and save us and comfort us. . . .

[In] a time of war, we look a little differently at our veterans, too. We pay tributes on Veterans Day, today, and they're made with . . . greater feeling, because Americans have seen the terrible harm that an enemy can inflict. And it has left us deeply grateful for the men and women who rise strongly in the defense of our nation. We appreciate the sacrifices that our military is making today. We appreciate the sacrifices that their families make with them.

When the call comes to defend our country, our military is ready, and is making us proud. Al Qaeda and the Taliban have made a serious mistake. And because our military is brave and prepared and courageous, they will pay a serious price.

America has always needed such bravery and such people, and we have always found them amongst us. Generations of our servicemen and women have not only fought for our country in the past, they have upheld our honorable traditions, and represented our country with courage and honor. And wherever our military has gone, they have brought pride to our own people and hope to millions of others.

One veteran of World War II recalled the spirit of the American military and the relief it brought to suffering peoples. America, he said, has sent the best of her young men around the world, not to conquer, but to liberate; not to terrorize, but to help.

And this is true in Afghanistan today. And this has always been true of the men and women who have served our nation. This nation is freedom's home, and freedom's defender. And we owe so much—so much—to the men and women, our veterans, who step forward to protect those freedoms.

Our veterans gave America some of the best years of their lives, and stood ready to give life itself. For all that, America's twenty-five million veterans have the deep respect of their fellow citizens, and the enduring gratitude of a nation they so nobly served.

May God bless our veterans, and may God continue to bless America.

### Excerpted Remarks by the President from Speech to Military Personnel
Fort Campbell, Kentucky
November 21, 2001

All Americans are especially grateful—especially grateful—for the sacrifice of our military families; the husbands and wives and sons and daughters, the mothers and dads. Some of you have loved ones that are deployed, or will be deployed, far from home in a war against terror and evil. And our nation and the world are counting on your loved ones. They're making us secure and they are making us proud.

Men and women of Fort Campbell, your country and your President are proud of you, as well. The 101st Airborneis living out its motto. Once again, you have a rendezvous with destiny. And so does our country; we're freedom's home and defender. And today we're the target of freedom's enemies.

Our enemies are evil and they're ruthless. They have no conscience. They have no mercy. They have killed thousands of our citizens,and seek to kill many more. They seek to overthrow friendly governments to force America to retreat from the world.

They seek weapons of mass destruction. But we're seeking them. We're fighting them. And one by one, we're bringing them to justice. We fight now—this great nation fights now—to save ourselves and our children from living in a world of fear.

We fight now because we will not permit the terrorists, these vicious and evil men, to hijack a peaceful religion and to impose their will on America and the world. We fight now, and we will keep on fighting, until our victory is complete. We cannot know every turn this war will take. But I'm confident of the outcome. I believe in the strong resolve of the American people. I believe good triumphs over evil. And I believe in the fearless hearts of the United States military.

We fight the terrorists and we fight all of those who give them aid. America has a message for the nations of the world: If you harbor terrorists, you are terrorists. If you train or arm a terrorist, you are a terrorist. If you feed a terrorist or fund a terrorist, you're a terrorist, and you will be held accountable by the United States and our friends.

The Taliban know that. Our military forces and the forces of our allies, and many Afghans seeking a better future are liberating Afghanistan. And the Afghan people are celebrating. Today, twenty-seven of thirty Afghanistan provinces are no longer under Taliban control. We've got the Taliban and terrorists' lines of communications, and they're on the run.

We've made a good start in Afghanistan; yet, there is still a lot to be done. There are still terrorists on the loose in Afghanistan, and we will find and destroy their network, piece by piece. The most difficult steps in this mission still lie ahead, where enemies hide in sophisticated cave complexes, located in some of the most mountainous and rugged territory. These hideouts are heavily fortified and defended by fanatics who will fight to the death.

Unlike efforts to liberate a town or destroy Taliban equipment, success against these cells may come more slowly. But we'll prevail. We'll prevail with a combination of good information, decisive action, and great military skill.

The enemy hopes they can hide until we tire. But we're going to prove them wrong. We will never tire. And we will hunt them down. The Afghan people deserve a just and stable government. And we will work with the United Nations to help them build it. Our diplomats in the region, in Europe, in New York, and in Washington are in communications with all parties. We're urging them to move quickly toward a government that is broadly based, multi-ethnic, and protects the rights and dignity of all Afghan citizens, including women.

Winter is coming. And years of drought and Taliban misrule have placed many Afghans on the brink of starvation. We will work with the world to bring them food and medicine. While we fight evil, this great country will help those who suffer.

Afghanistan is just the beginning [of] the war against terror. There are other terrorists who threaten America and our friends, and there are other nations willing to sponsor them. We will not be secure as a nation until all of these threats are defeated. Across the world and across the years, we will fight these evil ones, and we will win.

Great causes are not easy causes. It was a long way from Bunker Hill to Yorktown. It was a long way for the 101st from Normandy to final victory over fascism in Europe. When wronged, our great nation has always been patient and determined and relentless. And that's the way we are today. We have defeated enemies of freedom before. And we will defeat them again.

And this struggle must be won at home, in our own cities, on our own soil. A lot of good people—police officers, FBI agents, intelligence agents and health officials—are working hard to protect Americans from new threats. And Americans are being vigilant themselves. No matter what lies ahead, we'll be alert, we'll be careful, and we'll never be intimidated. We're proud Americans and we'll live like Americans: We'll travel, we'll build on our prosperity, we'll live the lives of free people.

Yet, make no mistake about it: Wars are not won on the home front alone. Wars are won by taking the fight to the enemy. America is not waiting for terrorists to try to strike us again. Wherever they hide, wherever they plot, we will strike the terrorists.

This mission will require sacrifice by our men and women in uniform. America appreciates that sacrifice. And I make a promise in return: Our military will have everything [needed] to win in the long battle that lies ahead. You'll have every resource, every weapon, every possible tool to ensure full victory for the cause of freedom.

These have been hard months for Americans. Yet, this Thanksgiving we have so much to be thankful for. We're thankful for the love of our families. We're thankful for the goodness and generosity of our fellow citizens. We're thankful for the freedoms of our country. And we're so very thankful to you, the men and women who wear our uniform.

Thanks to you, the people of Afghanistan have the hope of a better life. Thanks to you, many Afghan women are walking in public again, and walking with dignity. Thanks to you, eight humanitarian aid workers—including two Americans—are free today, instead of sitting in a Taliban jail. Thanks to you, every nation is seeing what will happen if you cast your lot with the terrorists. Thanks to you, there is less fear in the world and more freedom, and more hope, and a better chance for peace.

Every one of you is dedicated to something greater than yourself. You put your country ahead of your comfort. You live by a code and you fight for a cause. And I'm honored to be your Commander-in-Chief.

AUDIENCE: USA! USA! USA!

THE PRESIDENT: I want to thank you all for such a warm greeting . . . [and for] your service to a great nation.

May God bless the men and women who wear our uniform, and may God bless America.

## Presidential Radio Address to the Nation
November 24, 2001

Good morning. Thanksgiving this year comes seventy-two days after a terrible national shock, an act of evil that caused, and continues to cause, so much suffering. Yet, the evil the terrorists intended has resulted in good they never expected. And this holiday season, Americans have much to be thankful for.

We're thankful for the character of our fellow citizens who are flying flags and donating to charity, and comforting those who grieve. Americans have aided the families of victims, and the starving children of Afghanistan, half a world away. This country has a good and generous heart.

We're thankful for the decency of the American people who have stood for the American tradition of tolerance and religious liberty—a tradition that has welcomed and protected generations of immigrants from every faith and background.

We are thankful for new heroes—police officers and firefighters and emergency workers, who have renewed our respect for public service and provided lasting lessons in courage.

We're thankful for the men and women of our military, who are defending our lives and liberty with such skill, honor, and success.

We're thankful, this year even more intensely, for our lives and our families, and the love of those around us. Americans are remembering what really matters—holding our children more closely, giving them more time.

And we're thankful to God, who turned suffering into strength, and grief into grace. Offering thanks in the midst of tragedy is an American tradition, perhaps because, in times of testing, our dependence on God is so clear.

The Pilgrims gave thanks even after the many deaths of a bitter winter. Abraham Lincoln proclaimed days of national thanksgiving even during a bloody Civil War. Lincoln asked God to heal the wounds of the nation and to restore it, as soon as it may be consistent with the divine purposes, to the full enjoyment of peace, harmony, tranquility. We pray for this goal, and we work for it.

In America, blessings are meant to be shared, and our Thanksgiving is revealed in concern for others. At this season, Laura and I hope you'll find ways to reach out and share your blessings and talents in your own communities—tutor or mentor a child; volunteer in a hospital; support our troops by becoming active in the USO; comfort those who feel afraid; show your kindness to a Muslim neighbor; help someone in need of shelter, or food, or words of hope; and continue to pray for America.

We will face difficult times ahead. The fight we have begun will not be quickly or easily finished. Our enemies hide and plot in many nations. They are devious and ruthless. Yet we are confident in the justice of our cause. We will fight for as long as it takes, and we will prevail.

May God grant us patience, resolve, and wisdom in all that is to come. Happy Thanksgiving, and thank you for listening.

### Excerpted Remarks by the President from
### Speech to the U.S. Attorneys Conference
Washington, D.C.
November 29, 2001

I want to welcome the new U.S. attorneys. I want to congratulate you. I must tell you that we set a high standard, and you met it. And for that, I hope you're proud. And I am grateful that you are willing to serve the country, particularly at this time.

I know you know this, but I want to remind you that you have . . . a significant commitment to the security and safety of the American people. We all do. That's our job. And it's a job we will keep. . . .

The safety and security of America also faces a new threat, and that is the threat of terror. It is the calling of our time, to rid the world of terror. And it is the calling of our time to protect the American people.

You know, it's interesting—I can't imagine what a speech like this would have been like prior to September the 11th, but I doubt I would have ever said you are now on the front line of war. And that's where you are. And make no mistake about it, we've got a war here just like we've got a war abroad. And we have a huge responsibility, and that's to defend America while protecting our great liberties. And I'm confident you can do the job; otherwise you wouldn't be sitting here.

Our enemies are resourceful, and they are incredibly ruthless. They hide and they plot, and they target freedom. They can't stand what America stands for. It must bother them greatly to know we're such a free and wonderful place—a place where all religions can flourish; a place where women are free; a place where children can be educated. It must grate on them greatly. But that's what we're going to keep doing, because that's what America is about.

And we owe it to the American people. We owe it to our citizens, to the families, to be relentless and methodical in tracking down terrorists and bringing each and every one of them to justice. That's our calling. It's the calling of the 21st century. And it's a calling that we will not tire [of]; it's a calling that we will keep in our minds. And you must keep it in your minds, because I can assure [you] I'm going to keep it in mine.

The government and the people are determined. And I have been able to travel our country some, and I know you can—if you were to report back to me, you would tell me you've seen the same determination, and the same patience, and the same unity to achieve this objective. I like to remind people that the evil ones have roused a mighty nation, and they will pay a serious price.

Abroad, our military and our alliance is making good progress—good, steady, significant progress. We're disrupting their cash flows. We're finding their bankers. And we're shutting them down.

And it's not just America. There are a lot of other countries who have participated with us, and that's heartening. We've got great intelligence-sharing now, around the world. I've been able to say to a lot of leaders, face to face, you tell us when they're coming. And if we find out something about you, we'll let you know, too. And that's important. It's important to know as much information as possible about the enemy. It's important to try to figure out where they hide, and their intentions. It helps to have a vast coalition willing to share that kind of information.

And we're bringing a lot of terrorists to justice around the world, as well. I think we've arrested over 300—we, the coalition, has arrested over 350 al Qaeda members and terrorists. I was able to thank President Aznar of Spain this week, for arresting eight terrorists, eight people who hate freedom are now in jail, where they should be. And hopefully they'll give us some information that we will share with other coalition members, to keep us all safe.

And as we speak, we're enforcing the doctrine that makes it plain that not only do we seek the terrorists, but we also hold governments that harbor them and feed them and house them and hide them accountable for their behavior, as well.

Afghanistan is the first overseas front in this war against terror. And I'm pleased to report the military is performing really well. In a short period of time, most of the country now is in the hands of our allies and friends. We've rescued the humanitarian-aid workers. We've destroyed the Taliban military. They're in total confusion. The government that used to hate women, and not educate its children, and disrupt humanitarian supplies, and destroy religious symbols of other religions is now in rout.

And we've got al Qaeda on the run, too. Now, they think they can hide, but they can't hide for long. And they think they can run, but they can't run forever, because we will patiently, diligently pursue them until they are brought to justice.

And on the home front, terrorist violence must be prevented, and must be defeated. And it will be, with vigilance, aggressive investigation, and certain punishment. Already, we've committed significant new resources to homeland security. We've improved our ability to detect and stop terrorist activity. But we've still got a lot of work to do.

I'm pleased to report the culture of the FBI is changing, the people you'll be working with in the field [are] changing. Now, one in four employees of the FBI [is] directly involved with the efforts to track down every lead and to disrupt the evil ones. And our new investigations are moving forward. And as we do so, our laws are being enforced fairly and in full.

We'll hear from material witnesses. We'll give them a chance to participate in the war against terror by telling us what they know. We will apply the immigration laws. We're interviewing people on a voluntary basis. We're saying, welcome to America. You have come to our country; why don't you help make us safe? Why don't you share information with us? Why don't you help us protect innocent people, women and children and men? Why don't you help us value life? As you enjoy the freedoms of our country, help us protect those freedoms.

But there is no doubt about our intentions, and there shouldn't be. Those who plot terror, and those who help them, will be held accountable in America. That's what we're going to do. Protecting the innocent against violence is a solemn duty of this country. It is our most important responsibility now. And all of us in this room accept that responsibility. And we will tell the American people plainly, we will fulfill that responsibility. . . .

I have also reserved the option of trial by military commission for foreign terrorists who wage war against our country. Non-citizens—non-U.S. citizens who plan and/or commit mass murder—are more than criminal suspects. They are unlawful combatants who seek to destroy our country and our way of life. And if I determine that it is in the national security interest of our great land to try by military commission those who make war on America, then we will do so.

We will act with fairness, and we will deliver justice, which is far more than the terrorists ever grant to their innocent victims.

Ours is a great land, and we'll always value freedom. We're an open society. But we're at war. The enemy has declared war on us. And we must not let foreign enemies use the forums of liberty to destroy liberty itself. Foreign terrorists and agents must never again be allowed to use our freedoms against us.

Many of you will play a crucial part in our victory against terrorism, and make no mistake, we're going to win the war. Decisions important to millions of Americans will be made in your offices. Your work in the cause of justice will help ensure the security of this nation. And as you join this fight, you will honor the Constitution. You will not only protect our people, but you will uphold our values.

Every federal prosecutor has the unique privilege of standing up in a court and telling the judge that you are there on behalf of the United States. In a time of war, these words are even more deeply felt, are even more significant.

Yours is a great trust, and one of the great professions. Today, you carry not only the confidence and respect of the American people, but you carry our deep gratitude as well. God bless.

# December 2001

**Excerpted Remarks by the President from Statement on
the Financial Fight Against Terror**
The White House
December 4, 2001

Good morning. Today we take another important step in the financial fight against terror. From the beginning of this fight I have said our enemies are terrorist networks of global reach; and all who harbor them and support them are our enemies as well. We began with al Qaeda and the Taliban. We identified some of al Qaeda's financial backers and we moved against their accounts.

In November, we advanced further and identified twenty-two more global terrorist organizations. And now we are moving against their financing as well.

At midnight yesterday the Treasury Department froze the assets and accounts of the Holy Land Foundation in Richardson, Texas, whose money is used to support the Hamas terror organization.

Earlier today, federal agents secured the offices and records of the Holy Land Foundation in Texas, California, New Jersey, and Illinois as a part of an ongoing investigation. At the same time, we have blocked the accounts of an Hamas-linked bank, an Hamas-linked holding company based in the West Bank.

The message is this: Those who do business with terror will do no business with the United States or anywhere else the United States can reach.

Hamas is an extremist group that calls for the total destruction of the State of Israel. It is one of the deadliest terrorist organizations in the world today.

Hamas openly claimed responsibility for this past weekend's suicide attacks in Israel that killed twenty-five innocent people, many of them teenagers, and wounded almost two hundred other people. Hamas is guilty of hundreds of other deaths over the years; and just in the past twelve months have killed two Americans. And today we act.

Hamas has obtained much of the money that it pays for murder abroad right here in the United States, money originally raised by the Holy Land Foundation. The Holy Land Foundation is registered with the IRS as a tax-exempt charity based in Richardson. It raised $13 million from people in America last year. The Holy Land Foundation claims that the money it solicits goes to care for needy Palestinians in the West Bank and Gaza. Money raised by the Holy Land Foundation is used by Hamas to support schools and indoctrinate children to grow up into suicide bombers. Money raised by the Holy Land Foundation is also used by Hamas to recruit suicide bombers and to support their families.

America has called on other nations to suppress the financing of terror. Today we take further steps to suppress it inside our borders. I am confident that most of the donors to the Holy Land Foundation, and perhaps even some of the individuals who are associated with the Foundation, had no idea how its money was being used. They wanted to relieve suffering in [a] region of the world that has suffered too much. But the facts are clear, the terrorists benefit from the Holy Land Foundation. And we're not going to allow it. Our action today is another step in the war on terrorism. It's not the final step. There are more terrorist networks of global reach, and more front groups who use deceit to support them. The net is closing. Today it just got tighter.

### Excerpted Remarks by the President from Speech at the Lighting of the National Christmas Tree
The Ellipse, Washington, D.C.
December 6, 2001

In a moment, we will light the National Christmas Tree, a tradition Americans have been celebrating since 1923. The history of this event has included some memorable moments, including sixty years ago, less than three weeks after the attack on Pearl Harbor, when Prime Minister Winston Churchill made an appearance with President Franklin Roosevelt to light the tree.

Now, once again, we celebrate Christmas in a time of testing, with American troops far from home. This season finds our country with losses to mourn and great tasks to complete. In all those tasks, it is worth recalling the words from a beautiful Christmas hymn—in the third verse of "Oh Holy Night" we sing, "His law is love, and His gospel is peace. Chaines He shall break, for the slave is our brother. And in His name all oppression shall cease."

America seeks peace, and believes in justice. We fight only when necessary. We fight so that oppression may cease. And even in the midst of war, we pray for peace on earth and goodwill to men.

This is a time of the year for families and friends to gather together. Not simply to celebrate the season, but to renew the bonds of love and affection that give fulfillment to our lives. And this is a year [when] we will not forget those who lost loved ones in the attacks on September the 11th and on the battlefield. They will remain in our prayers.

### Excerpted Remarks by the President from Speech
### Commemmorating Pearl Harbor Day
Aboard the *USS Enterprise*, Norfolk, Virginia
December 7, 2001

This is a fitting place to mark one of the most fateful days in American history. On December the 7th, 1941, the enemy attacked. Today is an anniversary of a tragedy for the United States Navy. Yet, out of that tragedy, America built the strongest Navy in the world. And there is no better symbol of that strength than the *USS Enterprise.*

What happened at Pearl Harbor was the start of a long and terrible war for America. Yet, out of that surprise attack grew a steadfast resolve that made America freedom's defender. And that mission—our great calling—continues to this hour, as the brave men and women of our military fight the forces of terror in Afghanistan and around the world. . . .

We are especially honored to share this anniversary with twenty-five living witnesses to Pearl Harbor on December the 7th, 1941. Thank you all for being here. They saw the attack and knew its victims by name. They can recall the last moments of peace, the first moments of war—and the faces of lost friends, forever young in memory. These veterans represent the noble history and traditions of the United States military. And I ask the Navy of today to please join me in honoring these fine men from the military of yesterday.

The attack on Pearl Harbor was plotted in secret, waged without mercy, taking the lives of 2,403 Americans. The shock and chaos came on a quiet Sunday morning. There were acts of great heroism amongst those who survived, and those who did not. Nine who fell that day had Navy ships named after them. In two hours' time, for bravery above and beyond the call of duty, fifteen men earned the Medal of Honor. And ten of them did not live to wear it.

Young sailors refused to abandon ship, even as the waters washed over the decks. They chose instead to stay and try to save their friends. A mess steward carried his commander to safety, and then manned a machine gun for the first time in his life. Two pilots ran through heavy fire to get into their P-40 fighters. They proceeded to chase and shoot down four enemy aircraft.

Those were among the scenes of December the 7th. On December the 8th, as the details became known, the nation's grief turned to resolution. During four years of war, no one doubted the rightness of our cause, no one wavered in the quest [for] victory. As a result of the efforts and sacrifice of the veterans who are with us today, and of millions like them, the world was saved from tyranny.

Many of you in today's Navy are the children and grandchildren of the generation that fought and won the Second World War. Now your calling has come. Each one of you is commissioned by history to face freedom's enemies.

When the *Enterprise* sailed out of Norfolk last April, we were a nation at peace. All of that changed on the morning of September the 11th. You were among the first to fight in the first war of the 21st century. You were ready. You performed with skill and honor. And you have made your nation proud.

On board this ship, when you returned to port four weeks ago, was a young man named Ruben Rodriguez. Two days later, Petty Officer Rodriguez lost his life in a plane crash. His wife and his family are in our thoughts and prayers. One of the last things this sailor did was to visit Ground Zero in New York City. He saw what the terrorists did to America, and he said to a friend, that's why I fought.

And that's why we are all fighting. We are fighting to protect ourselves and our children from violence and fear. We're fighting for the security of our people and the success of liberty. We're fighting against men without conscience, but full of ambition—to remake the world in their own brutal images. For all these reasons we're fighting to win—and win we will.

There is a great divide in our time—not between religions or cultures, but between civilization and barbarism. People of all cultures wish to live in safety and dignity. The hope of justice and mercy and better lives [is] common to all humanity. Our enemies reject these values—and by doing so, they set themselves not against the West, but against the entire world.

Our war against terror is not a war against one terrorist leader or one terrorist group. Terrorism is a movement, an ideology that respects no boundary of nationality or decency. The terrorists despise creative societies and individual choice—and thus they bear a special hatred for America. They desire to concentrate power in the hands of a few, and to force every life into grim and joyless conformity. They celebrate death, making a mission of murder and a sacrament of suicide. Yet, for some reason—for some reason, only young followers are ushered down this deadly path to paradise, while terrorist leaders run into caves to save their own hides.

We've seen their kind before. The terrorists are the heirs to fascism. They have the same will to power, the same disdain for the individual, the same mad global ambitions. And they will be dealt with in just the same way. Like all fascists, the terrorists cannot be appeased: They must be defeated. This struggle will not end in a truce or treaty. It will end in victory for the United States, our friends, and the cause of freedom.

The *Enterprise* has been part of this campaign. And when we need you again, I know you'll be ready. Our enemies doubt this. They believe that free societies are weak societies. But we're going to prove them wrong. Just as we were 60 years ago, in a time of war, this nation will be patient, we'll be determined, and we will be relentless in the pursuit of freedom.

This is becoming clear to al Qaeda terrorists and the Taliban. Not long ago, that regime controlled most of Afghanistan. Today, they control not much more than a few caves. Not long ago, al Qaeda's leader dismissed America as a paper tiger. That was before the tiger roared. Throughout history, other armies have sought to conquer Afghanistan, and they failed. Our military was sent to liberate Afghanistan, and [is] succeeding.

We're a long way from finished in Afghanistan. Much difficult and dangerous work is yet to come. Many terrorists are still hiding in heavily fortified bunkers in very rugged territory. They are said to be prepared for a long stay underground. (Laughter) But they are in for a sudden change of plans—because one by one, we're going to find them. And piece by piece, we'll tear their terrorist network apart.

As we fight the terrorists, we are also helping the people they have persecuted. We have brought tons of food and medicine to the Afghan people. They will need more help as winter comes, and we will provide it. Most of all, that country needs a just and stable government. America is working with all concerned parties to help form such a government. After years of oppression, the Afghan people—including women—deserve a government that protects the rights and dignity of all its people. America is pleased by the Afghan progress in creating an interim government—and we're encouraged by the inclusion of women in positions of authority.

And the war on terror continues beyond Afghanistan, with the closing of bank accounts and the arrests of known terrorists. We've put the terrorists and the nations in the world on notice: We will not rest until we stop all terrorists of global reach. And for every nation that harbors or supports terrorists, there will be a day of reckoning.

A few days from now, I will go to a great American institution, The Citadel, to describe the new capabilities and technologies we will need to wage this broad war on terrorism for years to come. We will need the intelligence to find the enemy where he dwells, and the means to strike swiftly across the world. We must have a military organized for decisive and total victory. And to you, the men and women of our military, I make this pledge: You will have every resource, every weapon, every tool you need to win the long battle that lies ahead.

This war came oh so suddenly, but it has brought out the best in our nation. We have learned a lot about ourselves and about our friends in the world. Nations stand with us, because this is civilization's fight. Today we take special pride that one of our former enemies is now among America's finest friends: We're grateful to our ally, Japan, and to its good people. Today, our two Navies are working side by side in the fight against terror.

The bitterness of sixty years ago has passed away. The struggles of our war in the Pacific now belong to history. For Americans who fought it, and suffered its losses, what remains is the lasting honor of service in a great cause, and the memory of the ones who fell.

Today, at Pearl Harbor, veterans are gathering to pay tribute to the young men they remember who never escaped the sunken ships. And over the years, some Pearl Harbor veterans have made a last request. They asked that their ashes be brought down and placed inside the *USS Arizona*. After the long lives given them, they wanted to rest besides the best men they ever knew.

Such loyalty and love remain the greatest strength of the United States Navy. And the might of our Navy is needed again. When America looks at you—the young men and women who defend us today—we are grateful. On behalf of the people of the United States, I thank you for your commitment, your dedication, and your courage.

## Presidential Proclamation Declaring
## Human Rights Day and Bill of Rights Week
December 9, 2001

By the President of the United States of America
A Proclamation

The terrible tragedies of September 11 served as a grievous reminder that the enemies of freedom do not respect or value individual human rights. Their brutal attacks were an attack on these very rights. When our essential rights are attacked, they must and will be defended.

Americans stand united with those who love democracy, justice, and individual liberty. We are committed to upholding these principles, embodied in our Constitution's Bill of Rights, that have safeguarded us throughout our history and that continue to provide the foundation of our strength and prosperity.

The heinous acts of terrorism committed on September 11 were an attack against civilization itself, and they have caused the world to join together in a coalition that is now waging war on terrorism and defending international human rights. Americans have looked beyond our borders and found encouragement as the world has rallied to join the American-led coalition. Civilized people everywhere have recognized that terrorists threaten every nation that loves liberty and cherishes the protection of individual rights.

Respect for human dignity and individual freedoms reaffirms a core tenet of civilized people everywhere. This important observance honoring our Bill of Rights and advocating human rights around the world allows all Americans to celebrate the universal principles of liberty and justice that define our dreams and shape our hopes as we face the challenges of a new era.

NOW THEREFORE I, GEORGE W. BUSH, President of the United States of America, by virtue of the authority vested in me by the Constitution and laws of the United States, do hereby proclaim December 10, 2001, as Human Rights Day; December 15, 2001, as Bill of Rights Day; and the week beginning December 9, 2001, as Human Rights Week. I call upon the people of the United States to honor the legacy of human rights passed down to us from previous generations and to resolve that such liberties will prevail in our Nation and throughout the world as we move into the 21st century.

IN WITNESS WHEREOF, I have hereunto set my hand this ninth day of

December, in the year of our Lord two thousand one, and of the Independence of the United States of America the two hundred and twenty-sixth.

GEORGE W. BUSH


**Excerpted Remarks by the President from Speech to Citadel Cadets**
Charleston, South Carolina
December 11, 2001

I have come to talk about the future security of our country, in a place where I took up this subject two years ago when I was candidate for President. In September 1999, I said here at The Citadel that America was entering a period of consequences that would be defined by the threat of terror, and that we faced a challenge of military transformation. That threat has now revealed itself, and that challenge is now the military and moral necessity of our time.

So, today, I will set forth the commitments essential to victory in our war against terror.

Four days ago, I joined the men and women of the *USS Enterprise* to mark the sixtieth anniversary of Pearl Harbor. December 7th, 1941, was a decisive day that changed our nation forever. In a single moment, America's "splendid isolation" was ended. And the four years that followed transformed the American way of war.

The age of battleships gave way to the offensive capability of aircraft carriers. The tank, once used only to protect infantry, now served to cut through enemy lines. At Guadalcanal, and Normandy, and Iwo Jima, amphibious warfare proved its worth. And by war's end, no one would ever again doubt the value of strategic air power.

Even more importantly, an American President and his successors shaped a world beyond a war. They rebuilt Europe with the Marshall Plan, formed a great alliance for freedom in NATO, and expressed the hope of collective security in the United Nations. America took the lead, becoming freedom's defender and assuming responsibilities that only we could bear.

September 11th, 2001—three months and a long time ago—set another dividing line in our lives and in the life of our nation. An illusion of immunity was shattered. A faraway evil became a present danger. And a great cause became clear: We will fight terror and those who sponsor it, to save our children from a future of fear.

To win this war, we have to think differently. The enemy who appeared on September 11th seeks to evade our strength and constantly searches for our weaknesses. So America is required once again to change the way our military thinks and fights. And starting on October 7th, the enemy in Afghanistan got the first glimpses of a new American military that cannot, and will not, be evaded.

When I committed U.S. forces to this battle, I had every confidence that they would be up to the task. And they have proven me right. The Taliban and the terrorists set out to dominate a country and intimidate the world. Today, from their caves, it's all looking a little different. And no cave is deep enough to escape the patient justice of the United States of America.

We are also beginning to see the possibilities of a world beyond the war on terror. We have a chance, if we take it, to write a hopeful chapter in human history. All at once, a new threat to civilization is erasing old lines of rivalry and resentment between nations. Russia and America are building a new cooperative relationship. India and the United States are increasingly aligned across a range of issues, even as we work closely with Pakistan. Germany and Japan are assuming new military roles, appropriate to their status as great democracies.

The vast majority of countries are now on the same side of a moral and ideological divide. We're making common cause with every nation that chooses lawful change over chaotic violence—every nation that values peace and safety and innocent life.

Staring across this divide are bands of murderers, supported by outlaw regimes. They are a movement defined by their hatreds. They hate progress, and freedom, and choice, and culture, and music, and laughter, and women, and Christians, and Jews, and all Muslims who reject their distorted doctrines. They love only one thing—they love power. And when they have it, they use it without mercy.

The great threat to civilization is not that the terrorists will inspire millions. Only the terrorists themselves would want to live in their brutal and joyless world. The great threat to civilization is that a few evil men will multiply their murders, and gain the means to kill on a scale equal to their hatred. We know they have this mad intent, and we're determined to stop them.

Our lives, our way of life, and our every hope for the world depend on a single commitment: The authors of mass murder must be defeated, and never allowed to gain or use the weapons of mass destruction.

America and our friends will meet this threat with every method at our disposal. We will discover and destroy sleeper cells. We will track terrorist movements, trace their communications, disrupt their funding, and take their network apart, piece by piece.

Above all, we're acting to end the state sponsorship of terror. Rogue states are clearly the most likely sources of chemical and biological and nuclear weapons for terrorists. Every nation now knows that we cannot accept—and we will not accept—states that harbor, finance, train, or equip the agents of terror. Those nations that violate this principle will be regarded as hostile regimes. They have been warned, they are being watched, and they will be held to account.

Preventing mass terror will be the responsibilities of Presidents far into the future. And this obligation sets three urgent and enduring priorities for America. The first priority is to speed the transformation of our military.

When the Cold War ended, some predicted that the era of direct threats to our nation was over. Some thought our military would be used overseas—not to win wars, but mainly to police and pacify, to control crowds and contain ethnic conflict. They were wrong.

While the threats to America have changed, the need for victory has not. We are fighting shadowy, entrenched enemies—enemies using the tools of terror and guerrilla war—yet we are finding new tactics and new weapons to attack and defeat them. This revolution in our military is only beginning, and it promises to change the face of battle.

Afghanistan has been a proving ground for this new approach. These past two months have shown that an innovative doctrine and high-tech weaponry can shape and then dominate an unconventional conflict. The brave men and women of our military are rewriting the rules of war with new technologies and old values like courage and honor. And they have made this nation proud.

Our commanders are gaining a real-time picture of the entire battlefield, and are able to get targeting information from sensor to shooter almost instantly. Our intelligence professionals and special forces have cooperated with battle-friendly Afghan forces—fighters who know the terrain, who know the Taliban, and who understand the local culture. And our special forces have the technology to call in precision air strikes—along with the flexibility to direct those strikes from horseback, in the first cavalry charge of the 21st century.

This combination—real-time intelligence, local allied forces, special forces, and precision air power—has really never been used before. The conflict in Afghanistan has taught us more about the future of our military than a decade of blue-ribbon panels and think-tank symposiums.

The Predator is a good example. This unmanned aerial vehicle is able to circle over enemy forces, gather intelligence, transmit information instantly back to commanders, then fire on targets with extreme accuracy.

Before the war, the Predator had skeptics, because it did not fit the old ways. Now it is clear the military does not have enough unmanned vehicles. We're entering an era in which unmanned vehicles of all kinds will take on greater importance—in space, on land, in the air, and at sea.

Precision-guided munitions also offer great promise. In the Gulf War, these weapons were the exception—while in Afghanistan, they have been the majority of the munitions we have used. We're striking with greater effectiveness, at greater range, with fewer civilian casualties. More and more, our weapons can hit moving targets. When all of our military can continuously locate and track moving targets—with surveillance from air and space—warfare will be truly revolutionized.

The need for military transformation was clear before the conflict in Afghanistan, and before September the 11th. Here at The Citadel in 1999, I spoke of keeping the peace by redefining war on our terms. The same recommendation was made in the strategic review that Secretary Rumsfeld briefed me on last August—a review that I fully endorse. What's different today is our sense of urgency—the need to build this future force while fighting a present war. It's like overhauling an engine while you're going at 80 miles an hour. Yet we have no other choice.

Our military has a new and essential mission. For states that support terror, it's not enough that the consequences be costly—they must be devastating. The more credible this reality, the more likely that regimes will change their behavior—making it less likely that America and our friends will need to use overwhelming force against them.

To build our future force, the Armed Services must continue to attract America's best people, with good pay and good living conditions. Our military culture must reward new thinking, innovation, and experimentation. Congress must give defense leaders the freedom to innovate, instead of micromanaging the Defense Department. And every service and every constituency of our military must be willing to sacrifice some of their own pet projects. Our war on terror cannot be used to justify obsolete bases, obsolete programs, or obsolete weapons systems. Every dollar of defense spending must meet a single test: It must help us build the decisive power we will need to win the wars of the future.

Our country is united in supporting a great cause—and in supporting those who fight for it. We will give our men and women in uniform every resource, every weapon, every tool they need to win the long battle that lies ahead.

America's next priority to prevent mass terror is to protect against the proliferation of weapons of mass destruction and the means to deliver them. I wish I could report to the American people that this threat does not exist— that our enemy is content with car bombs and box cutters—but I cannot.

One former al Qaeda member has testified in court that he was involved in an effort 10 years ago to obtain nuclear materials. And the leader of al Qaeda calls that effort "a religious duty." Abandoned al Qaeda houses in Kabul contained diagrams for crude weapons of mass destruction. And as we all know, terrorists have put anthrax into the U.S. mail, and used sarin gas in a Tokyo subway.

And almost every state that actively sponsors terror is known to be seeking weapons of mass destruction and the missiles to deliver them at longer and longer ranges. Their hope is to blackmail the United States into abandoning our war on terror, and forsaking our friends and allies and security commitments around the world. Our enemies are bound for disappointment. America will never be blackmailed, and we will never forsake our commitment to liberty.

To meet our new threats, I have directed my National Security Advisor and my Homeland Security Director to develop a comprehensive strategy on proliferation. Working with other countries, we will strengthen nonproliferation treaties and toughen export controls. Together, we must keep the world's most dangerous technologies out of the hands of the world's most dangerous people.

A crucial partner in this effort is Russia—a nation we are helping to dismantle strategic weapons, reduce nuclear material, and increase security at nuclear sites. Our two countries will expand efforts to provide peaceful employment for scientists who formerly worked in Soviet weapons facilities. The United States will also work with Russia to build a facility to destroy tons of nerve agent. I'll request an overall increase in funding to support this vital mission.

Even as we fight to prevent proliferation, we must prepare for every possibility. At home, we must be better prepared to detect, protect against, and respond to the potential use of weapons of mass destruction. Abroad, our military forces must have the ability to fight and win against enemies who would use such weapons against us. . . .

The attacks on our nation made it even more clear that we need to build limited and effective defenses against a missile attack. Our enemies seek every chance and every means to do harm to our country, our forces, and our friends. And we will not permit it.

Suppose the Taliban and the terrorists had been able to strike America or important allies with a ballistic missile. Our coalition would have become fragile, the stakes in our war much, much higher. We must protect Americans and our friends against all forms of terror, including the terror that could arrive on a missile.

Last week we conducted another promising test of our missile-defense technology. For the good of peace, we're moving forward with an active program to determine what works and what does not work. In order to do so, we must move beyond the 1972 Anti-Ballistic Missile Treaty, a treaty that was written in a different era, for a different enemy.

America and our allies must not be bound to the past. We must be able to build the defenses we need against the enemies of the 21st century.

Our third and final priority in the fight against mass terror is to strengthen the advantage that good intelligence gives our country. Every day I make decisions influenced by the intelligence briefing of that morning. To reach decisions, a President needs more than data and information. A President needs real and current knowledge and analysis of the plans, intentions, and capabilities of our enemies.

The last several months have shown that there is no substitute for good intelligence officers, people on the ground. These are the people who find the targets, follow our enemies, and help us disrupt their evil plans.

The United States must rebuild our network of human intelligence. And we will apply the best new technology to gather intelligence on the new threats. Sophisticated systems like Global Hawk, an unmanned surveillance plane, are transforming our intelligence capabilities. Our technological strengths produce great advantages, and we will build on them.

Our intelligence services and federal law-enforcement agencies must work more closely together, and share timely information with our state and local authorities. The more we know, the more terrorist plans we can prevent and disrupt, and the better we'll be able to protect the American people.

And in all they do, our intelligence agencies must attract the best people—the best collectors, the best analysts, the best linguists. We will give them the training they need and the compensation they deserve.

There have been times here in America when our intelligence services were held in suspicion, and even contempt. Now, when we face this new war, we know how much we need them. And for their dedication and for their service, America is grateful.

We're also grateful to you, the students of The Citadel. Your uniforms symbolize a tradition of honor and sacrifice, renewed in your own lives.

Many of you will enter our military—taking your place in the war against terror. That struggle may continue for many years, and it may bring great costs. But you will have chosen a great calling at a crucial hour for our nation.

The course we follow is a matter of profound consequence to many nations. If America wavers, the world will lose heart. If America leads, the world will show its courage. America will never waver. America will lead the world to peace.

Our cause is necessary. Our cause is just. And no matter how long it takes, we will defeat the enemies of freedom.

In all that is to come, I know the graduates of The Citadel will bring credit to America, to the military, and to this great institution. In the words of your school song, you will go where you've always gone—"in the paths our fathers showed us. Peace and Honor, God and Country—we will fight for thee."

### Excerpted Remarks by the President from Speech at the Signing Ceremony for the Afghan Women and Children Relief Act
The White House
December 12, 2001

Thank you all. For several years, the people of Afghanistan have suffered under one of the most brutal regimes in modern history; a regime allied with terrorists and a regime at war with women. Thanks to our military and our allies and the brave fighters of Afghanistan, the Taliban regime is coming to an end.

Yet, our responsibilities to the people of Afghanistan have not ended. We work for a new era of human rights and human dignity in that country. The agreement reached in Bonn last week means that in ten days, the international community will have a new partner, an interim government of a new Afghanistan.

We join those in the interim government who seek education and better health for every Afghan woman and child. And today, with the Afghan Women and Children Relief Act, we take an important step toward that goal. . . .

America is beginning to realize that the dreams of the terrorists and the Taliban were a waking nightmare for Afghan women and their children. The Taliban murdered teenagers for laughing in the presence of soldiers. They jailed children as young as ten years old, and tortured them for supposed crimes of their parents.

Afghan women were banned from speaking or laughing loudly. They were banned from riding bicycles, or attending school. They were denied basic health care, and were killed on suspicion of adultery. One news magazine reports, "It's hard to find a woman in Kabul who does not remember a beating at the hands of the Taliban."

In Afghanistan, America not only fights for our security, but we fight for values we hold dear. We strongly reject the Taliban way. We strongly reject their brutality toward women and children. They not only violate basic human rights, they are barbaric in their indefensible meting [out] of justice. It is wrong. Their attitude is wrong for any culture. Their attitude is wrong for any religion.

You know, life in Afghanistan wasn't always this way. Before the Taliban came, women played an incredibly important part of that society. Seventy percent of the nation's teachers were women. Half of the government workers in Afghanistan were women, and forty percent of the doctors in the capital of Kabul were women.

The Taliban destroyed that progress. And in the process, they offered us a clear image of the world they and the terrorists would like to impose on the rest of us.

The central goal of the terrorists is the brutal oppression of women—and not only the women of Afghanistan. The terrorists who help rule Afghanistan are found in dozens and dozens of countries around the world. And that is the reason this great nation, with our friends and allies, will not rest until we bring them all to justice.

America is so proud of our military and our allies, because like the rest of us here, we've seen the pictures of joy when we liberated city after city in Afghanistan. And none of us will ever forget the laughter and the music and the cheering and the clapping at a stadium that was once used for public execution.

Children now fly kites and they play games. Women now come out of their homes from house arrest, able to walk the streets without chaperons. "It feels like we've all been released from prison," said one young person in Kabul, "that the whole of Afghanistan has been released from prison."

This is an important achievement. Yet, a liberated Afghanistan must now be rebuilt so that it will never again practice terror at home or abroad. This work begins by ensuring the essential rights of all Afghans.

This week is Human Rights Week, when we celebrate the adoption of the Universal Declaration of Human Rights more than a half-century ago. The preamble to that document declares that the people of the world reaffirm their "faith in fundamental human rights, in the dignity and worth of the human person, and in equal rights of men and women."

This is a great goal, and that's why I'm so pleased that Afghanistan's new government will respect the rights of all people, women and men. America and our allies will do our part in the rebuilding of Afghanistan. We learned our lessons from the past. We will not leave until the mission is complete. We will work with international institutions on long-term development—on the long-term development of Afghanistan. We will provide immediate humanitarian assistance to the people of Afghanistan.

After years of civil war and misrule by the Taliban, this is going to be an incredibly difficult winter in Afghanistan. We're doing what we can to help alleviate the suffering. In the month of November, the United Nations World Food Program, with our strong support, provided enough supplies to feed 4.3 million Afghans. And the Defense Department will continue to make sure that food is delivered in remote regions of that impoverished, poor, starving country.

The bill I sign today extends and strengthens our efforts. The Afghan Women and Children Relief Act commits the United States to providing education and medical assistance to Afghan women and children, and to Afghan refugees in surrounding countries.

The overwhelming support for this legislation sends a clear message: As we drive out the Taliban and the terrorists, we are determined to lift up the people of Afghanistan. The women and children of Afghanistan have suffered enough. This great nation will work hard to bring them hope and help.

## Excerpted Remarks by the President from Speech Marking the Donation of the *Spirit of Louisiana* Fire Truck to New York City
The White House
December 19, 2001

This *Spirit of Louisiana* truck really does show the deep concern of the good folks of Louisiana. Everybody in our nation realized on September 11th, we were all affected. They might have hit right around the corner here and they might have hit in New York City, but it affected all of us. And the good people of Louisiana realize that.

I particularly love this story, about how [someone] decides to do something on behalf of fellow citizens. So he gets on the phone and calls a local radio personality—the Governor. (Laughter) And out of that came a huge volunteer effort in the state of Louisiana to provide help and aid to the good people of New York City.

And I think America needs to understand that this is the kind of story that makes our country so unique and so different. It's a story that makes me so proud to be the President of such a great land. . . .

I want to thank all the volunteers who worked on this project. I want to thank the firefighters and police officers from the state of Louisiana who have come. You obviously represent a noble profession and a profession that really knows no borders. And you're on your way to express your solidarity with people who fight fires—they may talk with a different accent, but they share the same dangers. . . .

One of the things I like to remind the enemy is, you thought you were going to change America when you hit us. You thought by your actions and by your attacks that somehow this nation was so soft that we didn't know how to respond. And they're paying a terrible price for their miscalculation. We're making great progress in the first theater of this long war to rout terror where it may exist. . . .

I know the Governor likes to hunt rabbits down in Louisiana. Sometimes those rabbits think they can hide from the Governor. But, eventually, he smokes them out and gets them. And that's exactly what is happening to Mr. bin Laden, and all the murderers that he's trying to hide in Afghanistan.

But the other thing that the terrorists [didn't] understand was the strength of America. They didn't understand that. And the strength of America is our citizens, citizens who love each other; citizens who are decent; citizens who when called upon can respond to any adversity. And that's exactly what's happening here on the White House lawn today. People from all walks of life . . . who probably have never been to New York City before, have said, what can I do to help? How can I help [those] whose lives have been adversely affected by the evil ones?

And behind me sits the answer—one beautiful, well-manufactured truck, made by an entrepreneur in Louisiana who asked his people to work overtime, and they did, to deliver it here today. I know I speak on behalf of all Americans: Thank you for what you're doing.

No, they roused a mighty nation. They roused a mighty nation. And we will not be stopped. We're not going to be stopped overseas—and we're sure not going to be stopped here at home.

I hope every family here and all the folks who volunteered to make this happen have a wonderful holiday season. May God bless your families, and may God continue to bless America.

# January 2002

**Excerpted Remarks by the President from Speech
to the Missouri Farmers Association**
Aurora, Missouri
January 14, 2002

If the role of government is to create an environment in which people are willing to take risk, one of the things government must do is to work hard to create confidence in the people. And at this moment in history, the best thing I can do, along with my administration, in order to build the confidence of the American people, is to prevent the evil ones from hitting us again.

The best way to make sure this economy recovers, and people can find work, is to have a homeland security system that runs down every hint that somebody might harm us; runs down every lead that we find. I want to assure you all that I spend a lot of time, as [does] my administration, on this top priority; that we're working with intelligence-gathering services from around the world to sniff out, to listen to, to find out who might be trying to harm us again; that we've got our law enforcement officers around our country—at the federal, state, and local level—[who] now understand that they must remain on alert, that there's still an enemy and we've got to stop them. The FBI's primary mission is homeland security, and we're working closely with folks in your communities to make sure that if there's any hint that somebody might try to harm America, we're going to act, and act now, and bring them to justice.

I'm proud of the efforts of many all around our country who are working endless hours to make America safe. But the best way to make America safe is to hunt the enemy down where he tries to hide and bring [him] to justice. And that's exactly what we're going to do.

I gave our military a mighty task, and they have responded. I want to thank those of you who have got relatives in the military—a brother or a sister, or a son or a daughter, or a mom or a dad—they have made me proud. And I hope they made you proud, as well.

We sent the military on a clear mission, and that is to bring the evil ones to justice. It's a mission, however, that I expanded to include this: That if you hide a terrorist, if you feed a terrorist, if you provide aid and comfort for a terrorist, you're just as guilty as the terrorist. That's why the Taliban is no longer ruling Afghanistan.

I think that one of the most joyous things for me is to see the faces of the Afghan women as they have been liberated from the oppression of the Taliban rule. Not only is our military destroying those who would harbor evil, destroying whatever military they had, destroying their defenses, but we're liberators. We're freeing women and children from incredible oppression.

The humanitarian aid workers are home—as part of the conditions I laid down for the Taliban. The Taliban is in total rout. But we haven't completed our mission yet. And we're now at a very dangerous phase of the war in the first theater, and that is sending our boys and troops into the caves. You see, we're fighting an enemy that's willing to send others to death, suicide missions in the name of religion, and they, themselves, want to hide in caves.

But you know something? We're not going to tire. We're not going to be impatient. We're going to do whatever it takes to find them and bring them to justice. They think they can hide, but they're not going to hide from the mighty reach of the United States and the coalition we have put together.

I see members of the FFA here. I want you to know that the cause that our military now wages is a just cause, it's an important cause; that I long for peace, but I also understand that this nation must lead the war against terror if you and your children and your grandchildren are going to grow up and understand the freedoms that we so enjoy in America. . . . If you and your children and grandchildren can grow up in a peaceful and hopeful world, now is the time for this country to lead. And lead we will.

### Excerpted Remarks by the President from Speech
### to the Reserve Officers Luncheon
Washington, D.C.
January 23, 2002

It's a high privilege to be here with the men and women of the Reserve Officers Association. For eighty years you stood up for America and the people who wear its uniform. Today, many Reserve officers are on duty in our campaign against terror. Today, the Guard and Reserve are fighting a two-front war—one in Central Asia, and one here at home.

The Air Force Reserve alone has flown more than three thousand sorties over Afghanistan, and more than eight hundred sorties to protect American cities. In this hour of need, America is depending on our Reserve officers. You are not letting us down, and America is grateful.

We're in a fight for freedom and for the security of the American people. We're in a fight for the values of civilization. And the terrorists, the evil ones who targeted America, are learning something—they picked the wrong enemy. Whatever it takes, whatever it costs, this patient, this resolved nation will win the first war of the 21st century. . . .

You know, it has been four and a half months since September the 11th. It's been four and a half months since we've been attacked. Sometimes it seems like a long time. But one thing is for certain—when you think about the nature of the war we face, four and a half months is not a very long time. And yet, we've done a lot. We've accomplished a lot.

One thing is for certain; this great nation has risen to the challenge. One of the most brutal and repressive regimes ever, the Taliban, is now out of business. We've smoked members of al Qaeda out of their caves. We've destroyed their bunkers. And the global network of terrorists has seen the first glimpse of their fate.

We've sent food and medical shipments to the suffering people of Afghanistan. We've helped them organize a new government that represents all the people. And this proud military, and this great nation has liberated people. We've liberated women and children who lived under the severe hand of the most repressive Taliban.

And these gains are a tribute to the United States military. There [was] no doubt in my mind that when I unleashed our great military, our men and women would perform bravely. They have not let us down. Our military is relentless—I mean, relentless—in pursuing the terrorists. And at the same time, we've shown great care in protecting innocent life.

They serve with skill and dedication. Our commanders are patient; they're not restless. They know that they've got the backing of the administration and the American people; that I'm patient; the people are patient. We all know that we've entered a difficult phase in our first theater in the war against terror; that while, in the first couple of months, we saw great success on the ground, we're now on a manhunt, one person at a time. No matter how long it takes, no matter where we have to look, our United States military will patiently and surely hunt down the murderers and killers and terrorists, and bring them, one by one, to justice.

Our fight against terrorism began in Afghanistan, but it's not going to end there. We still face a shadowy enemy who dwells in the dark corners of the earth. Dangers and sacrifices lie ahead. Yet, America will not rest, we will not tire until every terrorist group of global reach has been found, has been stopped, and has been defeated.

We have a special responsibility to defend freedom. And I accept that responsibility, and so does our military, and so do the American people. And I have the responsibility to prepare the nation for all that lies ahead. Next week I will go before Congress to lay out my priorities for the coming year. There will be no room for misunderstanding. The most basic commitment of our government will be the security of our country. We will win this war; we will protect our people; and we will work to renew the strength of our economy.

Our first priority is the military. The highest calling to protect the people is to strengthen our military. And that will be the priority of the budget I submit to the United States Congress. Those who review our budget must understand that we're asking a lot of our men and women in uniform, and we'll be asking more of them in the future. In return, they deserve every resource, every weapon needed to achieve the final and full victory. . . .

We will invest in more precision weapons, in missile defenses, in unmanned vehicles, in high-tech equipment for soldiers on the ground. The tools of modern warfare are effective. They are expensive. But in order to win this war against terror, they are essential. Buying these tools may put a strain on the budget, but we will not cut corners when it comes to the defense of our great land.

Another priority is to protect our people from future terrorist attacks. And so the second priority in my budget will be a major new increase in spending for homeland security. The federal government has already acted quickly to increase the number of sky marshals, to support the largest criminal investigation in U.S. history, to acquire antibiotics for large-scale treatment of anthrax, to deploy hundreds of Coast Guard cutters and aircraft and small boats to patrol ports, and to station 8,000 National Guardsmen in the nation's airports.

All this came in response to a sudden emergency. Now we must undertake a sustained strategy for homeland defense. In our next budget, we move forward to complete the hiring of 30,000 new federal airport-security workers. We will hire an additional three hundred FBI agents to help fight the war on terror. We'll purchase new equipment to improve the safety of the mail, and protect the men and women who deliver our mail. We'll begin a major program of research to combat the threat of bioterrorism. We'll modernize public-health labs throughout the country, improving their capacity to detect and treat outbreaks of disease. We will ensure that state and local firemen and police and rescue workers are prepared for terrorism. And we will do more to secure our borders.

The American people are on watch against future attacks. And so [is] their government. The truth of the matter is, though, in order to fully secure America and our allies, those of us who love and defend freedom, in order to make sure we're safe in the long run, we must find the terrorists wherever they think they can hide, and, as I like to say, get 'em.

Another priority of the budget is to fight the recession and work on the economic security of our people. You know, our country is united when it comes to fighting the war. We need to be united when it comes to battling recession as well. It's time to set aside all the politics, all the posturing, and figure out how to take care of workers whose lives were affected because of the attacks on 9/11.

But as we do so, always remember that people may want an unemployment check to help them through tough times, but what they really want is a permanent paycheck. And, therefore, jobs ought to be the central core of any economic-development plan that we can run out of the United States Congress.

So when I submit my budget to the United States Congress, these will be my priorities. We've made our choices, to match the great challenges and opportunities of our time. Our great challenge is to protect the American people. Our great opportunity is to advance the cause of justice and human dignity and freedom all across the world. In this cause, our military is showing the world America at its best.

And so, on behalf of an entire nation, I want to say thanks to the men and women who wear our uniform, and thanks to the Reserve Officers Association for your sacrifices and your support of our great land.

### Excerpted Remarks by the President from Speech at
### Southern Maine Technical College
Portland, Maine
January 25, 2002

I'll have other priorities in my budget. One of the biggest, of course, is to make sure the homeland is secure. You know, none of us ever dreamt that we'd have a two-front war to fight: One overseas and one at home. But we do. That's reality. And as a result, we must respond, and continue to respond, and stay on alert, and help defend America. The biggest chore I have, my biggest job, is to make sure our homeland is secure. . . .

[When] I speak to the Congress next Tuesday night and I submit my budget, one of the top priorities will be the security of the homeland. I've asked for a doubling of homeland security funds, to $38 billion a year, money that will be spent to make sure that the federal government and the state governments and the local governments—and I know some mayors are here—work in a cooperative way to make sure that our first-responders—the police, the fire, the emergency medical teams—have the best equipment, the best training, the best ability to communicate with each other to protect the American people. . . .

And under this budget, we're spending $11 billion for controlling our borders. It is so important for our nation to work with our friend to the north, Canada, and our friend to the south, Mexico, on border initiatives—that one doesn't tie up commerce but, on the other hand, prevents illegal drugs, terrorists, [and] arms from flowing across our border.

Tom Ridge went up to Canada . . . and we're talking about a new border initiative with our friends. We're analyzing every aspect of the border and making sure that the effort is seamless, the communication is real, that the enforcement is strong.

And so, to this end, I've got a twenty-nine percent increase in the budget of the INS, to make sure we modernize our reporting data, to know who comes [into] our country and who leaves our country. . . .

The INS estimates that forty percent of the people who are here illegally have overstayed their visa. Forty percent of the people who are here illegally came because of the generosity of America, were given a period of time in which they could stay, and then they didn't leave.

And one of the things we want to make sure of is [that] we find the forty percent to make sure they're not part of some al Qaeda network that wants to hit the United States. And so we're looking, we're listening, we're following every single lead. . . .

There is nothing more important for me and the federal government to do everything within the Constitution of the United States—and I emphasize we will not let the terrorists tear down our Constitution—we will do everything within the Constitution to protect the innocent Americans, the innocent moms and dads, the people who yearn for freedom and normalcy . . .

But I want to explain to the American people that we must be patient. We've just started, and there's a lot to do. We've entered into a dangerous phase of the first theater in the war against terror. And that is, we're now hunting them down.

We've got teams on the ground that are going cave-to-cave. You see, this enemy is one that's willing to send their young on suicide missions, while they themselves hide in caves. But there's no cave deep enough for the reach of the American military. We're patient, we're deliberate, and we're going to bring them to justice, one person at a time.

I want to remind you all that our mission is not one person, our mission is terror wherever it exists. I'm proud we've got a strong coalition, a coalition that our country leads, a coalition bound up to protect freedom, a coalition that I hope will take every step necessary to find terrorists where they live, and help us bring them to justice.

You know, when the enemy hit us, they must have not known what they were doing. I like to tell people, they must have been watching too much TV, because they didn't understand America. They were watching some of those shows, that one can get the wrong impression about how materialistic we might be, how selfish we might be as a people.

But that's not the way we are. Not only are we patient and determined and resolute to defend values we love, starting with the value of freedom, this good nation understands that in order to fight evil, you do so with acts of kindness and goodness. . . .

You see, the great strength of America is not only our military. The true strength of America is the million acts of kindness and decency and compassion that define the soul and character of our country on a daily basis.

No, when the enemy struck us, little did they realize that out of the terrible evil would come such good. Our job is not only to win the war overseas, our job is not only to protect the homeland, to make sure we can live peacefully; our job is to fight evil on a daily basis, by loving a neighbor just like you'd like to be loved yourself.

And that's what [is] happening all across the country. And for those of you who do that, I want to thank you from the bottom of my heart. And I want to thank you for giving me a chance to be the President of the greatest nation on the face of the earth.


## Excerpted Remarks from President's State of the Union Address
### January 29, 2002

Thank you very much. Mr. Speaker, Vice President Cheney, members of Congress, distinguished guests, fellow citizens: As we gather tonight, our nation is at war, our economy is in recession, and the civilized world faces unprecedented dangers. Yet the state of our Union has never been stronger.

We last met in an hour of shock and suffering. In four short months, our nation has comforted the victims, begun to rebuild New York and the Pentagon, rallied a great coalition, captured, arrested, and rid the world of thousands of terrorists, destroyed Afghanistan's terrorist training camps, saved a people from starvation, and freed a country from brutal oppression.

The American flag flies again over our embassy in Kabul. Terrorists who once occupied Afghanistan now occupy cells at Guantanamo Bay. And terrorist leaders who urged followers to sacrifice their lives are running for their own.

America and Afghanistan are now allies against terror. We'll be partners in rebuilding that country. And this evening we welcome the distinguished interim leader of a liberated Afghanistan: Chairman Hamid Karzai.

The last time we met in this chamber, the mothers and daughters of Afghanistan were captives in their own homes, forbidden from working or going to school. Today women are free, and are part of Afghanistan's new government. And we welcome the new Minister of Women's Affairs, Doctor Sima Samar.

Our progress is a tribute to the spirit of the Afghan people, to the resolve of our coalition, and to the might of the United States military. When I called our troops into action, I did so with complete confidence in their courage and skill. And tonight, thanks to them, we are winning the war on terror. The men and women of our Armed Forces have delivered a message now clear to every enemy of the United States: Even 7,000 miles away, across oceans and continents, on mountaintops and in caves—you will not escape the justice of this nation.

For many Americans, these four months have brought sorrow, and pain that will never completely go away. Every day a retired firefighter returns to Ground Zero, to feel closer to his two sons who died there. At a memorial in New York, a little boy left his football with a note for his lost father: Dear Daddy, Please take this to Heaven. I don't want to play football until I can play with you again some day.

Last month, at the grave of her husband, Michael, a CIA officer and Marine who died in Mazur-e-Sharif, Shannon Spann said these words of farewell: "Semper Fi, my love." Shannon is with us tonight.

Shannon, I assure you and all who have lost a loved one that our cause is just, and our country will never forget the debt we owe Michael and all who gave their lives for freedom.

Our cause is just, and it continues. Our discoveries in Afghanistan confirmed our worst fears, and showed us the true scope of the task ahead. We have seen the depth of our enemies' hatred in videos, where they laugh about the loss of innocent life. And the depth of their hatred is equaled by the madness of the destruction they design. We have found diagrams of American nuclear power plants and public water facilities, detailed instructions for making chemical weapons, surveillance maps of American cities, and thorough descriptions of landmarks in America and throughout the world.

What we have found in Afghanistan confirms that, far from ending there, our war against terror is only beginning. Most of the 19 men who hijacked planes on September the 11th were trained in Afghanistan's camps, and so were tens of thousands of others. Thousands of dangerous killers, schooled in the methods of murder, often supported by outlaw regimes, are now spread throughout the world like ticking time bombs, set to go off without warning.

Thanks to the work of our law-enforcement officials and coalition partners, hundreds of terrorists have been arrested. Yet, tens of thousands of trained terrorists are still at large. These enemies view the entire world as a battlefield, and we must pursue them wherever they are. So long as training camps operate, so long as nations harbor terrorists, freedom is at risk. And America and our allies must not, and will not, allow it.

Our nation will continue to be steadfast and patient and persistent in the pursuit of two great objectives. First, we will shut down terrorist camps, disrupt terrorist plans, and bring terrorists to justice. And, second, we must prevent the terrorists and regimes who seek chemical, biological, or nuclear weapons from threatening the United States and the world.

Our military has put the terror training camps of Afghanistan out of business, yet camps still exist in at least a dozen countries. A terrorist underworld—including groups like Hamas, Hezbollah, Islamic Jihad, Jaish-i-Mohammed—operates in remote jungles and deserts, and hides in the centers of large cities.

While the most visible military action is in Afghanistan, America is acting elsewhere. We now have troops in the Philippines, helping to train that country's armed forces to go after terrorist cells that have executed an American, and still hold hostages. Our soldiers, working with the Bosnian government, seized terrorists who were plotting to bomb our embassy. Our Navy is patrolling the coast of Africa to block the shipment of weapons and the establishment of terrorist camps in Somalia.

My hope is that all nations will heed our call, and eliminate the terrorist parasites who threaten their countries and our own. Many nations are acting forcefully. Pakistan is now cracking down on terror, and I admire the strong leadership of President Musharraf.

But some governments will be timid in the face of terror. And make no mistake about it: If they do not act, America will.

Our second goal is to prevent regimes that sponsor terror from threatening America or our friends and allies with weapons of mass destruction. Some of these regimes have been pretty quiet since September the 11th. But we know their true nature. North Korea is a regime arming with missiles and weapons of mass destruction, while starving its citizens.

Iran aggressively pursues these weapons and exports terror, while an unelected few repress the Iranian people's hope for freedom.

Iraq continues to flaunt its hostility toward America and to support terror. The Iraqi regime has plotted to develop anthrax, and nerve gas, and nuclear weapons for over a decade. This is a regime that has already used poison gas to murder thousands of its own citizens—leaving the bodies of mothers huddled over their dead children. This is a regime that agreed to international inspections—then kicked out the inspectors. This is a regime that has something to hide from the civilized world.

States like these, and their terrorist allies, constitute an axis of evil, arming to threaten the peace of the world. By seeking weapons of mass destruction, these regimes pose a grave and growing danger. They could provide these arms to terrorists, giving them the means to match their hatred. They could attack our allies or attempt to blackmail the United States. In any of these cases, the price of indifference would be catastrophic.

We will work closely with our coalition to deny terrorists and their state sponsors the materials, technology, and expertise to make and deliver weapons of mass destruction. We will develop and deploy effective missile defenses to protect America and our allies from sudden attack. And all nations should know: America will do what is necessary to ensure our nation's security.

We'll be deliberate, yet time is not on our side. I will not wait on events, while dangers gather. I will not stand by, as peril draws closer and closer. The United States of America will not permit the world's most dangerous regimes to threaten us with the world's most destructive weapons.

Our war on terror is well begun, but it is only begun. This campaign may not be finished on our watch—yet it must be and it will be waged on our watch.

We can't stop short. If we stop now—leaving terror camps intact and terror states unchecked—our sense of security would be false and temporary. History has called America and our allies to action, and it is both our responsibility and our privilege to fight freedom's fight.

Our first priority must always be the security of our nation, and that will be reflected in the budget I send to Congress. My budget supports three great goals for America: We will win this war; we'll protect our homeland; and we will revive our economy.

September the 11th brought out the best in America, and the best in this Congress. And I join the American people in applauding your unity and resolve. Now Americans deserve to have this same spirit directed toward addressing problems here at home. I'm a proud member of my party—yet as we act to win the war, protect our people, and create jobs in America, we must act, first and foremost, not as Republicans, not as Democrats, but as Americans.

It costs a lot to fight this war. We have spent more than a billion dollars a month—over $30 million a day—and we must be prepared for future operations. Afghanistan proved that expensive precision weapons defeat the enemy and spare innocent lives, and we need more of them. We need to replace aging aircraft and make our military more agile, to put our troops anywhere in the world quickly and safely. Our men and women in uniform deserve the best weapons, the best equipment, the best training—and they also deserve another pay raise.

My budget includes the largest increase in defense spending in two decades—because while the price of freedom and security is high, it is never too high. Whatever it costs to defend our country, we will pay.

The next priority of my budget is to do everything possible to protect our citizens and strengthen our nation against the ongoing threat of another attack. Time and distance from the events of September the 11th will not make us safer unless we act on its lessons. America is no longer protected by vast oceans. We are protected from attack only by vigorous action abroad, and increased vigilance at home.

My budget nearly doubles funding for a sustained strategy of homeland security, focused on four key areas: Bioterrorism, emergency response, airport and border security, and improved intelligence. We will develop vaccines to fight anthrax and other deadly diseases. We'll increase funding to help states and communities train and equip our heroic police and firefighters. We will improve intelligence collection and sharing, expand patrols at our borders, strengthen the security of air travel, and use technology to track the arrivals and departures of visitors to the United States.

Homeland security will make America not only stronger, but, in many ways, better. Knowledge gained from bioterrorism research will improve public health. Stronger police and fire departments will mean safer neighborhoods. Stricter border enforcement will help combat illegal drugs. And as government works to better secure our homeland, America will continue to depend on the eyes and ears of alert citizens.

A few days before Christmas, an airline flight attendant spotted a passenger lighting a match. The crew and passengers quickly subdued the man, who had been trained by al Qaeda and was armed with explosives. The people on that plane were alert and, as a result, likely saved nearly 200 lives. And tonight we welcome and thank flight attendants Hermis Moutardier and Christina Jones.

Once we have funded our national security and our homeland security, the final great priority of my budget is economic security for the American people. To achieve these great national objectives—to win the war, protect the homeland, and revitalize our economy—our budget will run a deficit that will be small and short-term, so long as Congress restrains spending and acts in a fiscally responsible manner. We have clear priorities and we must act at home with the same purpose and resolve we have shown overseas: We'll prevail in the war, and we will defeat this recession. . . .

During these last few months, I've been humbled and privileged to see the true character of this country in a time of testing. Our enemies believed America was weak and materialistic, that we would splinter in fear and selfishness. They were as wrong as they are evil.

The American people have responded magnificently, with courage and compassion, strength and resolve. As I have met the heroes, hugged the families, and looked into the tired faces of rescuers, I have stood in awe of the American people.

And I hope you will join me—I hope you will join me in expressing thanks to one American for the strength and calm and comfort she brings to our nation in crisis, our First Lady, Laura Bush.

None of us would ever wish the evil that was done on September the 11th. Yet after America was attacked, it was as if our entire country looked into a mirror and saw our better selves. We were reminded that we are citizens, with obligations to each other, to our country, and to history. We began to think less of the goods we can accumulate, and more about the good we can do.

For too long our culture has said, "If it feels good, do it." Now America is embracing a new ethic and a new creed: "Let's roll." In the sacrifice of soldiers, the fierce brotherhood of firefighters, and the bravery and generosity of ordinary citizens, we have glimpsed what a new culture of responsibility could look like. We want to be a nation that serves goals larger than self. We've been offered a unique opportunity, and we must not let this moment pass.

My call tonight is for every American to commit at least two years—4,000 hours over the rest of your lifetime—to the service of your neighbors and your nation. Many are already serving, and I thank you. If you aren't sure how to help, I've got a good place to start. To sustain and extend the best that has emerged in America, I invite you to join the new USA Freedom Corps. The Freedom Corps will focus on three areas of need: Responding in case of crisis at home; rebuilding our communities; and extending American compassion throughout the world.

One purpose of the USA Freedom Corps will be homeland security. America needs retired doctors and nurses who can be mobilized in major emergencies; volunteers to help police and fire departments; transportation and utility workers well-trained in spotting danger.

Our country also needs citizens working to rebuild our communities. We need mentors to love children, especially children whose parents are in prison. And we need more talented teachers in troubled schools. USA Freedom Corps will expand and improve the good efforts of AmeriCorps and Senior Corps to recruit more than 200,000 new volunteers.

And America needs citizens to extend the compassion of our country to every part of the world. So we will renew the promise of the Peace Corps, double its volunteers over the next five years, and ask it to join a new effort to encourage development and education and opportunity in the Islamic world.

This time of adversity offers a unique moment of opportunity—a moment we must seize to change our culture. Through the gathering momentum of millions of acts of service and decency and kindness, I know we can overcome evil with greater good. And we have a great opportunity during this time of war to lead the world toward the values that will bring lasting peace.

All fathers and mothers, in all societies, want their children to be educated, and live free from poverty and violence. No people on earth yearn to be oppressed, or aspire to servitude, or eagerly await the midnight knock of the secret police.

If anyone doubts this, let them look to Afghanistan, where the Islamic "street" greeted the fall of tyranny with song and celebration. Let the skeptics look to Islam's own rich history, with its centuries of learning and tolerance and progress. America will lead by defending liberty and justice because they are right and true and unchanging for all people everywhere.

No nation owns these aspirations, and no nation is exempt from them. We have no intention of imposing our culture. But America will always stand firm for the non-negotiable demands of human dignity: The rule of law; limits on the power of the state; respect for women; private property; free speech; equal justice; and religious tolerance.

America will take the side of brave men and women who advocate these values around the world, including the Islamic world, because we have a greater objective than eliminating threats and containing resentment. We seek a just and peaceful world beyond the war on terror.

In this moment of opportunity, a common danger is erasing old rivalries. America is working with Russia and China and India, in ways we have never before, to achieve peace and prosperity. In every region, free markets and free trade and free societies are proving their power to lift lives. Together with friends and allies from Europe to Asia, and Africa to Latin America, we will demonstrate that the forces of terror cannot stop the momentum of freedom.

The last time I spoke here, I expressed the hope that life would return to normal. In some ways, it has. In others, it never will. Those of us who have lived through these challenging times have been changed by them. We've come to know truths that we will never question: Evil is real, and it must be opposed. Beyond all differences of race or creed, we are one country, mourning together and facing danger together. Deep in the American character, there is honor, and it is stronger than cynicism. And many have discovered again that even in tragedy—especially in tragedy—God is near.

In a single instant, we realized that this will be a decisive decade in the history of liberty, that we've been called to a unique role in human events. Rarely has the world faced a choice more clear or consequential.

Our enemies send other people's children on missions of suicide and murder. They embrace tyranny and death as a cause and a creed. We stand for a different choice, made long ago, on the day of our founding. We affirm it again today. We choose freedom and the dignity of every life.

Steadfast in our purpose, we now press on. We have known freedom's price. We have shown freedom's power. And in this great conflict, my fellow Americans, we will see freedom's victory.

# February 2002

**Excerpted Remarks by the President from Speech to the
New York Police Department Personnel**
New York City
February 6, 2002

Thank you all. It's nice to be back in New York City, and I am so proud to stand here today with New York's Finest, and New York's Bravest.

I have a message for you from your fellow Americans: Police and firefighters of New York, you have this nation's respect, and you'll have this nation's support. . . .

Last week I reported to our Congress that the state of our union has never been stronger; that despite a war, a recession, despite continuing danger, we are strong, really strong, because our people are strong. And there's no stronger people than the men and women who wear the uniform here in New York. There's no stronger people than those who kind of set the new standard of courage and honor.

There's a new ethic in America—at least I think one's coming on—a new culture, a culture to replace "if it feels good, do it" with one of responsibility, with one defined by those brave words, "Let's roll."

But that's nothing new for the firefighters and the policemen of New York. That's been your ethic for a long, long time. That ethic's been around here way before September the 11th.

And a lot of people are lucky the ethic was around.

As you rebuild your ranks, every new recruit walks in the path of heroes. And as a result of some of the courageous action here, not only is a new ethic evolving, but there's some fantastic examples for young recruits to follow.

Peter Ganci—many of you knew him. He was the highest-ranking uniformed officer in the New York Fire Department. His deputy, Michael Regan, saw him for the last time on the morning of September the 11th, after the first building had collapsed and while the second building was still burning. Michael Regan recalled this: Peter directed every citizen and every firefighter to go north to safety; and he want south, directly into danger. Let's roll.

Brian McDonnell. Maybe you knew Brian well here. His wife called him a cop's cop. He was a former Army paratrooper. He was known for always putting his colleagues first. September the 11th, he was last seen charging into the south tower to help his fellow citizens.

On the worst day this city has ever known, we saw some of the finest people New York has ever produced. We mourn every loss. We remember every life. But they will not have died in vain.

I told our country and I told the world that we don't seek revenge, we seek justice. And I want to assure you all, those who have been touched by this terrible tragedy, justice will be meted out. I unleashed the mighty United States military and they have not let us down. In five short months, in a brief period of time, we have completely routed the Taliban. I said loud and clear, if you harbor a terrorist, if you feed a terrorist, you're just as guilty as the terrorist, and the Taliban found out what we meant.

This is a patient nation. We are a determined nation. We're a nation that will not rest until we have brought justice not only on the al Qaeda killers and governments which support and house them, but on terrorism everywhere. Now we must seize the moment. History has called this nation into action; history has given us a chance to defend freedom, to fight tyranny. And that's exactly what this country is going to do. We defend freedom.

Not only do we owe it to those whose lives were lost on September the 11th, but we owe it to the living, as well. We owe it to our children and our children's children, to protect a way of life, to defend freedom, to defend our values, to fight evil. And we will not tire, nor will we rest, until justice is done.

Oh, some around the world may grow weary. Some may grow exhausted by our drive for freedom. But not me, not our government, and not our nation.

I have submitted a budget that recognizes that Afghanistan is only the first theater in the war against terror. We significantly [increased] the budget for national defense. After all, it is our number-one priority. It is the largest increase since the presidency of Ronald Reagan, whose 91st birthday we celebrate today. His budgets helped rebuild the military power of the United States. And for that our nation should be grateful.

But what was true in his day is true today—that whatever it costs to defend our security, and whatever it costs to defend our freedom, we must pay it. I ask Congress to pass this budget. Our men and women who wear the uniform of the United States military deserve the best training, the best equipment, another pay raise, the best support of the United States of America.

And for those of you who have a relative who wear the uniform of the United States military—the moms and dads, brothers and sisters, sons and daughters—on behalf of a grateful nation, I want to thank you very much.

I'm fully aware of the task at hand. I know that in order to defend America in the long-term, we've got to be successful overseas; that the best homeland defense is to rout out terror wherever it exists. I know that. And I know some of them are going to try to hide in caves, but there is no cave deep enough. . . . They're going to try to run, but they can't run forever. They cannot run forever. And in the meantime, until we achieve our objective—no matter how long that takes—we will secure our homeland.

I have the great honor of going into the Oval Office as your President. Every morning that I walk in there, I'm thrilled and honored. I take the dog in with me, and she seems to be thrilled and honored, too. (Laughter) I sit down at the fantastic desk—it's a desk that the Roosevelts used; it's a desk John Kennedy used; Reagan used; it's a desk I'm honored to use. And the first thing I do is, I look at threats to the United States of America.

They're still out there. The enemy still wants to get us. And I want to assure you all we're doing everything in our power to prevent them from doing that; that my main job—and the main job of Ridge and the FBI and Kelly and everybody else involved with law enforcement is to protect the American people, is to keep American families safe. And we're pouring all our energy into doing our job, which is the security of the country.

We've changed the attitude of the FBI. I mean, we're interested in spies; we're more interested in al Qaeda killers. We're going to run down white-collar criminals; but our focus is on finding any cell that may exist in our country and getting them. We're going to run down every piece of evidence we find and share it with state and local authorities. We're on the hunt. We're on the hunt, and we're not going to rest. We're just not going to rest. The American people need to know we're doing everything in our power to strengthen the security at home.

And we're preparing responses. Yesterday, Tom [Ridge] and I went over to Pittsburgh and talked about a bioterrorism response as a part of our homeland security package. We're loading up with medicines. We're going to have the health services communicate better with each other. We're getting ready.

We're doing a better job of securing our borders. We're going to figure out who's coming into our country and who's leaving our country, to make sure that people—(applause) Listen, we're a great nation. We welcome people in. We just want to know why you're here. (Laughter) And if you're not supposed to be here more than a period of time, then maybe you ought to just go on home. It's important—(applause)—it's important that we have good information so we can secure the homeland. It's important that our airports be secure.

And so, we worked with Congress to get a bill out to make air travel more safe. And it's important that we understand that in the first minutes and hours after attack, that's the most hopeful time to save lives. And so that's why we're focusing on the heroic efforts of those [first] responders. That's why we want to spend money to make sure equipment is there, strategies are there, communications are there, to make sure that you have whatever it takes . . . to respond.

But the interesting thing about making sure our homeland is more secure is that, as a result of focusing on first responders, neighborhoods will be more safe in the long run. As a result of focusing on bioterrorism, perhaps we'll develop vaccines and medicines and cures for other diseases. As [we] focus on making sure our health systems talk better, we'll leave behind a better health-care system. As [we're] making sure that our borders are more secure, we'll have a stronger Coast Guard. And so, [in] the short run, we're focusing on attacks; [in] the long run, the country will be better off for the doubling of the homeland security budget that I submitted to the United States Congress.

And part of making sure we're secure is to make sure there's economic security, for New Yorkers and for the country. Obviously, I'm deeply concerned about the recession. And I understand the shocks to our economy, what 9/11 did. And I'm worried about the fact that many New Yorkers aren't working, and we want them to work. And that's why I am committed to defeating not only terrorists, but the recession.

I want you to know something: When I say I'm going to do something, I'm going to do it. I told the people of New York that we will work to provide at least $20 billion to help New York rebuild . . . And that includes money apart from the Victims Compensation Fund. And when I say $20 billion, I mean $20 billion.

FEMA is on the spot. And we're now spending a lot of money here to help New York and the emergency side of things. And we need to restore the infrastructure. We need to quickly rebuild the highways. And you know what else we need? We need the Liberty Zone in lower Manhattan. We need to provide job incentives, incentives to create jobs in the area that was affected by the attack. Congress needs to put the Liberty Zone, the Liberty Bonds, in a stimulus package and get it to my desk so I can sign it for the good of New York City.

It is important that New York City be vibrant and strong. It's important when people not only here at home, but around the world, look at this fantastic city, they see economic vitality and growth. I'm confident we can recover together. It's going to take federal and state effort. I'm here to tell you the federal help is coming.

You know, I don't know what went through the enemy's mind when they attacked us. I think they thought we were soft. I like to needle them by saying they must have been watching too much daytime TV. (Laughter) They probably thought that, oh, we'll attack and [America will] just kind of roll over, gnash our teeth a little bit, wring our hands, mourn for the dead, and forget. Boy, they really miscalculated.

See, they don't understand America. They don't understand us. We're understanding more about ourselves as a result of what went on. We understand heroism. We understand now what it means to recite a prayer, tell your wife, "I love you," on the phone, and drive a plane into the ground to save others' lives. We're beginning to understand more about sacrifice, personal responsibility.

See, I believe out of this terrible evil can come some great good. I believe there's a better understanding of the sacrifice the policemen and firefighters make. And that's good for America. I believe there is a different culture evolving, one that says each of us need to be responsible for the decisions we make . . . There's a different culture evolving as moms and dads now understand their most important job is to love their children with all their heart and all their soul.

People ask me all the time what can I do to help fight terror, fight the evil ones. Well, I believe since this is a struggle between evil and good, the best way to do it is to do some good in your neighborhood; is to mentor a child who may be lost; is to help a shut-in; is to walk across the street to a neighbor in need and say, what can I do to help you?

Many of you are already doing that—by loving the widows and the children of those who lost their lives. It's these thousands and millions of acts of kindness all across America on a daily basis that define the character of our nation. The way you fight evil is with millions of acts of good. It's the cumulative effect of the heart and soul of America that stands tall against the evil ones. Not only will we prevail militarily in the long run, but we will have overcome evil by being a nation that is more compassionate, more decent, more loving to our fellow citizens.

I'm so proud of how America has responded. I'm proud of New York City and the strength and character you have shown. I loved it when our pilots found on some of the munitions this simple sign, "I LOVE NEW YORK." America loves New York. We love your strength. We love your resolve. We've loved your courage in the face of incredible difficulty.

Keep on, and my God bless you all.


### Excerpted Remarks by the President from Speech at the National Prayer Breakfast
Washington, D.C.
February 7, 2002

I'm particularly grateful to Lisa Beamer for her reading and for her example. I appreciate her example of faith made stronger in trial. In the worst moments of her life, Lisa has been a model of grace—her own, and the grace of God. And all America welcomes into the world Todd and Lisa's new daughter, Morgan Kay Beamer.

Since we met last year, millions of Americans have been led to prayer. They have prayed for comfort in time of grief; for understanding in a time of anger; for protection in a time of uncertainty. Many, including me, have been on bended knee. The prayers of this nation are a part of the good that has come from the evil of September the 11th, more good than we could ever have predicted. Tragedy has brought forth the courage and the generosity of our people.

None of us would ever wish on anyone what happened on that day. Yet, as with each life, sorrows we would not choose can bring wisdom and strength gained in no other way. This insight is central to many faiths, and certainly to faith that finds hope and comfort in a cross.

Every religion is welcomed in our country; all are practiced here. Many of our good citizens profess no religion at all. Our country has never had an official faith. Yet we have all been witnesses these past 21 weeks to the power of faith to see us through the hurt and loss that [have] come to our country.

Faith gives the assurance that our lives and our history have a moral design. As individuals, we know that suffering is temporary, and hope is eternal. As a nation, we know that the ruthless will not inherit the earth. Faith teaches humility, and with it, tolerance. Once we have recognized God's image in ourselves, we must recognize it in every human being.

Respect for the dignity of others can be found outside of religion, just as intolerance is sometimes found within it. Yet for millions of Americans, the practice of tolerance is a command of faith. When our country was attacked, Americans did not respond with bigotry. People from other countries and cultures have been treated with respect. And this is one victory in the war against terror.

At the same time, faith shows us the reality of good, and the reality of evil. Some acts and choices in this world have eternal consequences. It is always, and everywhere, wrong to target and kill the innocent. It is always, and everywhere, wrong to be cruel and hateful, to enslave and oppress. It is always, and everywhere, right to be kind and just, to protect the lives of others, and to lay down your life for a friend.

The men and women who charged into burning buildings to save others, those who fought the hijackers, were not confused about the difference between right and wrong. They knew the difference. They knew their duty. And we know their sacrifice was not in vain.

Faith shows us the way to self-giving, to love our neighbor as we would want to be loved ourselves. In service to others, we find deep human fulfillment. And as acts of service are multiplied, our nation becomes a more welcoming place for the weak, and a better place for those who suffer and grieve.

For half a century now, the National Prayer Breakfast has been a symbol of the vital place of faith in the life of our nation. You've reminded generations of leaders of a purpose and a power greater than their own. In times of calm, and in times of crisis, you've called us to prayer.

In this time of testing for our nation, my family and I have been blessed by the prayers of countless Americans. We have felt their sustaining power and we're incredibly grateful. Tremendous challenges await this nation, and there will be hardships ahead. Faith will not make our path easy, but it will give us strength for the journey.

The promise of faith is not the absence of suffering, it is the presence of grace. And at every step we are secure in knowing that suffering produces perseverance, and perseverance produces character, and character produces hope—and hope does not disappoint.

May God bless you, and may God continue to bless America.

## Excerpted Remarks by the President from Speech to Military Personnel in Alaska
Anchorage, Alaska
February 16, 2002

You know, I can't wait to take our message overseas. We're going to Japan and South Korea and China, where I'm going to continue to work with the leaders of those countries in our mutual concerns, starting with fighting the war against terror; making it clear that the resolve of this nation is steady and strong—to be able to look these leaders in the eye and say, when it comes to defending freedom, the United States of America will not blink.

And I look forward to sharing with them my passionate belief in the values that we hold dear here in America: Freedom—freedom to worship, freedom to speak, freedom to achieve your dreams. And it's those very values that came under attack on September the 11th. The good news is, our mighty military was ready.

You know, when we were attacked, it seemed like the people in the U.S. military took it personally. A reporter asked an Air Force pilot if he had any direct connection to any of the victims of September the 11th. And he said, you know, I think we all do; they're all Americans. You see, when you strike one American, you strike all Americans. And those terrorists are going to hear from us.

It's hard for me to figure out what was going through the minds of those who planned and attacked America. They must have thought we were soft—

AUDIENCE MEMBER: They were wrong!

THE PRESIDENT: Yes, they were. They thought we were so materialistic that we didn't understand sacrifice and honor and duty. They must have been watching some lousy movies. (Laughter) They didn't know that this great nation would rise up in unison to send a clear message that we will do whatever it takes to defend our freedoms; that this great nation is resolved to find the killers, one by one, and bring them to justice.

But this cause is more than just an individual. Oh, I know sometimes the people on the airwaves like to say, well, someone is—bin Laden's hiding here and he's hiding there. But this cause is much bigger than a single person. This is about fighting terror wherever it hides. This is about defending America and our friends and allies, defending values. The world must understand that this nation won't rest until we have destroyed terrorism, until we have denied the threat of global terrorism.

I can't tell you how passionate I feel on the subject. I look around and see your children and your grandchildren. This is an opportunity to defend freedom for them. This is a chance to say that your kids can grow up in a secure and peaceful America. And if they work hard and get a good education, they can realize their dreams in a peaceful world. We long for peace, but we understand that the terrorists must be brought to justice in order to achieve that peace.

Thanks to our military, we're making good progress, and it hasn't taken very long. If you think about it, we've been at this for a little less than six months, and we're achieving our objectives.

First, I mentioned the coalition the Secretary of State's working on. And we sent a clear message: Either you're with us or you're against us. Either you stand for freedom, or you stand with tyranny. And the good news is, many, many, many nations have heard that message. And I'm proud to report they stand squarely with the United States in the defense of freedom.

And you all also may remember that early on I said if you hide a terrorist, if you feed a terrorist, if you provide comfort to a terrorist, you're just as guilty as the terrorist. The Taliban now knows what we mean. They're gone. And, guess what? People in Afghanistan don't miss them one bit.

I am proud that our military has fulfilled our mission, our military mission. But, in so doing, we liberated a people. We freed women and children from the clutches of one of the most barbaric regimes in the history of mankind.

But there's more to do in Afghanistan. We're entering a difficult phase of the first theater in the war against terror. They've got a lot of caves over there, but they can't hide long. . . . See, we're patient, and we're determined, and we're a steadfast nation. We're steady in our resolve. And that's so important, because we're trying to run down some people that, on the one hand, send youngsters to their death, and they, themselves, try to hide in caves. But there is no cave deep enough to hide from the long arm of justice of the United States military. We're going to run them down, one by one. And it doesn't matter where they try to hide, there is no calendar, there is no deadline. . . . That's not the way it works. Now that they have laid down the gauntlet, we're going to pursue them. And we're going to get 'em. And when we do, the world will be a safer place.

But we've got a bigger task than that. One of the most dangerous things that can happen to the future of our nation is that these kind of terrorist organizations hook up with nations that develop weapons of mass destruction. One of the worst things that could possibly happen to freedom-loving people, whether it be the United States or our friends or allies, is to allow nations that have got a dark history and an ugly past to develop weapons of mass destruction like nuclear weapons, or chemical weapons, or biological weapons, which could, for example, be delivered by long-range missile, to become a part of the terrorist network. And there are such nations in the world.

Of course, we'd like for them to change their ways, and we'll continue to pressure them to do so. We'd like for them to conform to normal ways of treating their own people, plus their neighborhood, plus the world. We expect there to be transparency. People who have got something to hide make us nervous, particularly those who have gassed their own citizens in the past, for example.

And so we expect them—and so do other freedom-loving countries—to change their behavior. But if they do not, the United States will do what it takes to defend our freedom. Make no mistake about it.

This is a grand and noble cause, and it's going to require a strong and modern military. I sent a budget up to Congress. The good news is, I don't have to worry about the two United States Senators and the member of the House of Representatives from the state of Alaska.

The budget I submitted is the largest single increase in military spending in a generation. If we're going to fight for freedom, we have to pay the cost to fight for freedom. And it's worth it. And I also believe that any time we send our military into harm's way, they should have the best equipment, the best training, the best possible support. A grateful nation owes it to the United States military. And one other thing, you need another pay raise.

You hear a lot of talk about homeland security. And I want to assure you all, the moms and dads and everybody else here, that we are doing everything in our power to secure the homeland. I mean, we're chasing down every lead, every hint, every possible cell member. . . .

I can make no guarantees; I do know the enemy wants to hit us again. But every day, my administration discusses how best to make America a more difficult target. Every day, the FBI Director talks about how he has changed the culture of the FBI. We've got thousands of FBI agents working to protect the American people. We're making our borders more secure. We've now got a bioterrorism initiative we're starting. We're doing a lot, and I'm proud of the efforts of people who are working overtime, constantly working to make the homeland secure. . . .

As you [have] probably figured out by now, I view this current conflict as . . . us versus them, and evil versus good. And there's no in between. There's no hedging. And if you want to join the war against evil, do some good. If you want to be a part of our nation's stand against those who murder innocent people for the sake of murder, for those who believe in tyranny, for those who hijack a noble religion—if you want to take a stand, love a neighbor like you'd like to be loved yourself.

If you want to be a part of the war, walk across the street and say to a shut-in elderly person, what can I do to help you? Or mentor a child. Or get into your public schools here in Anchorage. Or provide support for people. Or go to your church or synagogue or mosque and walk out with a program that says, I want to help somebody in need. Feed the hungry. If you want to be a part of the war against terror, remember that it's the gathering momentum of millions and millions of acts of kindness that take place in America that stands squarely in the face of evil.

The enemy hit us, and they made a huge mistake. Not only will our nation seek justice, but out of the evil will come incredible goodness. Out of the evil will [come an] America more resolved not only to defend freedom, more resolved to sacrifice, if necessary, to defend freedom, but [an] America resolved to show the world our true strength, which is the compassionate, decent heart of the American people.

It is such an honor to be the President of the greatest nation on the face of the Earth. Thank you for coming out to say hello to Laura and me. And God bless.

## Excerpted Remarks by the President from Speech to Military Personnel Stationed in the Demilitarized Zone
Dorasan, Republic of Korea
February 20, 2002

We gather today surrounded by reminders of the challenges to peace and stability on the Korean Peninsula. President Kim has just shown me a road he built—a road for peace. And he's shown me where that road abruptly ends, right here at the DMZ. That road has the potential to bring the peoples on both sides of this divided land together, and for the good of all the Korean people, the North should finish it.

Traveling south on that road, the people of the North would see not a threat, but a miracle of peaceful development, Asia's third largest economy that has risen from the ruins of war. The people of the North would see more than physical wealth, they would see the creativity and spiritual freedom represented here today. They would see a great and hopeful alternative to stagnation and starvation. And they would find friends and partners in the rebuilding of their country.

South Korea is more than a successful nation, it is an example to the world. When nations embrace freedom, they find economic and social progress. When nations accept the rules of the modern world, they find the benefits of the modern world. And when nations treat men and women with dignity, they find true greatness.

When satellites take pictures of the Korean Peninsula at night, the South is awash in light. The North is almost completely dark. Kim Dae-jung has put forward a vision that can illuminate the whole Peninsula. We want all the Koreans to live in the light.

My vision is clear: I see a Peninsula that is one day united in commerce and cooperation, instead of divided by barbed wire and fear. Korean grand-parents should be free to spend their final years with those they love. Korean children should never starve while a massive army is fed. No nation should be a prison for its own people. No Korean should be treated as a cog in the machinery of the state.

And as I stated before the American Congress just a few weeks ago, we must not permit the world's most dangerous regimes to threaten us with the world's most dangerous weapons.

I speak for these convictions even as we hope for dialogue with the North. America provides humanitarian food assistance to the people of North Korea, despite our concerns about the regime. We're prepared to talk with the North about steps that would lead to a better future, a future that is more hopeful and less threatening. But like this road left unbuilt, our offer has gone unanswered.

Some day we all hope the stability of this Peninsula will be built on the reconciliation of its two halves. Yet today, the stability of this Peninsula is built on the great alliance between the Republic of Korea and the United States.

All of Asia, including North Korea, knows that America will stand firm-ly—will stand firmly—with our South Korean allies. We will sustain our obligations with honor. Our forces and our alliance are strong, and this strength is the foundation of peace on the Peninsula.

American forces receive generous support from our South Korean hosts, and we are very grateful. Today we are increasing the effectiveness of our military forces, even as U.S. troops become a less intrusive presence in Korea itself.

Americans are also very grateful for the tremendous outpouring of sym-pathy and support shown by the South Korean people following the terror of September the 11th. Today, both our nations are cooperating to fight against terror, proving that our alliance is both regional and global.

The United States and South Korea are bound by common interests. Our alliance is defined by common values. We deeply value our own liberty and we care about the liberty of others. Like the United States, South Korea has become a beacon of freedom, showing to the world the power of human liberty to bring down walls and uplift lives.

Today, across the mines and barbed wire, that light shines brighter than ever. It shines not as a threat to the North, but as an invitation. People on both sides of this border want to live in freedom and want to live in dignity, without the threat of violence and famine and war. I hope that one day soon this hope will be realized. And when that day comes, all the people of Korea will find in America a strong and willing friend.

### Excerpted Remarks by the President from Speech to Military Personnel Stationed at Osan Air Base
Seoul, Republic of Korea
February 21, 2002

I want to thank my fellow citizens, the members of the United States military, for being strong and steady, to keep the peace. It is such an honor to be traveling in Asia, representing our country. This is an important journey. We're stopping in the capitals of Japan and South Korea, and then in a couple of hours, in China. All three governments are lending their support in our war against terror.

It gives me a chance to look the leaders in the eye, to thank them on behalf of a grateful nation for their steady and strong support, as this nation leads a coalition to defend freedom. My trip was scheduled here for October, but we changed it after America came under attack. We had to change our plans. But since then, the killers and the government that sponsored them had to change their plans, too.

A few months ago, al Qaeda and the terrorists occupied Afghanistan. Now some of them are in cells in Guantanamo Bay. Not long ago they were urging their followers to sacrifice their lives. Now they're running for their own. Those who attacked us, and those who still want to try to hurt us, are beginning to realize they picked the wrong enemy. They thought we were soft. They thought we were so materialistic that we would not be willing to sacrifice. They didn't realize that we're a patient nation, that we're a deliberate nation.

And they're now beginning to realize that we're resolved to find the terrorists, wherever they hide, and rout them out. And as my fellow Americans, you need to know that we won't stop until the threat of global terrorism has been destroyed. We have been called to history. We must not stop. After all, we defend civilization itself. We didn't ask for this war, we're a peaceful nation. But we will do everything in our power to defend freedom and the universal values that are so important to our nation, and so important to a peaceful world. I made this message clear to our enemy, and the mighty United States military is delivering it.

I'm proud to report America and our allies are committed to this cause. If you haven't been back to America lately, I want to tell you, our nation is strongly united. This isn't a matter of political parties. We're talking about national purpose. The people of America understand it's going to take a while, but they're ready. We've accepted new responsibilities.

There's a new way of thinking in America. It was defined by the actions on Flight 93, when several people aboard an airplane got the word that that airplane might be headed to the Capitol, or the White House—but certainly headed to hurt [fellow Americans]. They were on the telephone with their loved ones. They told them they loved them. They said a prayer. And then they said: "Let's roll."

There is a new spirit of sacrifice in America that understands that we must, in life, serve something greater than ourselves. And we're now called to defend freedom, and our allies understand that. And the United States military understands that. And freedom we will defend with all our might.

And that's what you're doing here on the Korean Peninsula, a free and peaceful nation, and its 47 million people count on you every day. And in this duty the United States has a steady and courageous partner in the Republic of Korea.

During the years of partnership between our two countries, South Korea has become prosperous, and it has become strong. Its vibrant economy is an example of what free people and free institutions can achieve. And it shows the importance of America's presence in Asia.

The United States is a Pacific nation. History has led us here. Ties of commerce and friendship keep us here. And our friends and allies can be certain that we will always stand beside them. When America says we're your friend, we mean it.

We hope for a day when the stability of the Korean Peninsula is built on peaceful reconciliation of North and South. Today, however, the stability of this Peninsula is built on the military might of our great alliance. In our dealings with North Korea, we've laid down a clear marker. We will stand by the people of South Korea. We will maintain our presence here. And as I told the Congress and the world in my State of the Union message, we will not permit the world's most dangerous regimes to threaten us or our friends or our allies with weapons of mass destruction.

Those of you who are stationed here in Korea and members of our military throughout the world spend every day training and testing and preparing for any mission that may come. That's your responsibility, and you're the best in the world. And as your Commander-in-Chief, I have responsibilities to you to give clear orders, to set clear objectives, and to make sure you have everything you need to do your job. . . .

I'm so grateful many of you have brought your families, who are here. A grateful nation not only thanks those who wear the uniform, but we thank the wives and husbands and sons and daughters and family members who sacrifice along with you. But in order to make sure that sacrifice is not quite such a hill to climb, in the budget that I've [sent] to Congress I'm asking for another pay raise for the people who wear the uniform. It is necessary, it is the right course of action because in the months and years to come, our nation is going to be asking more of the United States military. And you have my confidence, because you've earned it. You earn it every day, in the difficulties you accept and the dangers you face. You're each here to serve your country, and your country is grateful. You're here because you believe in America, and America will always believe in you.

## Statement by the President on the Confirmation of the Death of Daniel Pearl
### Beijing, People's Republic of China
### February 22, 2002

Laura and I, and the American people, are deeply saddened to learn about the loss of Daniel Pearl's life. And we're really sad for his wife and his parents, and his friends and colleagues, who have been clinging to hope for weeks that he be found alive. We are especially sad for his unborn child, who will now know his father only through the memory of others.

All Americans are sad and angry to learn of the murder. All around the world, American journalists and humanitarian aid workers and diplomats and others do important work in places that are sometimes dangerous. Those who would threaten Americans, those who would engage in criminal, barbaric acts, need to know that these crimes only hurt their cause and only deepen the resolve of the United States of America to rid to world of these agents of terror. May God bless Daniel Pearl.

# March 2002

**Excerpted Remarks by the President from Speech to
Iowa Republican Party Victory Luncheon**
Des Moines, Iowa
March 1, 2002

This nation has sent men and women who wear our uniform into battle to defend freedom. And they have performed brilliantly. But if we send them into battle, they deserve the best training, the best supplies, the best equipment. They deserve another pay raise. And Congress needs to fully fund the military and defense budget I sent up to both the Senate and the House.

Because we're in for a long struggle. You know, I told the American people that this was a new kind of war. The enemy hit us. We've never been attacked like that before on the continental Forty-Eight. And we realized that we're in a new era. And that it's going to require patience of the American people. Because we're chasing down a kind of a faceless enemy; an enemy who sends young men to die on suicide missions and they, themselves, try to hide in caves.

But you need to know how determined I am to defend America and our freedom. It doesn't matter how deep the cave is. It doesn't matter where the cave is. We're going to find them. We're going to slowly but surely hunt them down and bring them to justice.

In the course of this war, I laid out some doctrines that are pretty darned clear. One of them is, if you harbor a terrorist, if you feed a terrorist, if you provide aid or comfort to a terrorist, you are just as guilty as the terrorist. And the Taliban found out exactly what we meant.

Our military took on a tough mission, to uphold that doctrine, and it was a dangerous mission, and they performed brilliantly. We're not conquerors, we showed the world; we're liberators. We liberated people from the clutches of one of the most barbaric regimes in the history of mankind. I cannot tell you how proud I was to see the joy on the faces of women and little girls in Afghanistan with the realization that this mighty nation has freed them to realize their dreams.

I also made it clear to the world that either you are with us or you're against us. That either you're with the United States in defending freedom, or you're not with the United States in defending freedom. And a lot of people have heard that [message] and they're proud to sign up with us. And we've got a vast coalition, as we're hunting down al Qaeda.

We've had over one thousand arrests in places outside of Afghanistan. I mean, we're slowly but surely doing what we need to do to protect the homeland. And the coalition understands our determination, and they see our resolve.

I'm proud of the patience of the American people. The American people recognize the new type of war we're in. They understand that sometimes they'll see the action of the United States government and sometimes [they] won't. But they also understand we must be strong and diligent as we defend freedom, because that's what we defend.

I made it clear that this is a war beyond just a single individual. One guy thinks he can hide, but he's not going to. We haven't heard much from him lately, by the way. (Laughter)

But we fight terror wherever it exists. And this is for the good of our children. History has called us into action, and we must not and we will not blink. It's a chance to define freedom for future generations.

I made it clear that a scenario which I will not let stand is one in which a terrorist organization could team up with a nation that has had a history of mistreating her people, a nontransparent nation perhaps, a nation that is known to be developing weapons of mass destruction.

We cannot let, for the sake of our children and grandchildren, terrorist organizations team up with nations that want to develop weapons that can be delivered from long distances that will hurt ourselves, our friends, and our allies. We're not going to let the world's worst regimes develop the worst weapons and threaten the United States of America.

We're doing everything at home to defend the homeland. We've got a good strategy in place. It starts, by the way, with having the best intelligence possible, gathering intelligence from all around the world, disseminating [it] on a quick basis, and following every lead and every hint.

If we get any kind of whiff that somebody is trying to do something to the American people, we're moving. We've got thousands of FBI agents whose major task, primary focus, is on preventing an attack. We're doing a much better job of coordinating with state and local authorities. We've got a national strategy in place to make our borders more secure, to make our nation more responsive to a potential bioterrorist attack. . . .

We're making good progress, and our budget reflects that. But the best way to secure the homeland is to be relentless in our pursuit [of] terrorists, and that's exactly what's going to happen, so long as I'm the President of the United States. . . .

I, like everybody else in America, was heartsick on 9/11. I can't tell you how sad I was, just like you. And then I got a little angry. And then I realized upon reflection that out of this evil was going to come some good, and it has.

Out of this terrible evil, we have a chance to keep the peace for a long time coming, and we will. And out of this evil, this nation has shown the world what a compassionate, kind people we are.

I always used to say that one of my hopes was that this nation's culture would shift from one that said, if it feels good, just go ahead and do it, and if you've got a problem go ahead and blame somebody else, to a culture which says [we] are responsible for the decisions we make in life. Unbeknownst to the evildoers, I think they've helped accelerate that cultural change.

I know millions of Americans are asking the question, what can I do to fight terror? What is it I can do to fight evil? And they're beginning to realize what I know, that in order to fight evil, do something good. In order to stand square in the face of evil, this good nation, through the millions of acts of kindness that take place on a daily basis, stands opposite of evil. And as a result of neighbors looking after neighbors, of people caring for somebody in need, of somebody loving their neighbor like they'd like to be loved themselves, people understand there's a new responsibility to be had.

Mothers and dads know that the most important job they will ever have is to love their children. Churches and synagogues and mosques who have these fantastic neighborhood healing programs need to be unleashed in America through the faith-based initiative that I have proposed.

You see, government shouldn't fear faith. We ought to welcome faith and the power of faith to change people's lives in a very positive way.

You know, I was working the rope line over there at the retirement-plan ceremony and I ran into a guy I met in Colfax, Iowa, from Teen Challenge. It was a fantastic experience during the course of the caucuses because it gave me a chance to explain to people . . . how faith changes life. But I'll never forget the heroin addict from Chicago standing up and saying he was clean because a power greater than himself entered into his heart.

These kinds of programs government can't create. But these kind of programs exist in America because of the goodness of America. And this society is changing, as we unleash this compassion, as people understand that part of being responsible is not only [being] responsible for your own family but responsible for loving a neighbor. And it's taking place in the country and it's so powerful and positive, it leads me to say that out of this evil is going to come a stronger, more decent, more humble society.

There [are] defining moments that take place in our history, and I think a defining moment was Flight 93, when people on an airplane, on cell phones, told their wives they loved them, said a prayer, and drove a plane into the ground to save somebody's life, to serve something greater than [themselves].

It's the ultimate testimony to the American character and the American spirit which defines this nation for what it is, the greatest nation on the face of the earth. And I am really proud to be its President. God bless.

### Remarks by the President from Speech on the Six-Month Anniversary of the September 11th Attacks
The White House
March 11, 2002

Diplomatic representatives of the coalition of nations; members of the Congress, the Cabinet, the Supreme Court; members of the American Armed Forces; military-coalition members from around the world; distinguished guests; and ladies and gentlemen. Welcome to the White House.

We have come together to mark a terrible day, to reaffirm a just and vital cause, and to thank the many nations that share our resolve and will share our common victory.

Six months separate us from September the 11th. Yet, for the families of the lost, each day brings new pain; each day requires new courage. Your grace and strength have been an example to our nation. America will not forget the lives that were taken, and the justice their death requires.

We face an enemy of ruthless ambition, unconstrained by law or morality. The terrorists despise other religions and have defiled their own. And they are determined to expand the scale and scope of their murder. The terror that targeted New York and Washington could next strike any center of civilization. Against such an enemy, there is no immunity, and there can be no neutrality.

Many nations and many families have lived in the shadows of terrorism for decades—enduring years of mindless and merciless killing. September the 11th was not the beginning of global terror, but it was the beginning of the world's concerted response. History will know that day not only as a day of tragedy, but as a day of decision—when the civilized world was stirred to anger and to action. And the terrorists will remember September 11th as the day their reckoning began.

A mighty coalition of civilized nations is now defending our common security. Terrorist assets have been frozen. Terrorist front groups have been exposed. A terrorist regime has been toppled from power. Terrorist plots have been unraveled, from Spain to Singapore. And thousands of terrorists have been brought to justice, are in prison, or are running in fear of their lives.

With us today are representatives from many of our partners in this great work, and we're proud to display their flags at the White House this morning. From the contributions these nations have made—some well known, others not—I am honored to extend the deepest gratitude of the people of the United States.

The power and vitality of our coalition have been proven in Afghanistan. More than half of the forces now assisting the heroic Afghan fighters, or providing security in Kabul, are from countries other than the United States. There are many examples of commitment: Our good ally, France, has deployed nearly one-fourth of its navy to support Operation Enduring Freedom, and Great Britain has sent its largest naval task force in twenty years. British and American special operations forces have fought beside teams from Australia, Canada, Norway, Denmark, and Germany. In total, seventeen nations have forces deployed in the region. And we could not have done our work without critical support from countries . . . like Pakistan and Uzbekistan.

Japanese destroyers are refueling coalition ships in the Indian Ocean. The Turkish air force has refueled American planes. Afghans are receiving treatment in hospitals built by Russians, Jordanians, and Spanish, and have received supplies and help from South Korea.

Nations in our coalition have shared in the responsibilities and sacrifices of our cause. On the day before September the 11th, I met with Prime Minister John Howard of Australia, who spoke of the common beliefs and shared affection of our two countries. We could not have known that bond was about to be proven again in war, and we could not have known its human cost. Last month, Sergeant Andrew Russell of the Australian Special Air Service died in Afghanistan. He left behind his wife, Kylie, and their daughter, Leisa, just eleven days old. Friends said of Sergeant Russell, "You could rely on him never to let you down."

This young man, and many like him, have not let us down. Each life taken from us is a terrible loss. We have lost young people from Germany, and Denmark, and Afghanistan, and America. We mourn each one. And for their bravery in a noble cause, we honor them.

Part of that cause was to liberate the Afghan people from terrorist occupation, and we did so. Next week, the schools reopen in Afghanistan. They will be open to all—and many young girls will go to school for the first time in their young lives. Afghanistan has many difficult challenges ahead—and yet, we've averted mass starvation, begun clearing mine fields, rebuilding roads, and improving health care. In Kabul, a friendly government is now an essential member of the coalition against terror.

Now that the Taliban are gone and al Qaeda has lost its home base for terrorism, we have entered the second stage of the war on terror—a sustained campaign to deny sanctuary to terrorists who would threaten our citizens from anywhere in the world.

In Afghanistan, hundreds of trained killers are now dead. Many have been captured. Others are still on the run, hoping to strike again. These terrorist fighters are the most committed, the most dangerous, and the least likely to surrender. They are trying to regroup, and we'll stop them. For five months in Afghanistan, our coalition has been patient and relentless. And more patience and more courage will be required. We're fighting a fierce battle in the Shahikote Mountains, and we're winning. Yet it will not be the last battle in Afghanistan. And there will be other battles beyond that nation.

For terrorists fleeing Afghanistan—for any terrorist looking for a base of operations, there must be no refuge, no safe haven. By driving terrorists from place to place, we disrupt the planning and training for further attacks on America and the civilized world. Every terrorist must be made to live as an international fugitive, with no place to settle or organize, no place to hide, no governments to hide behind, and not even a safe place to sleep.

I have set a clear policy in the second stage of the war on terror: America encourages and expects governments everywhere to help remove the terrorist parasites that threaten their own countries and peace of the world. If governments need training, or resources to meet this commitment, America will help.

We are helping right now in the Philippines, where terrorists with links to al Qaeda are trying to seize the southern part of the country to establish a militant regime. They are oppressing local peoples, and have kidnapped both American and Filipino citizens. America has sent more than 500 troops to train Philippine forces. We stand with President Arroyo, who is courageously opposing the threat of terror.

In the Republic of Georgia, terrorists working closely with al Qaeda operate in the Pankisi Gorge near the Russian border. At President Shevardnadze's request, the United States is planning to send up to 150 military trainers to prepare Georgian soldiers to reestablish control in this lawless region. This temporary assistance serves the interests of both our countries.

In Yemen, we are working to avert the possibility of another Afghanistan. Many al Qaeda recruits come from near the Yemen-Saudi Arabian border, and al Qaeda may try to reconstitute itself in remote corners of that region. President Saleh has assured me that he is committed to confronting this danger. We will help Yemeni forces with both training and equipment to prevent that land from becoming a haven for terrorists.

In the current stage of the war, our coalition is opposing not a nation, but a network. Victory will come over time, as that network is patiently and steadily dismantled. This will require international cooperation on a number of fronts: Diplomatic, financial, and military. We will not send American troops to every battle, but America will actively prepare other nations for the battles ahead. This mission will end when the work is finished—when terror networks of global reach have been defeated. The havens and training camps of terror are a threat to our lives and to our way of life, and they will be destroyed.

At the same time, every nation in our coalition must take seriously the growing threat of terror on a catastrophic scale—terror armed with biological, chemical, or nuclear weapons. America is now consulting with friends and allies about this greatest of dangers, and we're determined to confront it.

Here is what we already know: Some states that sponsor terror are seeking or already possess weapons of mass destruction; terrorist groups are hungry for these weapons, and would use them without a hint of conscience. And we know that these weapons, in the hands of terrorists, would unleash blackmail and genocide and chaos.

These facts cannot be denied, and must be confronted. In preventing the spread of weapons of mass destruction, there is no margin for error, and no chance to learn from mistakes. Our coalition must act deliberately, but inaction is not an option. Men with no respect for life must never be allowed to control the ultimate instruments of death.

Gathered here today, we are six months along—a short time in a long struggle. And our war on terror will be judged by its finish, not by its start. More dangers and sacrifices lie ahead. Yet America is prepared. Our resolve has only grown, because we remember. We remember the horror and heroism of that morning—the death of children on a field trip, the resistance of passengers on a doomed airplane, the courage of rescuers who died with strangers they were trying to save. And we remember the video images of terrorists who laughed at our loss.

Every civilized nation has a part in this struggle, because every civilized nation has a stake in its outcome. There can be no peace in a world where differences and grievances become an excuse to target the innocent for murder. In fighting terror, we fight for the conditions that will make lasting peace possible. We fight for lawful change against chaotic violence, for human choice against coercion and cruelty, and for the dignity and goodness of every life.

Every nation should know that, for America, the war on terror is not just a policy, it's a pledge. I will not relent in this struggle for the freedom and security of my country and the civilized world.

And we'll succeed. There will be a day when the organized threat against America, our friends, and allies is broken. And when the terrorists are disrupted and scattered and discredited, many old conflicts will appear in a new light—without the constant fear and cycle of bitterness that terrorists spread with their violence. We will see then that the old and serious disputes can be settled within the bounds of reason, and goodwill, and mutual security. I see a peaceful world beyond the war on terror, and with courage and unity, we are building that world together.

Any nation that makes an unequivocal commitment against terror can join this cause. Every nation of goodwill is welcome. And, together, we will face the peril of our moment, and seize the promise of our times.

May God bless our coalition.

### Excerpted Remarks by the President from Speech to Citizens and Military Personnel in North Carolina
Fayetteville, North Carolina
March 15, 2002

One week ago this coliseum was the scene of graduation ceremonies for the latest group of soldiers to have earned the right to wear the Green Beret. In doing so, they will join the ranks of some of the best and bravest citizens we have. The soldiers and sailors and airmen of the U.S. Special Operations Command are the best in the world, and the world is seeing how tough and how brave they are today.

Our Special Operations forces know the danger that awaits them. This is a dangerous battle that we face, a dangerous war. And I'm proud of the courage, not only of the soldiers who volunteer for battle, but [of] the loved ones who remain behind. Not only am I proud of our soldiers, I am proud of the wives and husbands and sons and daughters and moms and dads. And, on behalf of a grateful nation, we thank you, as well. We appreciate your courage and your sacrifice.

Two young men from the Special Forces were recently laid to rest, Chief Warrant Officer Stanley Harriman and Air Force Tech Sergeant John Chapman. I want their families to know that we pray with them, that we honor them, and [that] they died in a just cause of defending freedom, and that they will not have died in vain.

Because of such soldiers, a vicious regime has been toppled in Afghanistan, and an entire people has been liberated from oppression. Because of American soldiers and our brave allies and friends who have fought beside them, the Taliban is out of business.

At the beginning of this war, I made it very clear—as clear as a fellow from Texas could make it—either you're with us or you're against us. And if you harbor a terrorist, if you feed a terrorist, if you try to hide a terrorist, you are just as guilty as the murderers who killed innocent Americans on September the 11th. And thanks to the mighty United States military, the Taliban found out exactly what I meant.

But the world has seen we are not conquerors; we're liberators. We fight for freedom, and at the same time, we have saved a people from mass starvation. We fight for freedom, but at the same time we're clearing away minefields, rebuilding roads, and opening up hospitals. We fight for freedom, and yet, next week, schools will reopen in Afghanistan and . . . many young girls will go to school for the first time in their lives.

We haven't been at this struggle very long. I know it seems like a long time for those of you whose loved ones are overseas. But we've been at it for six months, and we've made a lot of progress. And you know what? The terrorists have now figured out they picked on the wrong people. They must have thought we were soft. They must have thought we were so materialistic that we wouldn't fight for values that we loved. They must have thought that we were so self-absorbed, that the word *sacrifice* had left the American vocabulary. And my, were they wrong.

Thousands of terrorists have been brought to justice. But I want you to know, my fellow citizens, we will not relent. We will not slow down until the threat of global terrorism has been destroyed.

I have made this message clear to the American people. I have made this message clear to our vast coalition. And I've made this message clear to our enemies—and our military has delivered the message.

We have finished the first phase of our war against terror. You see, when we routed out the Taliban, we completed that phase. And now we're entering a second stage of what I think will be a long war. It's a sustained campaign, a tireless, relentless campaign, to deny sanctuary, to deny safe haven to terrorists who would threaten citizens anywhere in the world, threaten our way of life, threaten our friends, threaten our allies. These terrorists are now on the run. And we intend to keep them on the run.

We know their strategy. They want to try to regroup, and they want to hit us. We're doing everything we can to stop them. . . . We know their strategy. We also know they're the most committed, the most dangerous, the least likely to surrender. Folks, these are trained killers who hate freedom. And so long as they're on the loose, we're in danger. And, therefore, in order to keep them from harming any of our citizens again, we're going to hunt 'em down, one by one. This mighty nation will not blink. We will not yield. We will defend the innocent lives of the American people by bringing terrorist killers to justice.

Obviously, as you well know, we found some of them bunched up in the Shahikote Mountains. And we sent our military in. And they're not bunched up anymore. (Laughter) And when we find them bunched up again, we'll send our military in, and the same thing will happen. You know, they've got these leaders that are so bold that they're willing to send youngsters to their suicide while they try to hide in deep caves. But they're going to find out there is not a cave deep enough to escape the long arm of American justice.

And so as fellow citizens, you need to know the strategy of this new phase is this: We want every terrorist to be made to live like an international fugitive, on the run, with no place to settle, no place to organize, no place to hide, no governments to hide behind, not even a safe place to sleep. And we're going to stay at it. You watch, we're going to stay at it for however long it takes. And the good news is, the American people are united and patient and understand the nature of the struggle ahead. And for that I'm grateful, and so are the men and women who wear the uniform of the United States military.

At the same time, the civilized world must take seriously the growing threat of terror on a catastrophic scale. We've got to prevent the spread of weapons of mass destruction, because there is no margin for error and there is no chance to learn from any mistake. The United States and her allies will act deliberately—we'll be deliberate—but inaction is not an option. Men who have no respect for life must never be allowed to control the ultimate instruments of death. I have made it clear that we will not let the most dangerous regimes in the world team up with killers and, therefore, hold this great nation hostage. Whatever it takes to defend the liberty of America, this administration will do.

I want you to know that, even though we have made great progress in six short months, I am aware that history will judge us not based upon the beginning of this campaign, but [upon] how it ends. Great challenges lie ahead, and we're in for a long struggle. And therefore, we must make sure that our United States military must have everything it needs to meet the objective.

And just like our military has responsibilities, I have responsibilities as the Commander-in-Chief to the military. At every stage of the war on terror, I can assure you our actions will be carefully planned and carefully prepared. Our objectives will be clear. We will be deliberate, but when we act, we'll be decisive. I will give clear orders, and I will make sure that you have every tool you need to do your job.

I've asked Congress for a one-year increase of more than $48 billion for national defense. This is the largest defense increase in a generation—because we're at war, and Congress needs to pass this budget. And, by the way, it includes another pay raise for people who wear the uniform.

Nothing is more important than the national security of our country, nothing is more important. So nothing is more important than our defense budget. I've heard some of them talking about, it's too big up there. Let me just make this as clear as I can make it: The price for freedom is high, but it's never too high, as far as I'm concerned.

As you know, if you follow the budget process, oftentimes Congress waits until the last days of the fiscal year in order to pass the defense budget. That's bad budgeting practices in times of peace. It's really bad budgeting practices in times of war. I expect the United States Congress to not only pass the budget as I submitted: I expect [Congress] to make it the first order of business, so we can plan for this war.

Now is not the time to play politics with the defense budget. . . . We need to send that clear message that not only are we in this for the long haul, but the elected representatives of the United States people understand it, as well. I'm proud of the bipartisan spirit that exists in our war against terror. Now, let's just make sure we've got some good budgeting practices to go along with it.

We're working hard to make sure the homeland is secure. I'll never forget, right after September the 11th I went to see some high-school kids. . . . And it dawned on me that—obviously on them, too—that this is the first high school class that had ever seen an attack on the homeland like this, at least on the forty-eight states that are contiguous. And it reminded me then, and I've never forgotten it, that oceans no longer matter when it comes to making us safe; that we have a giant obligation, an obligation I take very seriously here at home, to make sure we do everything we can to protect innocent life.

So you need to know that any time we get a hint [that] somebody may be thinking about doing something, we're on them. Every time we get a scintilla of evidence that somebody might be trying to get in here or burrow into our society, we're doing everything we can, everything we can, to protect the American people. We honor our Constitution, but we're on alert. And so are many of you all, and I want to thank you for that.

We've got a good first-responders initiative. We've got a great initiative on bioterrorism. We're making our borders more secure. We want to make sure we know who's coming in and who's [going] out. We want to make sure the INS is reformed. (Laughter and applause) As you could tell by the news that day, I was plenty hot—(laughter)—when I read about the bureaucratic inefficiency of this agency. We're going to do everything we can to reform it. We want to button up the homeland as best as we can.

But my attitude is this: The best way to secure the homeland is to unleash the mighty United States military and hunt them down and bring them to justice. And the best way to fight evil at home is to love your neighbor like you'd like to be loved yourself. The best way to stand squarely in the face of those who hijacked a good religion is to live a life that helps people in need.

You know, the true strength of our country is much greater than our military. The true strength of America are the hearts and souls of loving American citizens. And we have an obligation in our free society to work to make our society as compassionate and as kind as it can possibly be. . . .

I'm proud to be the President of a nation that is dedicated and firm in our defense of liberty, that will stand strong when we defend freedom, and not blink or tire. And likewise, I'm proud to be the President of a nation whose true strength [is] the hearts and souls of citizens from all walks of life.

May God bless you all, and may God bless America.

## Presidential Easter Message
March 27, 2002

I send greetings to everyone observing Easter this year. During this joyful season of new life and renewal, Christians around the world celebrate the central event of their faith—the Resurrection of Jesus Christ, whom Christians believe is the Messiah, the Son of God.

The life and teachings of Jesus have inspired people throughout the ages to strive for a better world and a more meaningful life. Jesus' death stands out in history as the perfect example of unconditional love.

The four Gospels of the Christian Bible recount Jesus' amazing life, his miraculous death, Resurrection, and Ascension, and his unending offer of salvation to all. The story of Jesus' wondrous Resurrection comes alive again for Christians each year at Easter.

Easter Sunday commemorates in song and celebration the joy and promise of Christ's triumph over evil and death.

Christians around the world gather together to sing well-loved hymns to God's glory, remembering the signs and wonders of God's grace revealed in Jesus. And they again will hear Gospel readings such as Saint Luke's rendering of that first Easter morning when the Angel asked: "Why do you look for the living among the dead? He is not here; He has risen!"

Easter's message of renewal is especially meaningful now during this challenging time in our nation's history. On September 11, 2001, America suffered devastating loss.

In the wake of great evil, however, Americans responded with strength, compassion, and generosity. As we fight to promote freedom around the world and to protect innocent lives in America, we remember the call of "The Battle Hymn of the Republic": "As He died to make men holy, let us live to make men free."

Laura joins me in sending best wishes for a wonderful Easter.

# April 2002

**Excerpted Remarks by the President from Speech to the
George C. Marshall ROTC Award Seminar on National Security
at the Virginia Military Institute**
Lexington, Virginia
April 17, 2002

As Army Chief of Staff, General Marshall became the architect of America's victory in the Second World War. He fought tenaciously against our enemies, and then worked just as hard to secure the peace. President Truman considered George C. Marshall the greatest man he knew. Above all, said Winston Churchill, Marshall "always fought victoriously against defeatism, discouragement, and disillusionment." The key to morale and to victory, Marshall said, is "steadfastness and courage and hope."

And, today, we are called to defend freedom against ruthless enemies. And, once again, we need steadfastness, courage, and hope. The war against terror will be long. And as George Marshall so clearly understood, it will not be enough to make the world safer. We must also work to make the world better.

In the days just after September the 11th, I told the American people that this would be a different war, fought on many fronts. Today, around the world, we make progress on the many fronts. In some cases, we use military force. In others, we're fighting through diplomacy, financial pressure, or special operations. In every case, we will defeat the threats against our country and the civilized world.

Our progress is measured day by day, terrorist by terrorist. We recently apprehended one of al Qaeda's top leaders, a man named Abu Zabaydah. He was spending a lot of time as one of the top operating officials of al Qaeda, plotting and planning murder. He's not plotting and he's not planning anymore. He's under lock and key, and we're going to give him some company. We're hunting down the killers one by one.

We're learning a lot about al Qaeda operations and their plans. As our enemies have fled their hideouts in Afghanistan, they left some things behind. We found laptop computers, drawings, and maps. And through them, we're gaining a clearer picture of the terrorist targets and their methods.

Our international coalition against these killers is strong and united and active. European nations have frozen almost $50 million in suspected terrorist assets, and that's important. Many European states are taking aggressive and effective law-enforcement action to join us in rounding up these terrorists and their cells. We're making good progress.

Yet, it's important for Americans to know this war will not be quick and this war will not be easy. The first phase of our military operation was in Afghanistan, where our armed forces continue to perform with bravery and with skill. You've got to understand that as we routed out the Taliban, they weren't sent in to conquer; they were sent in to liberate. And they succeeded. And our military makes us proud.

The battles in Afghanistan are not over. American and allied troops are taking risks today in what we call Operation Mountain Lion—hunting down the al Qaeda and Taliban forces, and keeping them on the run. Coalition naval forces, in the largest combined flotilla since World War II, are patrolling escape routes and intercepting ships to search for terrorists and their supplies.

As the spring thaw comes, we expect cells of trained killers to try to regroup, to murder, create mayhem, and try to undermine Afghanistan's efforts to build a lasting peace. We know this from not only intelligence, but from the history of military conflict in Afghanistan. It's been one of initial success, followed by long years of floundering and ultimate failure. We're not going to repeat that mistake.

In the United States of America, the terrorists have chosen a foe unlike [any that they have] faced before. They've never faced a country like ours before: We're tough, we're determined, we're relentless. We will stay until the mission is done.

We know that true peace will only be achieved when we give the Afghan people the means to achieve their own aspirations. Peace will be achieved by helping Afghanistan develop its own stable government. Peace will be achieved by helping Afghanistan train and develop its own national army. And peace will be achieved through an education system for boys and girls which works.

We're working hard in Afghanistan. We're clearing minefields. We're rebuilding roads. We're improving medical care. And we will work to help Afghanistan to develop an economy that can feed its people without feeding the world's demand for drugs.

And we [are helping] the Afghan people recover from the Taliban rule. And as we do so, we find mounting horror, evidence of horror. In the Hazarajat region, the Red Cross has found signs of massacres committed by the Taliban last year, victims who lie in mass graves. This is the legacy of the first regime to fall in the war against terror. These mass graves are a reminder of the kind of enemy we have fought and have defeated. And they are the kind of evil we continue to fight.

By helping to build an Afghanistan that is free from this evil and is a better place in which to live, we are working in the best traditions of George Marshall. Marshall knew that our military victory against enemies in World War II had to be followed by a moral victory that resulted in better lives for individual human beings.

After 1945, the United States of America was the only nation in the world strong enough to help rebuild a Europe and a Japan that had been decimated by World War II. Today, our former enemies are our friends. And Europe and Japan are strong partners in the rebuilding of Afghanistan.

This transformation is a powerful testimony to the success of Marshall's vision, and a beacon to light the path that we, too, must follow.

In the second phase of the war on terror, our military and law-enforcement intelligence officers are helping countries around the world in their efforts to crack down on terror within their borders. Global terrorism will be defeated only by global response. We must prevent al Qaeda from moving its operations to other countries. We must deny terrorists the funds they need to operate. We must deny them safe havens to plan new horrors and indoctrinate new recruits.

We're working with Yemen's government to prevent terrorists from reassembling there. We sent troops to help train local forces in the Philippines, to help them defeat terrorists trying to establish a militant regime. And in the Republic of Georgia, we provide temporary help to its military, as it routs out a terrorist cell near the Russian border. Wherever global terror threatens the civilized world, we and our friends and our allies will respond and will respond decisively.

Every nation that joins our cause is welcome. Every nation that needs our help will have it. And no nation can be neutral. Around the world, the nations must choose. They are with us, or they're with the terrorists.

And in the Middle East, where acts of terror have triggered mounting violence, all parties have a choice to make. Every leader, every state must choose between two separate paths: The path of peace or the path of terror. In the stricken faces of mothers, Palestinian mothers and Israeli mothers, the entire world is witnessing the agonizing cost of this conflict. Now, every nation and every leader in the region must work to end terror.

All parties have responsibilities. These responsibilities are not easy, but they're clear. And Secretary of State Powell is helping make them clear. I want to thank Secretary Powell for his hard work at a difficult task. He returns home having made progress towards peace.

We're confronting hatred that is centuries old, disputes that have lingered for decades. But I want you to know, I will continue to lead toward a vision of peace.

We will continue to remind folks they have responsibilities in the short run to defuse the current crisis. The Palestinian Authority must act, must act on its words of condemnation against terror. Israel must continue its withdrawals. And all Arab states must step up to their responsibilities.

The Egyptians and Jordanians and Saudis have helped in the wider war on terrorism. And they must help confront terrorism in the Middle East. All parties have a responsibility to stop funding or inciting terror. And all parties must say clearly that a murderer is not a martyr; he or she is just a murderer.

And all parties must realize that the only vision for a long-term solution is for two states—Israel, Palestine—to live side by side in security and in peace. That will require hard choices and leadership by Israelis, Palestinians, and their Arab neighbors. The time is now for all to make the choice for peace.

And, finally, the civilized world faces a grave threat from weapons of mass destruction. A small number of outlaw regimes today possess and are developing chemical and biological and nuclear weapons. They're building missiles to deliver them, and at the same time cultivating ties to terrorist groups. In their threat to peace, in their mad ambitions, in their destructive potential, and in the repression of their own people, these regimes constitute an axis of evil and the world must confront them.

America, along with other nations, will oppose the proliferation of dangerous weapons and technologies. We will proceed with missile defenses to protect the American people, our troops, and our friends and allies. And America will take the necessary action to oppose emerging threats.

We'll be deliberate and we will work with our friends and allies. And, as we do so, we will uphold our duty to defend freedom. We will fight against terrorist organizations in different ways, with different tactics, in different places. And we will fight the threat from weapons of mass destruction in different ways, with different tactics, in different places.

Yet, our objective is always the same: We will defeat global terror, and we will not allow the world's most dangerous regimes to threaten us with the world's most dangerous weapons.

America has a much greater purpose than just eliminating threats and containing resentment, because we believe in the dignity and value of every individual. America seeks hope and opportunity for all people in all cultures. And that is why we're helping to rebuild Afghanistan. And that is why we've launched a new compact for development for the Millennium Challenge Account. And that is why we work for free trade, to lift people out of poverty throughout the world.

A better world can seem very distant when children are sent to kill other children, and old hatreds are stoked and carefully passed from one generation to another, and a violent few love death more than life. Yet hatred [and] fanaticism are not the way of the future, because the hopes of humanity are always stronger than its hatreds.

And these hopes are universal in every country and in every culture. Men and women everywhere want to live in dignity to create and build and own, to raise their children in peace and security.

The way to a peaceful future can be found in the non-negotiable demands of human dignity. Dignity requires the rule of law, limits on the power of the state, respect for women, private property, equal justice, religious tolerance. No nation owns these principles. No nation is exempt from them.

Sixty years ago, few would have predicted the triumph of these values in Germany and Japan. Fifteen years ago, few would have predicted the advance of these values in Russia. Yet, Americans are not surprised. We know that the demands of human dignity are written in every heart.

The demands have a power and momentum of their own, defying all pessimism. And they are destined to change lives and nations on every continent. America has acted on these hopes throughout our history. General George Marshall is admired for the war he fought, yet best remembered for the peace he secured.

The Marshall Plan, rebuilding Europe and lifting up former enemies, showed that America is not content with military victory alone. Americans always see a greater hope and a better day. And America sees a just and hopeful world beyond the war on terror.

Many of you will help achieve this better world. At a young age, you've taken up a great calling. You'll serve your country and our values. You'll protect your fellow citizens. And, by your effort and example, you will advance the cause of freedom around the world. And so I'm here to thank you for your commitment and congratulate you on the high honor you have received.

May God bless you all, and may God bless America.

# May 2002

**Excerpted Remarks by the President from Speech upon Signing the
Enhanced Border Security and Visa Entry Reform Act**
Washington, D.C.
May 14, 2002

I [am reminded] of what was done to us there on September 11th, and how
important it is that we remain tough and strong and diligent, as we seek justice—as we chase down these killers one by one, and bring them to justice.

And that's a major responsibility of all of [us], and it's a responsibility we
take seriously. The country is united in our drive for justice. This nation is
determined, and we're patient, much to the chagrin of the enemy. It must
make them really worried to know that we don't have a calendar that says, on
such and such a date we're going to quit; that when it comes to defending our
freedoms, and securing our homeland, and protecting . . . innocent
Americans, and never forgetting what happened on September the 11th, we
are some kind of tough. And that's the way it's going to be.

We've got responsibilities here at home, as well, and it starts with our
borders. Our borders process an incredibly huge number of people. It may
come as a surprise to some of you, but there's—over 500 million people a
year enter America, and half of those are our own citizens that may have been
traveling. We have 11 million trucks come across our borders. We have
51,000 foreign ships call into our ports. It reminds us that no nation can be
totally secure, or more secure, unless we're well-protected, and unless our
borders are well-screened. We must know who's coming into our country and
why they're coming. We must know what our visitors are doing and when
they leave. That's important for us to know. It's knowledge necessary to make
our homeland more secure.

America is not a fortress; no, we never want to be a fortress. We're a free country; we're an open society. And we must always protect the rights of law-abiding citizens from around the world who come here to conduct business or to study or to spend time with their family. That's what we're known for. We're known for respect.

But, on the other hand, we can do a better job of making our borders more secure, and make our borders smart. We must use technology and be wise about how we use technology, to speed the flow of commerce across our borders, and to identify frequent travelers who pose no risk. We should be directing resources to risk. We ought to be routing out smugglers and focusing on criminals—and, of course, stopping terrorists from coming into the country.

The bill I sign today enhances our ongoing efforts to strengthen our borders. The purpose of this bill is to help our country do a better job of border security. It authorizes 400 additional inspectors, investigators, and other staff on the INS over the next five years. We're adding manpower, obviously. It makes it easier for the INS and other federal agencies to get better information about people and products that come into America. It requires every foreign visitor desiring entrance into the United States to carry a travel document containing biometric identification—that would be fingerprints or facial recognition—that will enable us to use technology to better deny fraudulent entry into America.

It strengthens the requirements that all commercial passenger ships and airplanes entering the United States provide a list of passengers and crew before arrival, so that border authorities can act immediately to prevent someone from entering the country if he or she poses a threat to our citizens. It makes a lot of sense to do that. We should have probably been doing it a long time ago.

These new measures will only be effective if federal authorities have access to important information. One of the things we've learned is how to better share information. Right now, the FBI and the CIA do a good job of sharing information. Information is [being] better shared from the federal to the state to the local levels.

But we've got to do a better job of sharing information and expanding information to the INS and the State Department and Customs agents, and throughout the intelligence community. We've just got to do a better job. This bill enables us to modernize our communication, so the information flows freely and quickly. The legislation requires law-enforcement and intelligence communities to continue to develop a list of suspected terrorists, and to maintain that list, and to make it readily available, so that nobody is granted entry into the United States that's on the list.

In other words, we're beginning to gather information overseas in a much better way. We've got a vast coalition of nations that are still with us. They heard the message, either you're with us, or you're not with us. They're still with us. And we're sharing information. And we can better use that information with our own agencies here at home, to make sure that we really button this up, that we do our job, the job the American people expect. . . .

Commonsense measures will help us meet the goal, and that's important. [They] will help us meet the goals of legitimate commerce and important travel. And at the same time, [they] will help us keep the country secure. Basically what we're saying is, this is a legislative part of a national strategy. . . .

You know, sometimes in Washington we actually are able to put our political parties aside and focus on what's best for the country. And we're able to say, let's make sure America is the first priority of all of us. And this has happened in this bill.

So it's my honor to welcome both Republicans and Democrats from the legislative branch of government here as I sign this important legislation. Thank you all for coming. God bless.

### Excerpted Remarks by the President from Speech at the Annual Peace Officers Association Memorial Service
U.S. Capitol, Washington, D.C
May 15, 2002

Today, and every May 15th, the American flag flies at half-staff in grateful memory—in *grateful* memory—of thousands of fallen police officers. This year we pay special homage to 480 men and women whose names are being added to the National Law Enforcement Officers Memorial. We do so with enormous respect and appreciation for the courage and character of all who have answered the call to be a law-enforcement officer. . . .

So many family members of fallen officers have come to Washington for this service, and I want you to know we are honored by your presence. Standing by you today, and always, are brother and sister officers who are faithful to the memory of lost friends.

I thank all the officers in attendance, and the departments you represent. Thank you for your loyalty to one another and for your service to America. The loyalty of police officers is seen in the neighborhoods of America when our officers are on duty and whenever one of your comrades is suddenly taken from us. That happens on average about three times a week in the life of our nation. And each time we witness the powerful family that unites the police officers of America.

When an officer dies in the line of duty, an entire community will pause in sorrow and in admiration with the depth of feeling Americans reserve for people who protect us every day.

Last September the 11th, our entire nation grieved at the loss of seventy two police officers. It was a loss unlike any we have known before, all in one moment, all at one place. More than three hundred firefighters and rescue workers died . . . along with thousands they were trying to save. As the buildings fell, the sound, said one survivor, "was like the roar of the devil."

September the 11th was a day of great horror and great heroism. It was the first day of a long struggle against determined enemies. It was the first day in which this mighty nation will hunt down the killers and their like one by one and bring them to justice.

It's the saddest day in the history of law enforcement. In his final moments, trapped in rubble, Officer Dominick Pezzulo called out to one of his fellows, and he said, "Just remember me." The last voice he heard was Officer Will Jimeno, promising him they would never forget. So, Dominick, today we remember—we remember courage and bravery and sacrifice.

Sacrifice like that of Police Officer John Perry, who retired on September the 11th. Early that morning, he had turned in his badge at the 40th Precinct. A moment later, he heard the sound of the first attack and the radio traffic that followed. He put his badge back on and was last seen directing people to safety at the bottom of the tower.

I have the police shield of another officer who died on that day. His name was George G. Howard. His mother gave me this badge. She gave it to me in love for George, but she gave it to me because I'm confident she wanted her President never to forget what took place.

We call all those we honor today, those who lost their lives on 9/11 and those who lost their life before and after 9/11, heroes—because they are heroes. Their families are proud of them, and always will be. Yet there's not a husband or wife here today, or a parent or child, who would not trade the honor to have them back. In a eulogy for his son who died on September the 11th, one father said, "I know he's in good hands, but I wish he was in my hands." We know how you feel.

There are more than 700,000 sworn law officers across America. When the oath is administered they accept great responsibilities—and accept great risk. Even in the most routine moments on watch or patrol, you protect us.

Even on the quietest day, the next call may send you into extremes of danger. America is grateful. You just need to know, America is grateful.

We have confidence in our law enforcement because we know the kind of men and women we select and we know the nature of the men and women we train for the job. They're the ones who face down threats, who place themselves between the innocent and the guilty, who step into scenes of chaos and violence thinking only of whom they can help.

No one goes into police work for the money, nor does anybody put on the uniform expecting a life of ease. You take the job because you respect the law and you know that someone has to do the challenging work of enforcing it. Fortunately, this great country—America—has never been short of such men and women and your devoted service, and we are very grateful.

Every day in every place in America we can be thankful for the integrity and courage of our officers of the law. Today we give thanks for the special courage of the fallen—those whose watch ended with their lives. America cannot fully repay our debt to them and to their families. We can only acknowledge that debt, which we do today with pride and affection of an entire nation.

May God bless you all, and may God bless America.


**Excerpted Remarks by the President from**
**Speech to the German Bundestag**
Berlin, Germany
May 23, 2002


I am honored to visit this great city. The history of our time is written in the life of Berlin. In this building, fires of hatred were set that swept across the world. To this city, Allied planes brought food and hope during 323 days and nights of siege. Across an infamous divide, men and women jumped from tenement buildings and crossed through razor wire to live in freedom or to die in the attempt. One American President came here to proudly call himself a citizen of Berlin. Another President dared the Soviets to "tear down that wall." And on a night in November, Berliners took history into their hands, and made your city whole.

In a single lifetime, the people of this capital and this country endured twelve years of dictatorial rule, suffered forty years of bitter separation, and persevered through this challenging decade of unification. From all these trials, Germany has emerged a responsible, a prosperous and peaceful nation. More than a decade ago, as the President pointed out, my father spoke of Germany and America as partners in leadership—and this has come to pass. A new era has arrived—the strong Germany you have built is good for the world.

On both sides of the Atlantic, the generation of our fathers was called to shape great events—and they built the great transatlantic alliance of democracies. They built the most successful alliance in history. After the Cold War, during the relative quiet of the 1990s, some questioned whether our transatlantic partnership still had a purpose. History has given its answer. Our generation faces new and grave threats to liberty, to the safety of our people, and to civilization itself. We face an aggressive force that glorifies death, that targets the innocent, and [that] seeks the means to murder on a massive scale.

We face the global tragedy of disease and poverty that take uncounted lives and leave whole nations vulnerable to oppression and terror.

We'll face these challenges together. We must face them together. Those who despise human freedom will attack it on every continent. Those who seek missiles and terrible weapons are also familiar with the map of Europe. Like the threats of another era, this threat cannot be appeased or cannot be ignored. By being patient, relentless, and resolute, we will defeat the enemies of freedom.

By remaining united, we are meeting modern threats with the greatest resources of wealth and will ever assembled by free nations. Together, Europe and the United States have the creative genius, the economic power, the moral heritage, and the democratic vision to protect our liberty and to advance our cause of peace.

Different as we are, we are building and defending the same house of freedom—its doors open to all of Europe's people, its windows looking out to global challenges beyond. We must lay the foundation with a Europe that is whole and free and at peace for the first time in its history. This dream of the centuries is close at hand.

From the Argonne Forest to the Anzio beachhead, conflicts in Europe have drawn the blood of millions, squandering and shattering lives across the earth. There are thousands of monuments in parks and squares across my country to young men of 18 and 19 and 20 whose lives ended in battle on this continent. Ours is the first generation in a hundred years that does not expect and does not fear the next European war. And that achievement—your achievement—is one of the greatest in modern times.

When Europe grows in unity, Europe and America grow in security. When you integrate your markets and share a currency in the European Union, you are creating the conditions for security and common purpose. In all these steps, Americans do not see the rise of a rival, we see the end of old hostilities. We see the success of our allies, and we applaud your progress.

The expansion of NATO will also extend the security on this continent, especially for nations that knew little peace or security in the last century. We have moved cautiously in this direction. Now we must act decisively.

As our summit in Prague approaches, America is committed to NATO membership for all of Europe's democracies that are ready to share in the responsibilities that NATO brings. Every part of Europe should share in the security and success of this continent. A broader alliance will strengthen NATO—it will fulfill NATO's promise.

Another mission we share is to encourage the Russian people to find their future in Europe, and with America. Russia has its best chance since 1917 to become a part of Europe's family. Russia's transformation is not finished; the outcome is not yet determined. But for all the problems and challenges, Russia is moving toward freedom—more freedom in its politics and its markets; freedom that will help Russia to act as a great and a just power. A Russia at peace with its neighbors, respecting the legitimate rights of minorities, is welcome in Europe.

A new Russian-American partnership is being forged. Russia is lending crucial support in the war on global terror. A Russian colonel now works on the staff of U.S. Army General Tommy Franks, commander of the war in Afghanistan. And in Afghanistan itself, Russia is helping to build hospitals and a better future for the Afghan people.

America and Europe must throw off old suspicions and realize our common interests with Russia. Tomorrow in Moscow, President Putin and I will again act upon these interests.

The United States and Russia are ridding ourselves of the last vestiges of Cold War confrontation. We have moved beyond an ABM treaty that prevented us from defending our people and our friends. Some warned that moving beyond the ABM treaty would cause an arms race. Instead, President Putin and I are about to sign the most dramatic nuclear-arms reduction in history. Both the United States and Russia will reduce . . . nuclear arsenals by about two-thirds—to the lowest levels in decades.

Old arms agreements sought to manage hostility and maintain a balance of terror. This new agreement recognizes that Russia and the West are no longer enemies.

The entire transatlantic alliance is forming a new relationship with Russia. Next week in Rome, Chancellor Schroeder, NATO allies, and I will meet as equal partners with President Putin at the creation of the NATO-

Russia Council. The Council gives us an opportunity to build common security against common threats. We will start with projects on nonproliferation, counterterrorism, and search-and-rescue operations. Over time, we will expand this cooperation, even as we preserve the core mission of NATO. Many generations have looked at Russia with alarm. Our generation can finally lift this shadow from Europe by embracing the friendship of a new, democratic Russia.

As we expand our alliance, as we reach out to Russia, we must also look beyond Europe to gathering dangers and important responsibilities. As we build the house of freedom, we must meet the challenges of a larger world. And we must meet them together.

For the United States, September the 11th, 2001, cut a deep dividing line in our history—a change of eras as sharp and clear as Pearl Harbor, or the first day of the Berlin Blockade. There can be no lasting security in a world at the mercy of terrorists—for my nation, or for any nation.

Given this threat, NATO's defining purpose—our collective defense—is as urgent as ever. America and Europe need each other to fight and win the war against global terror. My nation is so grateful for the sympathy of the German people, and for the strong support of Germany and all of Europe.

Troops from more than a dozen European countries have deployed in and around Afghanistan, including thousands from this country—the first deployment of German forces outside of Europe since 1945. German soldiers have died in this war, and we mourn their loss as we do our own. German authorities are on the trail of terrorist cells and finances. And German police are helping Afghans build their own police force. And we're so grateful for the support.

Together, we oppose an enemy that thrives on violence and the grief of the innocent. The terrorists are defined by their hatreds: They hate democracy and tolerance and free expression and women and Jews and Christians and all Muslims who disagree with them. Others killed in the name of racial purity, or the class struggle. These enemies kill in the name of a false religious purity, perverting the faith they claim to hold. In this war we defend not just America or Europe; we are defending civilization itself.

The evil that has formed against us has been termed the "new totalitarian threat." The authors of terror are seeking nuclear, chemical, and biological weapons. Regimes that sponsor terror are developing these weapons and the missiles to deliver them. If these regimes and their terrorist allies were to perfect these capabilities, no inner voice of reason, no hint of conscience would prevent their use.

Wishful thinking might bring comfort, but not security. Call this a strategic challenge; call it, as I do, *axis of evil*; call it by any name you choose, but let us speak the truth. If we ignore this threat, we invite certain blackmail, and place millions of our citizens in grave danger.

Our response will be reasoned, and focused, and deliberate. We will use more than our military might. We will cut off terrorist finances, apply diplomatic pressure, and continue to share intelligence. America will consult closely with our friends and allies at every stage. But make no mistake about it, we will and we must confront this conspiracy against our liberty and against our lives.

As it faces new threats, NATO needs a new strategy and new capabilities. Dangers originating far from Europe can now strike at Europe's heart—so NATO must be able and willing to act whenever threats emerge. This will require all the assets of modern defense—mobile and deployable forces, sophisticated special operations, the ability to fight under the threat of chemical and biological weapons. Each nation must focus on the military strengths it can bring to this alliance, with the hard choices and financial commitment that requires. We do not know where the next threat might come from, we really don't know what form it might take. But we must be ready, as full military partners, to confront threats to our common security.

One way to make ourselves more secure is to address the regional conflicts that enflame violence. Our work in the Balkans and Afghanistan shows how much we can achieve when we stand together. We must continue to stand for peace in the Middle East. That peace must assure the permanent safety of the Jewish people. And that peace must provide the Palestinian people with a state of their own.

In the midst of terrorist violence in the Middle East, the hope of a lasting accord may seem distant. That's how many once viewed the prospect of peace between Poland and Germany, Germany and France, France and England, Protestant and Catholic. Yet, after generations of traded violence and humiliation, we have seen enemies become partners and allies in a new Europe. We pray the same healing, the same shedding of hatred, might come to the Middle East. And we will be unrelenting in our quest for that peace.

We must recognize that violence and resentment are defeated by the advance of health, and learning, and prosperity. Poverty doesn't create terror—yet terror takes root in failing nations that cannot police themselves or provide for their people. Our conscience and our interests speak as one: To achieve a safer world, we must create a better world.

The expansion of trade in our time is one of the primary reasons for our progress against poverty. At Doha, we committed to build on this progress, and we must keep that commitment. Trans-Atlantic nations must resolve the small, disputed portion of our vast trading relationship within the rules and settlement mechanisms of the World Trade Organization—whether those disputes concern tax law, steel, agriculture, or biotechnology.

For all nations to gain the benefit of global markets, they need populations that are healthy and literate. To help developing nations achieve these goals, leaders of wealthy nations have a duty of conscience—we have a duty to share our wealth generously and wisely. Those who lead poor nations have a duty to their own people . . . to pursue reforms that turn temporary aid into lasting progress.

I've proposed that new American aid be directed to nations on that path of reform. The United States will increase our core development assistance by fifty percent over the next three budget years. It will be up to a level of $5 billion a year, above and beyond that which we already contribute to development.

When nations are governed justly, the people benefit. When nations are governed unjustly, for the benefit of a corrupt few, no amount of aid will help the people in need. When nations are governed justly, investing in education and health, and encouraging economic freedom, they will have our help. And more importantly, these rising nations will have their own ability and, eventually, the resources necessary to battle disease and improve their environment, and build lives of dignity for their people.

Members of the Bundestag, we are joined in very serious purposes on which the safety of our people and the fate of our freedom now rest. We build a world of justice, or we will live in a world of coercion. The magnitude of our shared responsibilities makes our disagreements look so small. And those who exaggerate our differences play a shallow game and hold a simplistic view of our relationship.

America and the nations in Europe are more than military allies, we're more than trading partners; we are heirs to the same civilization. The pledges of the *Magna Carta*, the learning of Athens, the creativity of Paris, the unbending conscience of Luther, the gentle faith of St. Francis—all of these are part of the American soul. The New World has succeeded by holding to the values of the Old.

Our histories have diverged, yet we seek to live by the same ideals. We believe in free markets, tempered by compassion. We believe in open societies that reflect unchanging truths. We believe in the value and dignity of every life.

These convictions bind our civilizations together and set our enemies against us. These convictions are universally true and right. And they define our nations and our partnership in a unique way. And these beliefs lead us to fight tyranny and evil, as others have done before us.

One of the greatest Germans of the 20th century was Pastor Dietrich Bonhoeffer, who left the security of America to stand against Nazi rule. In a dark hour, he gave witness to the Gospel of life, and paid the cost of his discipleship, being put to death only days before his camp was liberated.

"I believe," said Bonhoeffer, "that God can and wants to create good out of everything, even evil."

That belief is proven in the history of Europe since that day—in the reconciliation and renewal that have transformed this continent. In America, very recently, we have also seen the horror of evil and the power of good. In the tests of our time, we are affirming our deepest values and our closest friendships. Inside this chamber, across this city, throughout this nation and continent, America has valued friends. And with our friends we are building that house of freedom—for our time and for all time.

May God bless.

# June 2002

**Excerpted Remarks by the President from Speech at the
Graduation Exercises of the United States Military Academy**
West Point, New York
June 1, 2002

In every corner of America, the words "West Point" command immediate respect. This place where the Hudson River bends is more than a fine institution of learning. The United States Military Academy is the guardian of values that have shaped the soldiers who have shaped the history of the world. . . .

You walk in the tradition of Eisenhower and MacArthur, Patton and Bradley—the commanders who saved a civilization. And you walk in the tradition of second lieutenants who did the same, by fighting and dying on distant battlefields. . . .

Every West Point class is commissioned to the Armed Forces. Some West Point classes are also commissioned by history, to take part in a great new calling for their country. Speaking here to the class of 1942—six months after Pearl Harbor—General Marshall said, "We're determined that before the sun sets on this terrible struggle, our flag will be recognized throughout the world as a symbol of freedom on the one hand, and of overwhelming power on the other."

Officers graduating that year helped fulfill that mission, defeating Japan and Germany, and then reconstructing those nations as allies. West Point graduates of the 1940s saw the rise of a deadly new challenge—the challenge of imperial Communism—and opposed it from Korea to Berlin, to Vietnam, and in the Cold War, from beginning to end. And as the sun set on their struggle, many of those West Point officers lived to see a world transformed.

History has also issued its call to your generation. In your last year, America was attacked by a ruthless and resourceful enemy. You graduate from this Academy in a time of war, taking your place in an American military that is powerful and is honorable. Our war on terror is only begun, but in Afghanistan it was begun well.

I am proud of the men and women who have fought on my orders. America is profoundly grateful for all who serve the cause of freedom, and for all who have given their lives in its defense. This nation respects and trusts our military, and we are confident in your victories to come.

This war will take many turns we cannot predict. Yet I am certain of this: Wherever we carry it, the American flag will stand not only for our power, but for freedom. Our nation's cause has always been larger than our nation's defense. We fight, as we always fight, for a just peace—a peace that favors human liberty. We will defend the peace against threats from terrorists and tyrants. We will preserve the peace by building good relations among the great powers. And we will extend the peace by encouraging free and open societies on every continent.

Building this just peace is America's opportunity, and America's duty. From this day forward, it is your challenge as well, and we will meet this challenge together. You will wear the uniform of a great and unique country. America has no empire to extend or utopia to establish. We wish for others only what we wish for ourselves—safety from violence, the rewards of liberty, and the hope for a better life.

In defending the peace, we face a threat with no precedent. Enemies in the past needed great armies and great industrial capabilities to endanger the American people and our nation. The attacks of September the 11th required a few hundred thousand dollars in the hands of a few dozen evil and deluded men. All of the chaos and suffering they caused came at much less than the cost of a single tank. The dangers have not passed. This government and the American people are on watch, we are ready, because we know the terrorists have more money and more men and more plans.

The gravest danger to freedom lies at the perilous crossroads of radicalism and technology. When the spread of chemical and biological and nuclear weapons, along with ballistic missile technology—when that occurs, even weak states and small groups could attain a catastrophic power to strike great nations. Our enemies have declared this very intention, and have been caught seeking these terrible weapons. They want the capability to blackmail us, or to harm us, or to harm our friends—and we will oppose them with all our power.

For much of the last century, America's defense relied on the Cold War doctrines of deterrence and containment. In some cases, those strategies still apply. But new threats also require new thinking. Deterrence—the promise of massive retaliation against nations—means nothing against shadowy terrorist networks with no nation or citizens to defend. Containment is not possible when unbalanced dictators with weapons of mass destruction can deliver those weapons on missiles or secretly provide them to terrorist allies.

We cannot defend America and our friends by hoping for the best. We cannot put our faith in the word of tyrants, who solemnly sign non-proliferation treaties, and then systemically break them. If we wait for threats to fully materialize, we will have waited too long.

Homeland defense and missile defense are part of stronger security, and they're essential priorities for America. Yet the war on terror will not be won on the defensive. We must take the battle to the enemy, disrupt his plans, and confront the worst threats before they emerge. In the world we have entered, the only path to safety is the path of action. And this nation will act.

Our security will require the best intelligence, to reveal threats hidden in caves and growing in laboratories. Our security will require modernizing domestic agencies such as the FBI, so they're prepared to act, and act quickly, against danger. Our security will require transforming the military you will lead—a military that must be ready to strike at a moment's notice in any dark corner of the world. And our security will require all Americans to be forward-looking and resolute, to be ready for preemptive action when necessary to defend our liberty and to defend our lives.

The work ahead is difficult. The choices we will face are complex. We must uncover terror cells in 60 or more countries, using every tool of finance, intelligence, and law enforcement. Along with our friends and allies, we must oppose proliferation and confront regimes that sponsor terror, as each case requires. Some nations need military training to fight terror, and we'll provide it. Other nations oppose terror, but tolerate the hatred that leads to terror—and that must change. We will send diplomats where they are needed, and we will send you, our soldiers, where you're needed.

All nations that decide for aggression and terror will pay a price. We will not leave the safety of America and the peace of the planet at the mercy of a few mad terrorists and tyrants. We will lift this dark threat from our country and from the world.

Because the war on terror will require resolve and patience, it will also require firm moral purpose. In this way our struggle is similar to the Cold War. Now, as then, our enemies are totalitarians, holding a creed of power with no place for human dignity. Now, as then, they seek to impose a joyless conformity, to control every life and all of life.

America confronted imperial communism in many different ways—diplomatic, economic, and military. Yet moral clarity was essential to our victory in the Cold War. When leaders like John F. Kennedy and Ronald Reagan refused to gloss over the brutality of tyrants, they gave hope to prisoners and dissidents and exiles, and rallied free nations to a great cause.

Some worry that it is somehow undiplomatic or impolite to speak the language of right and wrong. I disagree. Different circumstances require different methods, but not different moralities. Moral truth is the same in every culture, in every time, and in every place. Targeting innocent civilians for murder is always and everywhere wrong. Brutality against women is always and everywhere wrong. There can be no neutrality between justice and cruelty, between the innocent and the guilty. We are in a conflict between good and evil, and America will call evil by its name. By confronting evil and lawless regimes, we do not create a problem, we reveal a problem. And we will lead the world in opposing it.

As we defend the peace, we also have an historic opportunity to preserve the peace. We have our best chance since the rise of the nation state in the 17th century to build a world where the great powers compete in peace instead of prepare for war. The history of the last century, in particular, was dominated by a series of destructive national rivalries that left battlefields and graveyards across the earth. Germany fought France, the Axis fought the Allies, and then the East fought the West, in proxy wars and tense standoffs, against a backdrop of nuclear Armageddon.

Competition between great nations is inevitable, but armed conflict in our world is not. More and more, civilized nations find ourselves on the same side—united by common dangers of terrorist violence and chaos. America has, and intends to keep, military strengths beyond challenge—thereby making the destabilizing arms races of other eras pointless, and limiting rivalries to trade and other pursuits of peace.

Today the great powers are also increasingly united by common values, instead of divided by conflicting ideologies. The United States, Japan and our Pacific friends, and now all of Europe, share a deep commitment to human freedom, embodied in strong alliances such as NATO. And the tide of liberty is rising in many other nations.

Generations of West Point officers planned and practiced for battles with Soviet Russia. I've just returned from a new Russia, now a country reaching toward democracy, and our partner in the war against terror. Even in China, leaders are discovering that economic freedom is the only lasting source of national wealth. In time, they will find that social and political freedom is the only true source of national greatness.

When the great powers share common values, we are better able to confront serious regional conflicts together, better able to cooperate in preventing the spread of violence or economic chaos. In the past, great-power rivals took sides in difficult regional problems, making divisions deeper and more complicated. Today, from the Middle East to South Asia, we are gathering broad international coalitions to increase the pressure for peace. We must build strong and great-power relations when times are good; to help manage crisis when times are bad. America needs partners to preserve the peace, and we will work with every nation that shares this noble goal.

And finally, America stands for more than the absence of war. We have a great opportunity to extend a just peace, by replacing poverty, repression, and resentment around the world with hope of a better day. Through most of history, poverty was persistent, inescapable, and almost universal. In the last few decades, we've seen nations from Chile to South Korea build modern economies and freer societies, lifting millions of people out of despair and want. And there's no mystery to this achievement.

The 20th century ended with a single surviving model of human progress, based on non-negotiable demands of human dignity, the rule of law, limits on the power of the state, respect for women and private property and free speech and equal justice and religious tolerance. America cannot impose this vision—yet we can support and reward governments that make the right choices for their own people. In our development aid, in our diplomatic efforts, in our international broadcasting, and in our educational assistance, the United States will promote moderation and tolerance and human rights. And we will defend the peace that makes all progress possible.

When it comes to the common rights and needs of men and women, there is no clash of civilizations. The requirements of freedom apply fully to Africa and Latin America and the entire Islamic world. The peoples of the Islamic nations want and deserve the same freedoms and opportunities as people in every nation. And their governments should listen to their hopes.

A truly strong nation will permit legal avenues of dissent for all groups that pursue their aspirations without violence. An advancing nation will pursue economic reform, to unleash the great entrepreneurial energy of its people. A thriving nation will respect the rights of women, because no society can prosper while denying opportunity to half its citizens. Mothers and fathers and children across the Islamic world, and all the world, share the same fears and aspirations. In poverty, they struggle. In tyranny, they suffer. And as we saw in Afghanistan, in liberation, they celebrate.

America has a greater objective than controlling threats and containing resentment. We will work for a just and peaceful world beyond the war on terror.

The bicentennial class of West Point now enters this drama. With all in the United States Army, you will stand between your fellow citizens and grave danger. You will help establish a peace that allows millions around the world to live in liberty and to grow in prosperity. You will face times of calm, and times of crisis. And every test will find you prepared—because you're the men and women of West Point. You leave here marked by the character of this Academy, carrying with you the highest ideals of our nation.

Toward the end of his life, Dwight Eisenhower recalled the first day he stood on the plain at West Point. "The feeling came over me," he said, "that the expression 'the United States of America' would now and henceforth mean something different than it had ever before. From here on, it would be the nation I would be serving, not myself."

Today, your last day at West Point, you begin a life of service in a career unlike any other. You've answered a calling to hardship and purpose, to risk and honor. At the end of every day you will know that you have faithfully done your duty. May you always bring to that duty the high standards of this great American institution. May you always be worthy of the long gray line that stretches two centuries behind you.

On behalf of the nation, I congratulate each one of you for the commission you've earned and for the credit you bring to the United States of America. May God bless you all.

## Presidential Address to the Nation
June 6, 2002

Good evening. During the next few minutes, I want to update you on the progress we are making in our war against terror, and to propose sweeping changes that will strengthen our homeland against the ongoing threat of terrorist attacks.

Nearly nine months have passed since the day that forever changed our country. Debris from what was once the World Trade Center has been cleared away in a hundred thousand truckloads. The west side of the Pentagon looks almost as it did on September the 10th. And as children finish school and families prepare for summer vacations, for many, life seems almost normal.

Yet we are a different nation today—sadder and stronger, less innocent and more courageous, more appreciative of life, and for many who serve our country, more willing to risk life in a great cause. For those who have lost family and friends, the pain will never go away—and neither will the responsibilities that day thrust upon all of us. America is leading the civilized world in a titanic struggle against terror. Freedom and fear are at war—and freedom is winning.

Tonight over 60,000 American troops are deployed around the world in the war against terror—more than 7,000 in Afghanistan; others in the Philippines, Yemen, and the Republic of Georgia, to train local forces. Next week Afghanistan will begin selecting a representative government, even as American troops, along with our allies, still continuously raid remote al Qaeda hiding places.

Among those we have captured is a man named Abu Zabedah, al Qaeda's chief of operations. From him, and from hundreds of others, we are learning more about how the terrorists plan and operate; information crucial in anticipating and preventing future attacks.

Our coalition is strong. More than 90 nations have arrested or detained over 2,400 terrorists and their supporters. More than 180 countries have offered or are providing assistance in the war on terrorism. And our military is strong and prepared to oppose any emerging threat to the American people.

Every day in this war will not bring the drama of liberating a country. Yet every day brings new information, a tip or arrest, another step, or two, or three in a relentless march to bring security to our nation and justice to our enemies.

Every day I review a document called the Threat Assessment. It summarizes what our intelligence services and key law-enforcement agencies have picked up about terrorist activity. Sometimes the information is very general—vague talk, bragging about future attacks. Sometimes the information is more specific, as in a recent case when an al Qaeda detainee said attacks were planned against financial institutions.

When credible intelligence warrants, appropriate law-enforcement and local officials are alerted. These warnings are, unfortunately, a new reality in American life—and we have recently seen an increase in the volume of general threats. Americans should continue to do what you're doing—go about your lives, but pay attention to your surroundings. Add your eyes and ears to the protection of our homeland.

In protecting our country, we depend on the skill of our people—the troops we send to battle, intelligence operatives who risk their lives for bits of information, law-enforcement officers who sift for clues and search for suspects. We are now learning that before September the 11th, the suspicions and insights of some of our front-line agents did not get enough attention.

My administration supports the important work of the intelligence committees in Congress to review the activities of law-enforcement and intelligence agencies. We need to know when warnings were missed or signs unheeded—not to point the finger of blame, but to make sure we correct any problems, and prevent them from happening again.

Based on everything I've seen, I do not believe anyone could have prevented the horror of September the 11th. Yet we now know that thousands of trained killers are plotting to attack us, and this terrible knowledge requires us to act differently.

If you're a front-line worker for the FBI, the CIA, some other law-enforcement or intelligence agency, and you see something that raises suspicions, I want you to report it immediately. I expect your supervisors to treat it with the seriousness it deserves. Information must be fully shared, so we can follow every lead to find the one that may prevent tragedy.

I applaud the leaders and employees at the FBI and CIA for beginning essential reforms. They must continue to think and act differently to defeat the enemy.

The first and best way to secure America's homeland is to attack the enemy where he hides and plans, and we're doing just that. We're also taking significant steps to strengthen our homeland protections—securing cockpits, tightening our borders, stockpiling vaccines, increasing security at water-treatment and nuclear power plants.

After September the 11th, we needed to move quickly, and so I appointed Tom Ridge as my Homeland Security Advisor. As Governor Ridge has worked with all levels of government to prepare a national strategy, and as we have learned more about the plans and capabilities of the terrorist network, we have concluded that our government must be reorganized to deal more effectively with the new threats of the 21st century. So tonight, I ask the Congress to join me in creating a single, permanent department with an overriding and urgent mission: Securing the homeland of America, and protecting the American people.

Right now, as many as a hundred different government agencies have some responsibilities for homeland security, and no one has final accountability. For example, the Coast Guard has several missions, from search and rescue to maritime treaty enforcement. It reports to the Transportation Department, whose primary responsibilities are roads, rails, bridges, and the airways. The Customs Service, among other duties, collects tariffs and prevents smuggling—and it is part of the Treasury Department, whose primary responsibility is fiscal policy, not security.

Tonight, I propose a permanent Cabinet-level Department of Homeland Security to unite essential agencies that must work more closely together: Among them, the Coast Guard, the Border Patrol, the Customs Service, Immigration officials, the Transportation Security Administration, and the Federal Emergency Management Agency. Employees of this new agency will come to work every morning knowing their most important job is to protect their fellow citizens. The Department of Homeland Security will be charged with four primary tasks. This new agency will control our borders and prevent terrorists and explosives from entering our country. It will work with state and local authorities to respond quickly and effectively to emergencies. It will bring together our best scientists to develop technologies that detect biological, chemical, and nuclear weapons, and to discover the drugs and treatments to best protect our citizens. And this new department will review intelligence and law-enforcement information from all agencies of government, and produce a single daily picture of threats against our homeland. Analysts will be responsible for imagining the worst, and planning to counter it.

The reason to create this department is not to [increase] the size of government, but to increase its focus and effectiveness. The staff of this new department will be largely drawn from the agencies we are combining. By ending duplication and overlap, we will spend less on overhead, and more on protecting America. This reorganization will give the good people of our government their best opportunity to succeed by organizing our resources in a way that is thorough and unified.

What I am proposing tonight is the most extensive reorganization of the federal government since the 1940s. During his presidency, Harry Truman recognized that our nation's fragmented defenses had to be reorganized to win the Cold War. He proposed uniting our military forces under a single Department of Defense, and creating the National Security Council to bring together defense, intelligence, and diplomacy. Truman's reforms are still helping us to fight terror abroad, and now we need similar dramatic reforms to secure our people at home.

Only the United States Congress can create a new department of government. So tonight, I ask for your help in encouraging your representatives to support my plan. We face an urgent need, and we must move quickly, this year, before the end of the congressional session. All in our government have learned a great deal since September the 11th, and we must act on every lesson. We are stronger and better prepared tonight than we were on that terrible morning—and with your help, and the support of Congress, we will be stronger still.

History has called our nation into action. History has placed a great challenge before us: Will America—with our unique position and power—blink in the face of terror, or will we lead . . . a freer, more civilized world? There's only one answer: This great country will lead the world to safety, security, peace, and freedom.


## Excerpted Remarks by the President from Speech at the Opening of Oak Park High School
Kansas City, Missouri
June 11, 2002

You know, I don't know what went through the minds of the enemy when they hit us. I can't imagine what they were thinking—what kind of thought process did they have? I guess they thought America was so materialistic and so self-absorbed and so selfish, that all we would do after the attack was maybe file a lawsuit or two. They didn't understand, we love freedom. And if somebody tries to take our freedoms away, or if somebody tries to frighten us because of our freedoms, we'll respond.

And I'm proud to report this mighty nation has responded. We are fierce, and we're tough when it comes to defending our values.

I see a lot of you have brought your children; I want to thank you for that. And I want you, as moms and dads, and as grandparents, to make sure you tell your children that we fight not to seek revenge, but we do so because we seek justice; and that the overriding ambition of this country is to achieve long-lasting peace.

It's important our fellow citizens of all ages understand the goal and vision of a strong and tough America is a more peaceful world; that we long for a chance for our own children and children all across the globe to grow up in societies which tolerate people based on—and don't prejudice—based upon people's religious beliefs; that we honor freedom of religion, we respect other people's opinions, we honor the notion of being able to speak freely with political discourse. . . . .

It's important that when our children read about military movements or arrests that it's all done with a clear understanding that this is a peaceful nation, that we long for a freer day for everybody around the globe.

Our country is—I like to use the word *tough,* because we are. We are, we're a tough country. We've got a great military, and for those of you who have got relatives in the military, I want to thank you on behalf of a grateful nation, and thank them on behalf of a grateful nation, as well.

But we're also a patient nation. The American people understand that this is a new type of war. After all, we were attacked. We lost thousands of innocent citizens. Old wars used to be battle lines and tanks moving here and equipment moving there, and logistics. New wars are wars fought against shadowy enemies, people who hide in caves and then are willing to send youngsters to their [deaths]. And that kind of war's going to require patience and resolve. It's going to require us gathering the best intelligence we possibly can. It requires our great nation to assemble a vast coalition of freedom-loving people to join us as we're seeking these killers one by one. It requires us cutting off their money.

One of the things that the terrorists and the enemy can't stand is to have their money dried up. They operate on money, as well as they do on hate, and we're working with . . . financial institutions all over the world.

We've got over 60,000 American troops all around the world fighting terror. . . . Not only are they in Afghanistan to fight terror, they're also there to bring some order into a chaotic society. One of the things I was most proud of is that when we sent our troops, they arrived in Afghanistan, they weren't there to conquer a country; they went in to liberate a country from the clutches of one of the most barbaric regimes in the history of mankind. And thanks to the United States and our coalition, young girls now go to school for the first time in their lives.

This is an unusual kind of war. . . . Sometimes there will be moments of high drama and, of course, good reporters will be going—all kinds of hyperventilating about this action or that action. (Laughter) And sometimes you won't see a thing.

Interestingly enough, we've rounded up and detained over 2,400 terrorists, and that's good. It's not just us; our friends have as well. We're making progress. You probably read in the newspaper, the number's now 2,401.

And it's not very dramatic at times when that happens. But you need to know that we're steady and strong on the subject of keeping America free. I'm going to talk about homeland security, but the best way to secure our homeland is to hunt the killers down one by one and bring them to justice, and that is what we're going to do.

It also is a new kind of war, because we're going to be confronted with the notion that the shadowy terrorists could hook up with a nation that has got weapons of mass destruction, the nations that I labeled *axis of evil*, people who in one case have gassed their own people with a weapons of mass destruction. People aren't afraid to use these weapons; people who hate America because of our freedoms. And I made it clear that we will use all tools at our disposal. But one thing we are going to do is defend the American people, and make sure that these terrorist networks don't hook up with these nations that harbor bad designs on us, and at the same time develop the worst kind of weapons.

We owe it to our children to defend freedom. We owe it to our children to defend what we believe in, and we owe it to the world to speak clearly: Murder of innocent people is always wrong. Societies which mistreat women are always wrong. Religious intolerance is always wrong. And this country has a duty to speak out loud and clear. And when we see evil, I know it may hurt some people's feelings, it may not be what they call diplomatically correct, but I'm calling evil for what it is. Evil is evil, and we will fight it with all our might.

I recognize the best way to defend our homeland is to go on the offense, and we're going to. But we've got to do a pretty good job on defense, as well. And that's why I've called for the creation of the Department of Homeland Security, a new Cabinet agency. And I'd like to explain why I did so.

Right now, there are over one hundred agencies responsible for a part of homeland security—one hundred different entities at the federal level. I'm a person who believes in accountability. One reason I believe in accountability is because I understand who the American people are going to hold accountable if something happens. (Laughter) Me. (Laughter) And therefore, I'm the kind of fellow who likes to pick up the phone, and say, How we doing? How are we doing on implementing the strategy? I don't like the idea of calling one hundred different agencies; I like to call one, and say, here is the strategy, and what are you doing about it? And if you're not doing something about it, I expect you to. And if you don't, I'm going to find somebody else [who] will do something about it.

We've got to have accountability. In order to get good results, it's important to hold people accountable, and align authority and responsibility. And so that's part of my thinking—to take the functions and put them in one Cabinet agency. The idea, of course, is not to grow the size of government. I ran on, you know, making sure we didn't grow the size of government. The idea is to make government more effective and more efficient so we can do our job.

Within this Cabinet department, we're going to have four basic functions. [The first is] borders. We've got to do a better job of protecting the borders of the United States. We need to know who's coming in and why they're not going out. We need to know what they're here for and how long they say they're going to be here for. And that requires a management plan and focus and technology. And I'll be honest with you, we've got a long way to go to make sure that what they call the INS is working the way we want it to work. But we've got the strategy, we know what we need to do.

Secondly, we've got to support our first responders, the fine police and fire and emergency medical squads not only here in Kansas City, but all across the country. We need to help them with their strategy of responding if need be.

Thirdly, we've got to develop detection capability to be able to detect weapons of mass destruction—chemical, nuclear, biological weapons—and if they ever were to be used, figure out what to do about it. We've got to have a strategy to deal with bioterrorism, for example, here in America.

And finally, we must have the capacity to analyze all sources of intelligence so that we can imagine the worst and plan for it; so we can figure out how best to deal with the new threats that face America. And those are the four major categories.

And people say, well, can you give me some examples of why it's necessary. Well, I'll give you a couple. The Customs Department: Their job is to collect tariffs and to worry about people bringing things into our country, and yet they work for the Treasury Department. Well, the Treasury Department's job is to worry about fiscal matters, not the security of the homeland.

Or how about the Coast Guard? The Coast Guard can do a good job of patrolling our borders, and they do. The Coast Guard is a fine outfit. But guess who they report to? The Transportation Department. The Transportation Department is worried about highways and airplanes and railroads. And so I want to make sure that we [have] a strategy that works and a focus that is intense.

It's important to have these agencies that have . . . responsibility to defend our homeland under one leader, under one department. In other words, we've aligned functions, and that, in itself, will help change cultures within agencies. And that's an important aspect of making sure we defend our homeland. We've got to make sure agencies that have not been focused on defending the homeland change their culture, so that they do a more effective job. . . .

I'll give you one example of where things have changed in a positive direction—the Federal Bureau of Investigation, the FBI. And we've been reading a lot about the FBI lately. And I appreciate those who come forward and make suggestions as to how to better protect the homeland. But I wasn't surprised that the FBI wasn't fully prepared for the war against terror, because, after all, the FBI's major job up until September the 11th was to make cases against people who committed crimes already in America—white-collar crimes, spies. They really weren't focused on preventing attacks.

And so we needed to change the culture. The FBI man running it now, a guy named Robert Mueller, came on one week before September the 11th. That's when he started his job. He's had his hands full. (Laughter) But he's a good man. He knows what to do. And he discovered that we needed to change the attitude, the focus, the culture within the FBI, so that its major function now is to think about how best to prevent attack; is to chase down every lead, to run down every hint, to follow every possible terrorist activity and find out what they're up to, so that we can keep America safe. And it's happening, it's happening.

Now that's not to say they're still not going to have an important law-enforcement function, [that] they're not going to do what they used to do in the past. They are, of course. But the attitude in America has got to change, because we've got a new problem we're faced with. It's an enemy who is very tough, and smart, and determined. They're not as tough and smart and determined as we are, however.

The other thing we are doing a better job of is having the CIA, which collects information overseas, coordinate with the FBI. That's part of how you restructure agencies in order to better protect America. It used to be they didn't talk very much. There was kind of a—I guess a structural problem. You just need to know we've changed that. We've changed it. . . .

Every morning I meet with George Tenet, who's the head of the CIA; and then after I named Bob Mueller, right after September 11th, he comes in every day, as well. There's nothing like having face-to-face discussions with agency heads, to determine how we're doing, and whether or not people are talking to each other. And they are, and they are. And that's important. It's important that we link up the two.

And this new capacity at the Department of Homeland Security is going to be also important, where we'll have people whose job it is to analyze everything we see, and assess everything we hear. And it's to make sure it's all in one area, so we can get a clearer picture of what may or may not be happening to America.

As well, it is important for us to trust the local folks, to do a better job at recognizing in Washington [that] we don't have all the smarts, that we want to work with the mayors, people at the local level. We want to hear from the police and fire [departments]. We just came from one of the water-treatment plants here in the area, and we're pleased to see how secure the plant is. [EPA Administrator] Christie Todd Whitman was telling me how we're going to eventually have grant money for water-treatment facilities all around the country, to encourage them to make sure that there's a full assessment of the plant, to address any vulnerability that may exist. This one didn't appear very vulnerable, I want you to know. So I was looking. I was pleased to take a big gulp of water when I arrived here. (Laughter and applause)

But I want you to know we're making progress. We've got a good strategy, we do. It's going to be an interesting challenge to see if Congress responds.

I had a good meeting today with Speaker Hastert and Representative Gephardt from Missouri, as well as Senator Daschle and Senator Lott and all the leadership from both parties. And in our discussions, I made it clear to them that I don't view this as a political issue. I don't view it as a Republican issue or a Democrat issue. I think loving America is an American issue. It's important to elevate this debate way beyond political parties. And I was pleased with the meeting. I was pleased with the spirit of the meeting.

You know, sometimes there's a not-invented-here attitude in Washington. I don't care who gets the credit for putting this thing in. I just want it done right, and I want it done on behalf of the American people as quickly as possible.

It may seem kind of easy, but here's the problem. There's a hundred different agencies involved with homeland security. It means there's a lot of people in the Congress and in the Senate who have got jurisdiction over those agencies. In other words, that's what they call *turf*. And people like to defend their turf. And so, all of a sudden, when you're saying, well, you know, Mr. Chairman, we're going to have to take this away from you and put it in a single agency, you don't get to fund it anymore, it kind of makes the chairman nervous.

So . . . I need the help of the American people to remind the turf fighters not to be nervous, because we're talking about doing what's right for America.

I believe we can get it done, I really do. But I want your help . . . to talk to the members and the senators. Just let them know that you appreciate their efforts, their concerns about the homeland, but you hope that they will join the White House and work hard together to do what's right for the American people. I sincerely think this is right; otherwise I wouldn't have proposed it.

You know, I am an optimistic guy. I believe in this country. I know this country is a fabulous country. But I believe we've got great days ahead of us. I believe that by being strong and tough . . . we can achieve peace. I believe that. I sincerely, honestly believe it. And not only do I believe we can bring peace for America, I believe we can bring peace to parts of the world [where it] may not seem like there ever is going to be peace.

This country has got a great chance to lead the world toward a more peaceful tomorrow. I know they're watching us pretty carefully—that is, the other leaders and other countries. If America blinks, they'll probably go to sleep. But we're not blinking. We're not blinking.

America understands that history has really called us to action. Out of the evil is going to come some good. And it's going to be peace. And out of the evil is going to come some good at home, too. I believe that, as well. . . .

## Excerpted Remarks by the President from Speech at Ceremony Honoring Port Authority Heroes
### Port Elizabeth, New Jersey
### June 24, 2002

It is my high honor to be in the midst of so many great Americans, people who serve our country with dignity and honor, people who allow me to say: We're winning, and we're going to continue to win as we fight for our freedoms.

I'm honored to be here at the largest marine-cargo terminal on the east coast. I'm so impressed with the massive size of this operation and its obvious importance to the economy of our country—but not nearly as impressed as I have been and am by the way New Jersey firefighters and police officers and emergency rescue units and Port Authority officers responded on September the 11th and have continued to respond.

The country has come to appreciate so very much the dedication of our nation's first responders, thanks to the bravery of many in this audience and the continued hard work you do on behalf of all America. So on behalf of a grateful nation, I want to thank you for the job you're doing for the people of New Jersey and the people of New York. And, as importantly, for the people of this great land, your fellow Americans. . . .

I marvel at the strength of our country. It's an incredibly great country because the people are great. Today when I landed on Air Force One, I had the honor of meeting a young lady named Joanna Glick. She's a member of the USA Freedom Corps. Her brother, Jeremy, was one of the heroes on Flight 93. That was the flight where average citizens were flying across the country; they realized their airplane was to be used as a weapon to harm their fellow Americans. They told their loved ones good-bye on cell phones; they said a prayer; and they drove the airplane [into] the ground.

They served something greater than themselves in life. And Joanna and her classmates Kelly Bianco and Allison Cohen heard the call, the example of her brother to serve something greater than themselves in life. They understand that in order to defeat evil, you can do so by loving your neighbor like you'd like to be loved yourself. They started what they call the Teen Freedom Corps in their high school. They serve as a fabulous example for young and old alike to respond to the challenge of our country, by working to make somebody else's life better. Would you girls please rise, and thank you for being here. I'm real proud of you. Thank you. I'm really proud of your service and your leadership.

I also want to thank Arlene Howard for coming. Arlene is my friend, mother of George Howard, Port Authority policeman. She represents so many moms and dads and loved ones who mourn for the loss of a child or a husband or a wife. I appreciate your strength, Arlene. I love seeing you every time. She's always telling me what to do. (Laughter)

But being here reminds me that the country still continues to pay tribute to the heroism of 9/11, and we must. As we pay tribute to the heros, we pay tribute to America's character. And it's important for many to see the character of our country. One of those heroes was Fred Morrone. Many of you may have known Fred. He was the Port Authority Superintendent of Police and Director of Public Safety.

Immediately after the plane crashed into One World Trade Center, Fred raced from his Jersey City office to the Trade Center. He oversaw the evacuation of staff from the Port Authority's offices on the 67th floor. The plane crashes, he heads over, up to the 67th floor. Many were leaving—he's heading in. Evacuees heading downstairs saw the calm superintendent urging people to leave in an orderly fashion. He was posthumously awarded the Port Authority's Medal of Honor.

Eddie Calderon was a civilian employee of the Port Authority, a former Marine—you're never really a former Marine. Eddie was a Supervisor of the Trade Center's Operation Control Center. On the morning of September the 11th, Eddie stayed at his desk, speaking to people trapped in elevators, coordinating requests for information from firefighters. When a co-worker expressed concern about Eddie's own safety, here's what he said: "I'm a

Marine. I do not ever leave anybody behind." He, too, received the Port Authority Civilian Medal of Honor.

I know their loved ones are with us today. Our nation is extremely grateful for the dedication and example for others to see. God bless you all.

Altogether, seventy-five Port Authority employees were killed on September the 11th. And you need to know, no matter how long it takes, we're going to hunt their killers down, one by one, and bring them to justice.

This is a different kind of war, and it has placed many Americans on the front line of this war: America's firefighters and police officers and postal workers and all the folks who work here at the Port Authority [of] New York and New Jersey to keep America safe.

And we're working hard to make sure your job is easier, that the port is safer. Here's some examples of what's taking place. The Customs Service is working with overseas ports and shippers to improve its knowledge of container shipments, assessing risk so that we have a better feel of who we ought to look at, what we ought to worry about. Inspectors here can focus on high-risk shipments. America will be better protected.

The Port Authority of New York and New Jersey has been putting together a $60 million closed-circuit TV security system, with cameras all around sensitive areas here at the port. This will strengthen our ability to safeguard these facilities. Coast Guard inspectors and law-enforcement officials currently board targeted commercial vessels shortly before they enter the [port], and then they escort them safely to docks. Tomorrow, the Coast Guard's Deep Water Project will award a multi-year contract to replace aging ships and aircraft, and improve communications and information sharing.

The whole purpose is to push out our maritime borders, giving us more time to identify threats and more time to respond. The Coast Guard is also working on ways to better detect weapons of mass destruction. They've assembled strike teams, one of which I was able to meet today. . . .

We're better and stronger and wiser today than we were. We're working harder than ever before. As I travel our country, I remind our citizens there are thousands of people working as hard as they possibly can to keep America safe. Today I recognize I'm in the midst of that type of citizen, who's working hard to keep America safe. Thank you from a grateful nation.

We must constantly think of ways to improve our ability to protect the homeland, because these killers are still out there. Somebody asked me to describe them one time. I said, they're nothing but a bunch of cold-blooded killers. And they still hate the fact that we love freedom. And they really can't stand the fact that we're not backing down. See, they thought we'd probably just file a lawsuit or two. (Laughter) They didn't understand America. That's what they didn't know. They didn't understand our character. They don't have any idea about what makes the people right here tick.

And so we've got to continue to do everything we can to protect innocent lives. And that's why I think it is vital the federal government reorganize, so that we've got people involved with homeland security under a Cabinet office dedicated to homeland security. You see, we've got to change our priorities. We've got to focus our priorities. We've got to set clear goals. If cultures need to be changed within agencies, we'll change the cultures, because this new war of the 21st century requires a hundred percent focused effort to protect the homeland.

Now I know some are nervous about taking this from here and that from there. It is the right thing to do, to have the over one hundred agencies involved with homeland security under one authority, so that we can have accountability and responsibility in Washington, D.C. I want to thank the members of Congress who understand that it's important to put their own personal turf aside. It's also important to put our political parties in the background as we focus on doing what's right for the country.

I believe with hard work and a lot of effort, and a lot of reminding by the President that this is the right thing to do on behalf of the American people, we can get this new Cabinet agency up and running. It will make your jobs easier, for those of you involved with the agencies I'm talking about. It'll make our federal government more responsive. It will allow us to communicate better. It will allow all of you to make sure that the hard hours you're putting in are able to more secure the homeland.

But I want you to know that no matter what we do here in America, the best way to protect the homeland is to chase the killers down wherever they think they can hide, and bring them to justice. And we're making progress. Sometimes you'll read about it, and sometimes you won't. It's important for our country to understand this new war of the 21st century is really not like any other war we've fought. You see, we fight people who, on the one hand, send youngsters to their death, and they themselves try to hide in a cave. Those are the kind of people we fight. You know, they claim in the name of a great religion that death is justified. . . .

This country will take its time, because we defend freedom. This country will not blink, because we defend freedom. We love freedom. And we love our fellow Americans. The mighty United States military in step one performed brilliantly in Afghanistan. And I submitted a defense budget up in Washington—that's big, no question about it—because anytime we commit our young into harm's way they deserve the best pay and the best training possible.

You know, the enemy would have loved to have seen a scrawny little budget up there. They'd have said, well, we were right, they're going to quit. We're not quitting. I don't care where the theater is, how long it takes, this mighty nation is going to track them down until we can say with certainty, our children and our grandchildren are free.

We've hauled in about 2,400 of them. This weekend I called Gloria Arroyo, the President of the Philippines, to congratulate her on her country's steadfast desire to rout out the Abu Zubaydah killer organization. This is the organization which captured the Burnhams. They're nothing but cold-blooded killers. . . . They may espouse some kind of doctrine; they have no regard for innocent life. I told Gloria early on in the fight that we'd help her—if she wanted us to take on the enemy without her, we'd be glad to do that, too. And she said, no, we'd like your help to train so we can go get them. And she did. So I guess it's 2,401. But we're making progress, one person at a time.

At the same time, we recognize that there are other threats that could face our country and our history—these nations which have no regard for human rights, and at the same time want to develop weapons of mass destruction. We're not going to let the world's worst leaders blackmail America with the world's worst weapons.

This country recognizes history has called us into action. History has given us an opportunity to lead the world to more freedom. And as far as I'm concerned, history will record this: The United States of America led a mighty coalition to freedom so that all freedom-loving people in every country could grow up in a peaceful environment; so children of all walks of life could grow up understanding what freedom means, in a peaceful way.

I think out of the evil done to America, the evil so many saw firsthand and had to live with, will come incredible good. I believe there will be peace in the world if America continues to lead and remain strong. And I believe here at home, thanks to the loving hearts of thousands of our fellow citizens, America can not only be a safer place, but a better place.

I want to thank you all for coming today. I want to thank you for giving me the chance to be the President of the greatest country on the face of the earth. God bless, and God bless America.

# September 2002

### Presidential Proclamation Establishing
### Patriot Day
September 4, 2002

By the President of the United States of America
A Proclamation

On this first observance of Patriot Day, we remember and honor those who perished in the terrorist attacks of September 11, 2001. We will not forget the events of that terrible morning, nor will we forget how Americans responded in New York City, at the Pentagon, and in the skies over Pennsylvania—with heroism and selflessness; with compassion and courage; and with prayer and hope. We will always remember our collective obligation to ensure that justice is done, that freedom prevails, and that the principles upon which our nation was founded endure.

Inspired by the heroic sacrifices of our firefighters, rescue, and law-enforcement personnel, military-service members, and other citizens, our Nation found unity, focus, and strength. We found healing in the national outpouring of compassion for those lost, as tens of millions of Americans participated in moments of silence, candlelight vigils, and religious services. From the tragedy of September 11 emerged a stronger nation, renewed by a spirit of national pride and a true love of country.

We are a people dedicated to the triumph of freedom and democracy over evil and tyranny. The heroic stories of the first responders who gave their all to save others strengthened our resolve. And our Armed Forces have pursued the war against terrorism in Afghanistan and elsewhere with valor and skill. Together with our coalition partners, they have achieved success.

Americans also have fought back against terror by choosing to overcome evil with good. By loving their neighbors as they would like to be loved, countless citizens have answered the call to help others. They have contributed to relief efforts, improved homeland security in their communities, and volunteered their time to aid those in need. This spirit of service continues to grow as thousands have joined the newly established USA Freedom Corps, committing themselves to changing America one heart at a time through the momentum of millions of acts of decency and kindness.

Those whom we lost last September 11 will forever hold a cherished place in our hearts and in the history of our nation. As we mark the first anniversary of that tragic day, we remember their sacrifice; and we commit ourselves to honoring their memory by pursuing peace and justice in the world and security at home. By a joint resolution approved December 18, 2001 (Public Law 107-89), the Congress has authorized and requested the President to designate September 11 of each year as "Patriot Day."

NOW THEREFORE I, GEORGE W. BUSH, President of the United States of America, do hereby proclaim September 11, 2002, as Patriot Day. I call upon the people of the United States to observe this day with appropriate ceremonies and activities, including remembrance services and candlelight vigils. I also call upon the Governors of the United States and the Commonwealth of Puerto Rico, as well as appropriate officials of all units of government, to direct that the flag be flown at half-staff on Patriot Day. Further, I encourage all Americans to display the flag at half-staff from their homes on that day and to observe a moment of silence beginning at 8:46 A.M. Eastern Daylight Time, or another appropriate commemorative time, to honor the innocent victims who lost their lives as a result of the terrorist attacks of September 11, 2001.

IN WITNESS WHEREOF, I have hereunto set my hand this fourth day of September, in the year of our Lord two thousand two, and of the Independence of the United States of America the two hundred and twenty-seventh.

GEORGE W. BUSH

## Excerpted Remarks by the President From Speech
## Marking the Observance of the September 11th Attacks
The Pentagon, Washington, D.C.
September 11, 2002

One year ago, men and women and children were killed here because they were Americans. And because this place is a symbol to the world of our country's might and resolve. Today, we remember each life. We rededicate this proud symbol and we renew our commitment to win the war that began here.

The terrorists chose this target hoping to demoralize our country. They failed. Within minutes, brave men and women were rescuing their comrades. Within hours, in this building, the planning began for a military response. Within weeks, commands went forth from this place that would clear terrorist camps and caves and liberate a nation. And within one year, this great building has been made whole once again.

Many civilian and military personnel have now returned to offices they occupied before the attack. The Pentagon is a working building, not a memorial. Yet the memories of a great tragedy linger here. And for all who knew loss here, life is not the same.

The 184 whose lives were taken in this place—veterans and recruits, soldiers and civilians, husbands and wives, parents and children—left behind family and friends whose loss cannot be weighed. The murder of innocence cannot be explained, only endured. And though they died in tragedy, they did not die in vain.

Their loss has moved a nation to action, in a cause to defend other innocent lives across the world. . . . We've captured more than 2,000 terrorists; a larger number of killers have met their end in combat. We've seized millions in terrorist assets. We're reorganizing the federal government to protect the homeland. Yet there's a great deal left to do. And the greatest tasks and the greatest dangers will fall to the armed forces of the United States.

I came to the presidency with respect for all who wear America's uniform. Every day as your Commander in Chief, my respect and that of our nation has deepened. I have great confidence in every man and woman who wears the uniform of the United States of America. I am proud of all who have fought on my orders, and this nation honors all who died in our cause.

Wherever our military is sent in the world, you bring hope and justice and promise of a better day. You are worthy of the traditions you represent, the uniform you wear, the ideals you serve. America is counting on you. And our confidence is well placed.

What happened to our nation on a September day set in motion the first great struggle of a new century. The enemies who struck us are determined and they are resourceful. They will not be stopped by a sense of decency or a hint of conscience—but they will be stopped.

A greater force is amassed against them. They are opposed by freedom-loving people in many lands. They are opposed by our allies who have fought bravely by our side. And as long as terrorists and dictators plot against our lives and our liberty, they will be opposed by the United States Army, Navy, Coast Guard, Air Force, and Marines.

We fight as Americans have always fought, not just for ourselves, but for the security of our friends, and for peace in the world. We fight for the dignity of life against fanatics who feel no shame in murder. We fight to protect the innocent, so that the lawless and the merciless will not inherit the earth.

In every turn of this war, we will always remember how it began, and who fell first—the thousands who went to work, boarded a plane, or reported to their posts.

Today, the nation pays our respects to them. Here, and in Pennsylvania, and in New York, we honor each name, and each life. We ask God to bring comfort to every home where they are loved and missed. And on this day, and on every day, may He watch over the United States of America.

## Presidential Address to the Nation Marking the Observance of the September 11th Attacks
Ellis Island, New York, N.Y.
September 11, 2002

Good evening. A long year has passed since enemies attacked our country. We've seen the images so many times they are seared on our souls, and remembering the horror, reliving the anguish, re-imagining the terror, is hard —and painful.

For those who lost loved ones, it's been a year of sorrow, of empty places, of newborn children who will never know their fathers here on earth. For members of our military, it's been a year of sacrifice and service far from home. For all Americans, it has been a year of adjustment, of coming to terms with the difficult knowledge that our nation has determined enemies, and that we are not invulnerable to their attacks.

Yet, in the events that have challenged us, we have also seen the character that will deliver us. We have seen the greatness of America in airline passengers who defied their hijackers and ran a plane into the ground to spare the lives of others. We've seen the greatness of America in rescuers who rushed up flights of stairs toward peril. And we continue to see the greatness of America in the care and compassion our citizens show to each other.

September 11, 2001, will always be a fixed point in the life of America. The loss of so many lives left us to examine our own. Each of us was reminded that we are here only for a time, and these counted days should be filled with things that last and matter: love for our families, love for our neighbors, and for our country; gratitude for life and to the Giver of life.

We resolved a year ago to honor every last person lost. We owe them remembrance and we owe them more. We owe them, and their children, and our own, the most enduring monument we can build: a world of liberty and security made possible by the way America leads, and by the way Americans lead [their] lives.

The attack on our nation was also attack on the ideals that make us a nation. Our deepest national conviction is that every life is precious, because every life is the gift of a Creator who intended us to live in liberty and equality. More than anything else, this separates us from the enemy we fight. We value every life; our enemies value none—not even the innocent, not even their own. And we seek the freedom and opportunity that give meaning and value to life.

There is a line in our time, and in every time, between those who believe all men are created equal, and those who believe that some men and women and children are expendable in the pursuit of power. There is a line in our time, and in every time, between the defenders of human liberty and those who seek to master the minds and souls of others. Our generation has now heard history's call, and we will answer it.

America has entered a great struggle that tests our strength, and even more our resolve. Our nation is patient and steadfast. We continue to pursue the terrorists in cities and camps and caves across the earth. We are joined by a great coalition of nations to rid the world of terror. And we will not allow any terrorist or tyrant to threaten civilization with weapons of mass murder. Now and in the future, Americans will live as free people, not in fear, and never at the mercy of any foreign plot or power.

This nation has defeated tyrants and liberated death camps, raised this lamp of liberty to every captive land. We have no intention of ignoring or appeasing history's latest gang of fanatics trying to murder their way to power. They are discovering, as others before them, the resolve of a great country and a great democracy. In the ruins of two towers, under a flag unfurled at the Pentagon, at the funerals of the lost, we have made a sacred promise to ourselves and to the world: We will not relent until justice is done and our nation is secure. What our enemies have begun, we will finish.

I believe there is a reason that history has matched this nation with this time. America strives to be tolerant and just. We respect the faith of Islam, even as we fight those whose actions defile that faith. We fight, not to impose our will, but to defend ourselves and extend the blessings of freedom.

We cannot know all that lies ahead. Yet, we do know that God [has] placed us together in this moment, to grieve together, to stand together, to serve each other and our country. And the duty we have been given—defending America and our freedom—is also a privilege we share.

We're prepared for this journey. And our prayer tonight is that God will see us through, and keep us worthy.

Tomorrow is September the 12th. A milestone is passed, and a mission goes on. Be confident. Our country is strong. And our cause is even larger than our country. Ours is the cause of human dignity; freedom guided by conscience and guarded by peace. This ideal of America is the hope of all mankind. That hope drew millions to this harbor. That hope still lights our way. And the light shines in the darkness. And the darkness will not overcome it. May God bless America.

## Presidential Radio Address to the Nation
September 13, 2002

Good morning. Today I'm meeting with Italian Prime Minister Silvio Berlusconi about the growing danger posed by Saddam Hussein's regime in Iraq, and the unique opportunity the U.N. Security Council has to confront it.

I appreciate the Prime Minister's public support for effective international action to deal with this danger. The Italian Prime Minister joins other concerned world leaders who have called on the world to act. Among them, Prime Minister Blair of Great Britain, Prime Minister Aznar of Spain, President Kwasniewski of Poland. These leaders have reached the same conclusion I have—that Saddam Hussein has made the case against himself.

He has broken every pledge he made to the United Nations and the world since his invasion of Kuwait was rolled back in 1991. Sixteen times the United Nations Security Council has passed resolutions designed to ensure that Iraq does not pose a threat to international peace and security. Saddam Hussein has violated every one of these 16 resolutions—not once, but many times.

Saddam Hussein's regime continues to support terrorist groups and to oppress its civilian population. It refuses to account for missing Gulf War personnel, or to end illicit trade outside the U.N.'s oil-for-food program. And although the regime agreed in 1991 to destroy and stop developing all weapons of mass destruction and long-range missiles, it has broken every aspect of this fundamental pledge.

Today this regime likely maintains stockpiles of chemical and biological agents, and is improving and expanding facilities capable of producing chemical and biological weapons. Today Saddam Hussein has the scientists and infrastructure for a nuclear weapons program, and has illicitly sought to purchase the equipment needed to enrich uranium for a nuclear weapon. Should his regime acquire fissile material, it would be able to build a nuclear weapon within a year.

The former head of the U.N. team investigating Iraq's weapons of mass destruction program, Richard Butler, reached this conclusion after years of experience: "The fundamental problem with Iraq remains the nature of the regime itself. Saddam Hussein is a homicidal dictator who is addicted to weapons of mass destruction."

By supporting terrorist groups, repressing its own people, and pursuing weapons of mass destruction in defiance of a decade of U.N. resolutions, Saddam Hussein's regime has proven itself a grave and gathering danger. To suggest otherwise is to hope against the evidence. To assume this regime's good faith is to bet the lives of millions and the peace of the world in a reckless gamble. And this is a risk we must not take.

Saddam Hussein's defiance has confronted the United Nations with a difficult and defining moment: Are Security Council resolutions to be honored and enforced, or cast aside without consequence? Will the United Nations serve the purposes of its founding, or will it be irrelevant?

As the United Nations prepares an effective response to Iraq's defense, I also welcome next week's congressional hearings on the threats Saddam Hussein's brutal regime poses to our country and the entire world. Congress must make it unmistakably clear that when it comes to confronting the growing danger posed by Iraq's efforts to develop or acquire weapons of mass destruction, the status quo is totally unacceptable.

The issue is straightforward: We must choose between a world of fear, or a world of progress. We must stand up for our security and for the demands of human dignity. By heritage and choice, the United States will make that stand. The world community must do so as well.

Thank you for listening.

# October 2002

**Excerpted Remarks by the President from Speech at
Massachusetts Victory 2002 Reception**
Boston, Massachusetts
October 4, 2002

I am optimistic about our economy, but we've got more work to do. And I want you to know that I will spend a lot of time working to strengthen this economy in any way I can.

Having said that, my number-one priority is to make America a safer place, because I understand there's still an enemy out there which hates America. And I want to tell you why they hate us, at least my opinion about why they hate us. They hate us for what we love. They hate us because we love freedom.

They hate us because we love the idea that people can worship an Almighty God any way he or she sees fit. They hate us because we love political discourse and a free society. They hate us because of our free press. They hate everything about us, because of our freedom.

And there are a lot of distinguishing features; but one of the most clear ones to me is this: We value life in America. We say everybody is precious, everybody counts, every life has worth, every life has dignity. They don't value life. They're willing to hijack a great religion and take innocent life in the name of that religion.

And they're still out there. And so long as they're out there, the number-one job of your government is to protect innocent life, is to [prevent] the enemy from hitting us again. You need to know there are a lot of good people working long hours to do everything in their power to disrupt, to find, to hunt down, to—anything we can do, within the United States Constitution, to protect the American people. . . .

But in order to make sure we do the job better, I have asked Congress to create what they call the Department of Homeland Security. And let me tell you why I asked them to do that. [There are] over a hundred agencies in Washington involved with homeland security. And they're scattered everywhere. . . . [I]n order to make sure that we align authority and responsibility, they ought to be under one boss. At least the functions for the homeland ought to be coordinated. If the number-one priority of the government is to protect you, we ought to have the ability to make sure that culture changes within agencies so it becomes the number-one priority.

And I asked Congress to join me. And the House passed a bill, and they still can't get it out of the Senate. They're fixing to go home, and they're still arguing over homeland security. And I'll tell you why: There are some up there who believe that they ought to micromanage the process.

And I'll give you an example. They want these work rules to make it difficult for the Secretary and the President, and future Secretaries and Presidents, to be able to move people to the right place at the right time in order to respond to an enemy. For example, if you're working for Customs, we thought it was a wise idea to have people wear radiation-detection devices in order to be able to determine whether somebody is trying to smuggle weapons of mass destruction into America. The union wanted to take that to collective bargaining. It would have taken over a year to determine whether or not people could carry detection devices. That doesn't make any sense to me.

We've got a border. We need to know who's coming in our country, what they're bringing in the country, why they're bringing what they're bringing into the country.

We've got three different agencies on the border, fine people, really good people working hard. I'm proud that I'm a federal employee with them. But we've got the Border Patrol and the INS and Customs. They wear different uniforms. In some sectors, they may have different strategies. They need to be able to be knitted up. They need to be able to work in concert. They need to be able to do everything they can to make sure that we understand our borders are functioning properly. . . .

I need the flexibility. We cannot leave a legacy behind of micro-management and unnecessary work rules and inflexible rules on managers. I'm all for public employees being able to bargain collectively if that's what they choose to do. But I'm also for making sure the President, in the name of national security, has the capacity to put people at the right place at the right time to protect America.

They need to get it done. They need to get something done up there. They need to get it to my desk before they go home.

But the best way to protect our homeland, in the short run and in the long run, is to hunt the killers down one person at a time and bring them to justice.

This is a different kind of war. I spent a lot of time talking to our fellow citizens about this, and it's important for America to understand. I think they do. This is a different kind of war. You don't measure progress in this war based upon the number of ships sunk, or the numbers of tanks dismantled, or the number of aircraft grounded.

You measure progress in this war by the number of killers brought to justice. And that's why I say hunting them down one person at a time, which is precisely the strategy we're employing.

It starts with upholding doctrine. The doctrine which says either you're with us, or you're with the enemy, still stands.

We still got this coalition of freedom-loving nations we're working together with. And we're hunting them down; the other day, one of them popped up, popped his head up, named bin al-Shibh. He's no longer a problem. He would have been a problem. This is the fellow that was bragging about the fact that had he gotten a visa, he would have been the twentieth killer that would have come to America and killed innocent lives. That's what he bragged about.

Thanks to the hard work of our intelligence folks and our United States military and our friends and allies, this guy is not a problem anymore, and neither are a couple of thousand of them just like him who have been detained. And about that many weren't as lucky.

Slowly but surely, slowly but surely, we're dismantling the al Qaeda network. Sometimes you'll see it on your TV screens, sometimes you won't.

I sent a significant increase in our defense spending, the largest since Ronald Reagan was the President, to the Congress for two reasons. One, any time we put our troops into harm's way, they deserve the best pay, the best training, and the best possible equipment.

And, secondly, I sent a message to friend and foe alike that, when it comes to the defense of our freedom [and] our desire to make the world more peaceful, there's no artificial deadline for America. . . . There's no quitting in this country because we love freedom, we love our peace. . . .

I asked Congress to get the defense bill to my desk. The House passed it, the Senate passed it, but they haven't come to a conclusion yet. They need to get it to my desk before they go home. I hope they will. I know there's a lot of good people from both parties working hard to get the bill done. But we're at war and, at the very minimum, they ought to get the defense bill passed in time of war, and get it to my desk before they go home.

I want to remind you all about what I said earlier. We value each life. Everybody counts. That is not just for American life, that's every life, by the way. That's what America thinks.

I want to remind you as well that when we upheld the doctrine that says, if you harbor a terrorist and feed one of them, you're just as guilty as the terrorist. And when we upheld that doctrine in Afghanistan, we went in not to conquer anybody, we went in to liberate people from the clutches of a barbaric regime.

You need to tell your children, you need to tell children who wonder about this war, about the nature of your country, that we love peace, that we're going to secure our homeland. And that, thanks to the United States of America in the first theater of the first war of the 21st century, many young girls now go to school for the first time; that this country loves freedom, and we value each and every life. We also must recognize threats when we see them, and deal with them.

See, September 11th taught us a new lesson about our vulnerabilities. Prior to that, it used to be that we could be protected by two oceans. And unrest or what was going on in a different part of the world—it might have been OK sometimes, because we were protected. No longer is that the case; we're now the battlefield, because of what we believe in and what we hold dear.

And since we're never going to relinquish those freedoms, or love for freedom, since we're never going to back down from the things we hold dear, we'll continue to be a battlefield until the world is more secure.

We've got a true threat facing us, a threat that faces our very homeland. And that is Saddam Hussein. And I want to explain to you about Saddam Hussein, just quickly, if I might.

This is a man who has used weapons of mass destruction. He used them on his own people. He used them on his neighbors.

This is a man who said he wouldn't have weapons of mass destruction. Yet he does. This is a man who, eleven years ago, said he wouldn't harbor terrorists, he wouldn't develop chemical or biological weapons. This is a man who said he would free prisoners.

He has lied and deceived and denied for eleven long years.

This is a man who continues to torture people in his own country who disagree with him. He's a cold-blooded killer. This is a man who I believe strongly thinks he can use terrorist networks to foster his own ambitions. . . . When [inspectors] went into Iraq the first time, it was discovered that he was a short period away from developing a nuclear weapon.

This is a man who has invaded two countries. This is a man who is a threat—he's a threat to the United States, he's a threat to Israel, he's a threat to neighbors of his. He is a threat.

My job is to protect the American people. My job is to anticipate. And so I went to the United Nations. I went to the United Nations because I want the United Nations to be effective. I went to the United Nations to remind them that for eleven years this man has defied 16 resolutions. Time and time and time again, he has ignored the United Nations.

I basically said, you can be an effective body to help us keep the peace, or you can be the League of Nations.

It's up to them. It's up to them. We will continue to work with our friends in the United Nations for peace to deal with threats, to not ignore reality. I want the United Nations to be effective, I want them to do their job of disarming Saddam Hussein.

The choice is theirs and the choice is also Mr. Saddam Hussein's. . . . There are no negotiations; there's nothing to negotiate. He said he wouldn't have weapons of mass destruction, and that's what those of us who love peace expect. We expect him not to have weapons of mass destruction.

But I want to tell you all, for the sake of our freedom, for the sake of peace, if the United Nations won't make the decision, if Saddam Hussein continues to lie and deceive, the United States will lead a coalition to disarm this man before he harms America and our friends.

The military's not my first choice. But peace is; peace is my first choice.

[What] I just told you is a sentiment that's becoming more and more shared in Washington. I was honored this week to stand on the steps of the Rose Garden with Speaker Hastert, Minority Leader Gephardt, Leader Lott, Senator Lieberman, Senator McCain, Senator Bayh, just to name a few of both Republicans and Democrats who are coming together to speak with one voice—a voice out of concern for the future of our country and for the future of our friends.

This country next week will be having a big debate on a really important, historic resolution. I welcome the debate. This is not a political debate. It's a debate about peace and security.

I also think it's a debate about responsibility for those of us who've been given high office. I believe we have a responsibility to speak clearly, to defend that which we hold dear, to be determined. And by doing so, we can achieve peace. We can achieve peace for America by speaking strongly against terror, by holding our line the values we hold of freedom.

We can achieve peace in the Middle East. We can achieve peace in South Asia. I know the enemy hit us, but out of the evil done to America that day has a chance to come a more peaceful world. . . . Out of the evil done to America that day can come a better world for America, too.

You know, I don't know what was on their mind. They probably thought that, after September the 11th, 2001, somebody might file a lawsuit or two. (Laughter) They didn't know. They didn't know who they're dealing with. They're dealing with a great country, a country which can be tough but a country which also can be compassionate.

See, in our midst of plenty, there are people who hurt in America, people who are addicted, people who are lost. When you say American Dream, they go, what the heck are you talking about American Dream. They don't know.

And when one of us hurts, we all got to realize all of us hurt in this country. We must do everything we can to eradicate those pockets of despair. And the best way to do so in my judgment is to unleash the character of our country. See, government can hand out money, and sometimes we do a pretty darn good job of it. (Laughter) But what government cannot do is put hope in people's hearts or a sense of purpose in people's lives.

That's done when a fellow American hears the universal call to love a neighbor just like you'd like to be loved yourself. If you want to fight evil here in America, do some good. You see, it's the millions of acts of kindness and compassion that really define the true character of our country and will enable us to defy the killers by making this country a more compassionate and decent place. Mentor a child, help a shut-in, start a Boys' Club or a Girls' Club. . . .

These acts of kindness don't have to be huge, they've just got to be significant enough to change America one person at a time. No, they hit us, they hit us—they didn't know what they were getting into. They had no idea what they were getting into.

I truly believe that this country is going to be a stronger and better place, because I understand the nature of America. See, a lot of us took a step back after what happened to us that day, and realized there's something more important in life than self, something more important in life than materialism. . . . [And that] being a patriot is somebody who does love a neighbor. . . .

You know, I first got into politics because I believed that I could make a difference in helping change a culture, from one which said, if it feels good, do it, and if you've got a problem, blame somebody else. See, I was hoping to help usher in a period of personal responsibility, when each of us understands we're responsible for the decisions we make in life.

If you're responsible, if you're a mother or dad, your most important responsibility is to love your child with all your heart and all your soul. If you're living in Boston, Massachusetts, you're responsible for helping people in need, not some faraway government. If you're running a corporation, you're responsible for telling the truth to your employees and your shareholders and the public.

It's happening. It's happening. Perhaps the most vivid example was Flight 93. People flying across the country; they heard from their loved ones that the plane was going to be used as a weapon.

They said good-bye. They used the word *love* a lot. They said a prayer. A guy said: "Let's roll." They took the plane into the ground, to serve something greater than themselves in life.

No, the enemy hit us. But see, they didn't know, they didn't know the character of this great country.

They didn't realize that this country is a country which will fight for peace, lead the world for peace. And this is a country which will make sure that everybody who lives here understands that the great American experience, the great hope of this country, is available for everybody. There's no doubt in my mind—we can accomplish these objectives because America is the greatest country, full of the finest people, on the face of the earth.

## Presidential Radio Address to the Nation
### October 5, 2002

Good morning. This week leaders of the Congress agreed on a strong bipartisan resolution authorizing the use of force if necessary to disarm Saddam Hussein and to defend the peace. Now both the House and the Senate will have an important debate and an historic vote. Speaker Hastert and Leader Gephardt and Leader Lott did tremendous work in building bipartisan support on this vital issue.

The danger to America from the Iraqi regime is grave and growing. The regime is guilty of beginning two wars. It has a horrible history of striking without warning. In defiance of pledges to the United Nations, Iraq has stockpiled biological and chemical weapons, and is rebuilding the facilities used to make more of those weapons. Saddam Hussein has used these weapons of death against innocent Iraqi people, and we have every reason to believe he will use them again.

Iraq has longstanding ties to terrorist groups, which are capable of and willing to deliver weapons of mass death. And Iraq is ruled by perhaps the world's most brutal dictator, who has already committed genocide with chemical weapons, ordered the torture of children, and instituted the systematic rape of the wives and daughters of his political opponents.

We cannot leave the future of peace and the security of America in the hands of this cruel and dangerous man. This dictator must be disarmed. And all the United Nations resolutions against his brutality and support for terrorism must be enforced.

The United States does not desire military conflict, because we know the awful nature of war. Our country values life, and we will never seek war unless it is essential to security and justice. We hope that Iraq complies with the world's demands. If, however, the Iraqi regime persists in its defiance, the use of force may become unavoidable. Delay, indecision, and inaction are not options for America, because they could lead to massive and sudden horror.

Should force be required to bring Saddam to account, the United States will work with other nations to help the Iraqi people rebuild and form a just government. We have no quarrel with the Iraqi people. They are the daily victims of Saddam Hussein's oppression, and they will be the first to benefit when the world's demands are met.

American security, the safety of our friends, and the values of our country lead us to confront this gathering threat. By supporting the resolution now before them, members of Congress will send a clear message to Saddam: His only choice is to fully comply with the demands of the world. And the time for that choice is limited. Supporting this resolution will also show the resolve of the United States, and will help spur the United Nations to act.

I urge Americans to call their members of Congress to make sure your voice is heard. The decision before Congress cannot be more consequential. I'm confident that members of both political parties will choose wisely.

Thank you for listening.

## Excerpted Remarks by the President from Speech at the Cincinnati Museum Center
Cincinnati, Ohio
October 7, 2002

Tonight I want to take a few minutes to discuss a grave threat to peace, and America's determination to lead the world in confronting that threat.

The threat comes from Iraq. It arises directly from the Iraqi regime's own actions—its history of aggression, and its drive toward an arsenal of terror. Eleven years ago, as a condition for ending the Persian Gulf War, the Iraqi regime was required to destroy its weapons of mass destruction, to cease all development of such weapons, and to stop all support for terrorist groups. The Iraqi regime has violated all of those obligations. It possesses and produces chemical and biological weapons. It is seeking nuclear weapons. It has given shelter and support to terrorism, and practices terror against its own people. The entire world has witnessed Iraq's eleven-year history of defiance, deception, and bad faith.

We also must never forget the most vivid events of recent history. On September the 11th, 2001, America felt its vulnerability—even to threats that gather on the other side of the earth. We resolved then, and we are resolved today, to confront every threat, from any source, that could bring sudden terror and suffering to America.

Members of the Congress of both political parties, and members of the United Nations Security Council, agree that Saddam Hussein is a threat to peace and must disarm. We agree that the Iraqi dictator must not be permitted to threaten America and the world with horrible poisons and diseases and gases and atomic weapons. Since we all agree on this goal, the issue is: How can we best achieve it?

Many Americans have raised legitimate questions: About the nature of the threat; about the urgency of action—why be concerned now?; about the link between Iraq developing weapons of terror, and the wider war on terror. These are all issues we've discussed broadly and fully within my administration. And tonight, I want to share those discussions with you.

First, some ask why Iraq is different from other countries or regimes that also have terrible weapons. While there are many dangers in the world, the threat from Iraq stands alone—because it gathers the most serious dangers of our age in one place. Iraq's weapons of mass destruction are controlled by a murderous tyrant who has already used chemical weapons to kill thousands of people. This same tyrant has tried to dominate the Middle East, has invaded and brutally occupied a small neighbor, has struck other nations without warning, and holds an unrelenting hostility toward the United States.

By its past and present actions, by its technological capabilities, by the merciless nature of its regime, Iraq is unique. As a former chief weapons inspector of the U.N. has said, "The fundamental problem with Iraq remains the nature of the regime itself. Saddam Hussein is a homicidal dictator who is addicted to weapons of mass destruction."

Some ask how urgent this danger is to America and the world. The danger is already significant, and it only grows worse with time. If we know Saddam Hussein has dangerous weapons today—and we do—does it make any sense for the world to wait to confront him as he grows even stronger and develops even more dangerous weapons?

In 1995, after several years of deceit by the Iraqi regime, the head of Iraq's military industries defected. It was then that the regime was forced to admit that it had produced more than 30,000 liters of anthrax and other deadly biological agents. The inspectors, however, concluded that Iraq had likely produced two to four times that amount. This is a massive stockpile of biological weapons that has never been accounted for, and [is] capable of killing millions.

We know that the regime has produced thousands of tons of chemical agents, including mustard gas, sarin nerve gas, VX nerve gas. Saddam Hussein also has experience in using chemical weapons. He has ordered chemical attacks on Iran, and on more than forty villages in his own country. These actions killed or injured at least 20,000 people, more than six times the number of people who died in the attacks of September the 11th.

And surveillance photos reveal that the regime is rebuilding facilities that it had used to produce chemical and biological weapons. Every chemical and biological weapon that Iraq has or makes is a direct violation of the truce that ended the Persian Gulf War in 1991. Yet Saddam Hussein has chosen to build and keep these weapons despite international sanctions, U.N. demands, and isolation from the civilized world.

Iraq possesses ballistic missiles with a likely range of hundreds of miles—far enough to strike Saudi Arabia, Israel, Turkey, and other nations—in a region where more than 135,000 American civilians and service members live and work. We've also discovered through intelligence that Iraq has a growing fleet of manned and unmanned aerial vehicles that could be used to disperse chemical or biological weapons across broad areas. We're concerned that Iraq is exploring ways of using these UAVs for missions targeting the United States. And, of course, sophisticated delivery systems aren't required for a chemical or biological attack; all that might be required are a small container and one terrorist or Iraqi intelligence operative to deliver it.

And that is the source of our urgent concern about Saddam Hussein's links to international terrorist groups. Over the years, Iraq has provided safe haven to terrorists such as Abu Nidal, whose terror organization carried out more than 90 terrorist attacks in 20 countries that killed or injured nearly 900 people, including 12 Americans. Iraq has also provided safe haven to Abu Abbas, who was responsible for seizing the *Achille Lauro* and killing an American passenger. And we know that Iraq is continuing to finance terror and gives assistance to groups that use terrorism to undermine Middle East peace.

We know that Iraq and the al Qaeda terrorist network share a common enemy—the United States of America. We know that Iraq and al Qaeda have had high-level contacts that go back a decade. Some al Qaeda leaders who fled Afghanistan went to Iraq. These include one very senior al Qaeda leader who received medical treatment in Baghdad this year, and who has been associated with planning for chemical and biological attacks. We've learned that Iraq has trained al Qaeda members in bomb-making and poisons and deadly gases. And we know that after September the 11th, Saddam Hussein's regime gleefully celebrated the terrorist attacks on America.

Iraq could decide on any given day to provide a biological or chemical weapon to a terrorist group or individual terrorists. Alliance with terrorists could allow the Iraqi regime to attack America without leaving any fingerprints.

Some have argued that confronting the threat from Iraq could detract from the war against terror. To the contrary; confronting the threat posed by Iraq is crucial to winning the war on terror. When I spoke to Congress more than a year ago, I said that those who harbor terrorists are as guilty as the terrorists themselves. Saddam Hussein is harboring terrorists and the instruments of terror, the instruments of mass death and destruction. And he cannot be trusted. The risk is simply too great that he will use them, or provide them to a terror network.

Terror cells and outlaw regimes building weapons of mass destruction are different faces of the same evil. Our security requires that we confront both. And the United States military is capable of confronting both.

Many people have asked how close Saddam Hussein is to developing a nuclear weapon. Well, we don't know exactly, and that's the problem. Before the Gulf War, the best intelligence indicated that Iraq was eight to ten years away from developing a nuclear weapon. After the war, international inspectors learned that the regime [had] been much closer—the regime in Iraq would likely have possessed a nuclear weapon no later than 1993. The inspectors discovered that Iraq had an advanced nuclear weapons development program, had a design for a workable nuclear weapon, and was pursuing several different methods of enriching uranium for a bomb.

Before being barred from Iraq in 1998, the International Atomic Energy Agency dismantled extensive nuclear weapons-related facilities, including three uranium-enrichment sites. That same year, information from a high-ranking Iraqi nuclear engineer who had defected revealed that despite his public promises, Saddam Hussein had ordered his nuclear program to continue.

The evidence indicates that Iraq is reconstituting its nuclear weapons program. Saddam Hussein has held numerous meetings with Iraqi nuclear scientists, a group he calls his "nuclear mujahideen"—his nuclear holy warriors. Satellite photographs reveal that Iraq is rebuilding facilities at sites that have been part of its nuclear program in the past. Iraq has attempted to purchase high-strength aluminum tubes and other equipment needed for gas centrifuges, which are used to enrich uranium for nuclear weapons.

If the Iraqi regime is able to produce, buy, or steal an amount of highly enriched uranium a little larger than a single softball, it could have a nuclear weapon in less than a year. And if we allow that to happen, a terrible line would be crossed. Saddam Hussein would be in a position to blackmail anyone who opposes his aggression. He would be in a position to dominate the Middle East. He would be in a position to threaten America. And Saddam Hussein would be in a position to pass nuclear technology to terrorists.

Some citizens wonder, after 11 years of living with this problem, why do we need to confront it now? And there's a reason. We've experienced the horror of September the 11th. We have seen that those who hate America are willing to crash airplanes into buildings full of innocent people. Our enemies would be no less willing, in fact they would be eager, to use [a] biological or chemical, or a nuclear weapon.

Knowing these realities, America must not ignore the threat gathering against us. Facing clear evidence of peril, we cannot wait for the final proof—the smoking gun—that could come in the form of a mushroom cloud. As President Kennedy said in October of 1962, "Neither the United States of America, nor the world community of nations can tolerate deliberate deception and offensive threats on the part of any nation, large or small. We no longer live in a world," he said, "where only the actual firing of weapons represents a sufficient challenge to a nation's security to constitute maximum peril."

Understanding the threats of our time, knowing the designs and deceptions of the Iraqi regime, we have every reason to assume the worst, and we have an urgent duty to prevent the worst from occurring.

Some believe we can address this danger by simply resuming the old approach to inspections, and applying diplomatic and economic pressure. Yet this is precisely what the world has tried to do since 1991. The U.N. inspections program was met with systematic deception. The Iraqi regime bugged hotel rooms and offices of inspectors to find where they were going next; they forged documents, destroyed evidence, and developed mobile weapons facilities to keep a step ahead of inspectors. Eight so-called presidential palaces were declared off-limits to unfettered inspections. These sites actually encompass twelve square miles, with hundreds of structures, both above and below the ground, where sensitive materials could be hidden.

The world has also tried economic sanctions—and watched Iraq use billions of dollars in illegal oil revenues to fund more weapons purchases, rather than providing for the needs of the Iraqi people.

The world has tried limited military strikes to destroy Iraq's weapons of mass destruction capabilities—only to see them openly rebuilt, while the regime again denies they even exist.

The world has tried no-fly zones to keep Saddam from terrorizing his own people—and in the last year alone, the Iraqi military has fired upon American and British pilots more than 750 times.

After eleven years during which we have tried containment, sanctions, inspections—even selected military action—the end result is that Saddam Hussein still has chemical and biological weapons and is increasing his capabilities to make more. And he is moving ever closer to developing a nuclear weapon.

Clearly, to actually work, any new inspections, sanctions, or enforcement mechanisms will have to be very different. America wants the U.N. to be an effective organization that helps keep the peace. And that is why we are urging the Security Council to adopt a new resolution setting out tough, immediate requirements. Among those requirements: The Iraqi regime must reveal and destroy, under U.N. supervision, all existing weapons of mass destruction. To ensure that we learn the truth, the regime must allow witnesses to its illegal activities to be interviewed outside the country—and these witnesses must be free to bring their families with them so they are beyond the reach of Saddam Hussein's terror and murder. And inspectors must have access to any site, at any time, without pre-clearance, without delay, without exceptions.

The time for denying, deceiving, and delaying has come to an end. Saddam Hussein must disarm himself—or, for the sake of peace, we will lead a coalition to disarm him.

Many nations are joining us in insisting that Saddam Hussein's regime be held accountable. They are committed to defending the international security that protects the lives of both our citizens and theirs. And that's why America is challenging all nations to take the resolutions of the U.N. Security Council seriously.

And these resolutions are clear. In addition to declaring and destroying all of its weapons of mass destruction, Iraq must end its support for terrorism. It must cease the persecution of its civilian population. It must stop all illicit trade outside the Oil for Food program. It must release or account for all Gulf War personnel, including an American pilot, whose fate is still unknown.

By taking these steps, and by only taking these steps, the Iraqi regime has an opportunity to avoid conflict. Taking these steps would also change the nature of the Iraqi regime itself. America hopes the regime will make that choice. Unfortunately, at least so far, we have little reason to expect it. And that's why two administrations—mine and President Clinton's—have stated that regime change in Iraq is the only certain means of removing a great danger to our nation.

I hope this will not require military action, but it may. And military conflict could be difficult. An Iraqi regime faced with its own demise may attempt cruel and desperate measures. If Saddam Hussein orders such measures, his generals would be well advised to refuse those orders. If they do not refuse, they must understand that all war criminals will be pursued and punished. If we have to act, we will take every precaution that is possible. We will plan carefully; we will act with the full power of the United States military; we will act with allies at our side, and we will prevail.

There is no easy or risk-free course of action. Some have argued we should wait—and that's an option. In my view, it's the riskiest of all options, because the longer we wait, the stronger and bolder Saddam Hussein will become. We could wait and hope that Saddam does not give weapons to terrorists, or develop a nuclear weapon to blackmail the world. But I'm convinced that is a hope against all evidence. As Americans, we want peace—we work and sacrifice for peace. But there can be no peace if our security depends on the will and whims of a ruthless and aggressive dictator. I'm not willing to stake one American life on trusting Saddam Hussein.

Failure to act would embolden other tyrants, allow terrorists access to new weapons and new resources, and make blackmail a permanent feature of world events. The United Nations would betray the purpose of its founding, and prove irrelevant to the problems of our time. And through its inaction, the United States would resign itself to a future of fear.

That is not the America I know. That is not the America I serve. We refuse to live in fear. This nation, in world war and in Cold War, has never permitted the brutal and lawless to set history's course. Now, as before, we will secure our nation, protect our freedom, and help others to find freedom of their own.

Some worry that a change of leadership in Iraq could create instability and make the situation worse. The situation could hardly get worse, for world security and for the people of Iraq. The lives of Iraqi citizens would improve dramatically if Saddam Hussein were no longer in power, just as the lives of Afghanistan's citizens improved after the Taliban. The dictator of Iraq is a student of Stalin, using murder as a tool of terror and control, within his own cabinet, within his own army, and even within his own family.

On Saddam Hussein's orders, opponents have been decapitated, wives and mothers of political opponents have been systematically raped as a method of intimidation, and political prisoners have been forced to watch their own children being tortured.

America believes that all people are entitled to hope and human rights, to the non-negotiable demands of human dignity. People everywhere prefer freedom to slavery; prosperity to squalor; self-government to the rule of terror and torture. America is a friend to the people of Iraq. Our demands are directed only at the regime that enslaves them and threatens us. When these demands are met, the first and greatest benefit will come to Iraqi men, women, and children. The oppression of Kurds, Assyrians, Turkomans, Shi'a, Sunnis, and others will be lifted. The long captivity of Iraq will end, and an era of new hope will begin.

Iraq is a land rich in culture, resources, and talent. Freed from the weight of oppression, Iraq's people will be able to share in the progress and prosperity of our time. If military action is necessary, the United States and our allies will help the Iraqi people rebuild their economy, and create the institutions of liberty in a unified Iraq at peace with its neighbors.

Later this week, the United States Congress will vote on this matter. I have asked Congress to authorize the use of America's military, if it proves necessary, to enforce U.N. Security Council demands. Approving this resolution does not mean that military action is imminent or unavoidable. The resolution will tell the United Nations, and all nations, that America speaks with one voice and is determined to make the demands of the civilized world mean something. Congress will also be sending a message to the dictator in Iraq: That . . . his only choice is full compliance, and the time remaining for that choice is limited.

Members of Congress are nearing an historic vote. I'm confident they will fully consider the facts, and their duties.

The attacks of September the 11th showed our country that vast oceans no longer protect us from danger. Before that tragic date, we had only hints of al Qaeda's plans and designs. Today in Iraq, we see a threat whose outlines are far more clearly defined, and whose consequences could be far more deadly. Saddam Hussein's actions have put us on notice, and there is no refuge from our responsibilities.

We did not ask for this present challenge, but we accept it. Like other generations of Americans, we will meet the responsibility of defending human liberty against violence and aggression. By our resolve, we will give strength to others. By our courage, we will give hope to others. And by our actions, we will secure the peace, and lead the world to a better day.

## President's Statement on Terrorist Attack in Bali
### October 13, 2002

Terrorists have once again targeted innocents—this time in Indonesia. At least 182 innocent men and women have been murdered and hundreds injured in a cowardly act designed to create terror and chaos.

On behalf of the people of the United States, I condemn this heinous act. I offer our heartfelt condolences to the families of all the murder victims from numerous countries and our wish for the swift and complete recovery of those injured in this attack.

I offer our sympathy to our friends, the people of Indonesia, for this terrible tragedy. Our prayers are also with our friends and allies, the people of Australia, who are suffering a grievous personal and national loss.

The world must confront this global menace—errorism. We must together challenge and defeat the idea that the wanton killing of innocents advances any cause or supports any aspirations. And, we must call this despicable act by its rightful name—murder.

The United States has offered its assistance to the government of Indonesia to help bring these murderers to justice.

# November 2002

**Excerpted Remarks by the President from a**
**Campaign Speech in South Dakota**
Sioux Falls, South Dakota
November 3, 2002

One of the values that I know John [Thune] holds dear to his heart is the value that his World War II fighter-pilot daddy taught him. And that is, sometimes you have to sacrifice for freedom; sometimes it's important to serve something greater than yourself to secure the freedom. And that means in the 21st century that we've got to sacrifice here in America to protect ourselves.

The most important responsibility John and I will have will be to work together to protect the homeland, to protect you from further attack; to prevent an enemy which hates America because we love freedom from hurting innocent life ever again.

There's a lot of good people working for you right now [at] the federal level and the state level and the local level, a lot of really decent people are running down any hint. Any time anybody kind of whispers that they may be thinking about doing something to America, you need to know we're moving on it. We're going to disrupt them and deny them any chance they have to hurt the American people.

But in order to make our job go better—and, by the way, this isn't just something that's going to take place next year. We've been protecting the homeland for a while. They're out there, and it's going to take a while for us to rout them out. And therefore, I thought that it would be best to have a Department of Homeland Security so we could better coordinate the agencies involved with your protection, so we could change cultures if need be, so people got the message: their number-one job in Washington is to protect you.

And I got a good bill out of the House of Representatives, thanks to John Thune. However, it is stuck in the United States Senate. And let me describe to you why it's stuck in the Senate. Because some senators are trying to take power away from the President—a power that every President has had since John F. Kennedy was the President. And that is the capacity to suspend collective-bargaining rules in any department of the federal government when national security is at stake.

In other words, if there are some work rules that stand in the way of [our] being able to protect the American people, for the sake of national security, I now have the right to suspend those rules, for your protection. But because of special interests in Washington, some senators are trying to take away this power. And I'm not going to let them. I refuse to stand for a lousy bill.

But the best way to secure our homeland is to chase these killers down one person at a time and bring them to justice. It's a different kind of war we fight. It's important for you to understand that. John understands that. You see, in the old days, if you destroyed tanks and airplanes, you knew you were making progress. These killers are hiding in caves. They send youngsters to their suicidal deaths. The only way to deal with them is to treat them like they are, international criminals, and hunt them down one person at a time.

I went to the Congress and said, why don't you give me a defense bill that shows our mettle, that speaks clearly about our intentions. Thankfully, they did. They passed the largest increase since Ronald Reagan was the President. And here's the message, the message that John Thune was taught by his daddy: Any time you put our troops into harm's way, they deserve the best pay, the best training, and the best possible equipment.

And the other message is this: It doesn't matter how long it takes to secure our freedom; it doesn't matter how long it takes to secure the homeland, we're staying the course. There's no quitting in America. There's not a calendar on my desk that says on such and such a date, bring them home. That's not how we think. That's not the lesson that John Thune learned from his dad or I learned from my dad or any of us learned from previous generations of people who sacrificed for our freedom.

No, we've been called into action. And we're making progress. Slowly but surely, we're dismantling the terrorist network which attacked America. Slowly but surely, we're hauling them in. See, that doctrine that says, either you're with us or you're with the enemy, it still stands. . . .

What's important for us as we work to secure the homeland is to remember the stakes have changed. After September the 11th, world changed. It changed for a lot of reasons. Perhaps the most profound reason on a foreign-policy perspective, or from a homeland security perspective, is that we're no longer protected by two big oceans. [It] used to be if there was a threat overseas we could deal with it if we chose to do so, but we didn't have to worry about something happening here at home. It used to be oceans could protect us from conflict and from threats.

But that's changed, and it's important to have people in the Senate who are clear-eyed realists. It's important to have people who see the world the way it is, not the way we hope it is. And the world is a dangerous place, particularly with people like Saddam Hussein in power.

Saddam Hussein is a man who told the world he wouldn't have weapons of mass destruction, but he's got them. He's a man who a while ago was close to having a nuclear weapon. Imagine if this madman had a nuclear weapon. [He's] a man who not only has chemical weapons, but he's used chemical weapons against some of his neighbors. He used chemical weapons, incredibly enough, against his own people. He can't stand America. He can't stand some of our closest friends.

And, not only that, he would like nothing better than to hook up with one of these shadowy terrorist networks like al Qaeda, provide some weapons and training to them, let them come and do his dirty work, and we wouldn't be able to see his fingerprints on his action.

No, he's a threat. And that's why I went to the United Nations. I went to the United Nations because, I said to that august body, you need to hold this man to account. For eleven years, in resolution after resolution after resolution, he's defied you. For the sake of keeping the peace, we want you to be effective. For the sake of keeping the world free, we want you to be an effective body. It's up to you, however. You can show the world whether you've got the backbone necessary to enforce your edicts or whether you're going to turn out to be just like the League of Nations; [it's] your choice to make.

And my message to Saddam Hussein is that, for the sake of peace, for the sake of freedom, you must disarm. . . . But my message to you all and to the country is this: For the sake of our future freedoms, and for the sake of world peace, if the United Nations can't act, and if Saddam Hussein won't act, the United States will lead a coalition of nations to disarm Saddam Hussein.

And that's the lesson John learned from his daddy, that this country sometimes must act and act decisively in the name of freedom and peace, in order to keep the peace. That when we see a gathering threat, we shouldn't shirk our duty and responsibility, but we must deal with it.

I want you to know that out of the evil done to America is going to come some great good. I truly believe that. I believe by being firm and strong, we can keep the peace. I know that if we remember our values, remember that freedom is not America's gift to the world, freedom is a God-given gift to the world— if we remember that value. [if] we remember our uniqueness and the values we hold dear, we can bring peace, and that's going to happen. And here at home, we'll have a better America, too. A better America. . . .

No, out of the evil done to this country is going to come some great good. And the American spirit is strong and alive. It's a spirit that says, when it comes to the defense of our freedoms, we'll defend them. It also says that being a patriot means you serve something greater than yourself.

Flight 93 comes to mind when I'm thinking about the American spirit. Citizens were flying across the country on that fateful day. They heard the air-plane was going to be used as a weapon. They realized this plane was going to crash into the ground and kill. They told their loved ones good-bye, they said a prayer; a guy said: "Let's roll." They took the plane into the ground to serve something greater than themselves in life. The American spirit is strong and alive in America today.

It is alive and well because of values such as those South Dakota values. It is alive and well. It allows me to boldly predict that, out of the evil done to America, will come peace in the world and a better, more hopeful America here at home.

And I can say that with certainty, because this is the greatest nation, full of the finest people on the face of this earth. I'm honored you'd be here tonight. Thank you for supporting John. May God bless you and may God bless America.


### Excerpted Remarks by the President from Speech at
### Metropolitan Police Operations Center
Washington, D.C.
November 11, 2002


I'm here to thank you all for your hard work. I'm here, as well, to tell all the first responders across the District, as well as around the country, how much our country is grateful for your service, your dedication, and remind you that we have not only a duty to prepare for emergencies, we have a duty in this country to prevent them from happening in the first place.

It's a new charge. It's a new charge because we learned on that fateful day that America is now a battlefield. It used to be that oceans would protect us. We didn't have to take certain threats seriously. We could say, well, we can deal if we want to deal with them. But we learned a tough lesson: that the old ways are gone, that the enemy can strike us here at home, and we all have new responsibilities. And I'm confident we can meet those responsibilities because I understand the nature of the people who wear the uniform all across America—fine, dedicated, honorable public servants who are willing to serve something greater than themselves. So, thank you for what you do.

And the federal government has got a job, as well. Our job—our government's greatest responsibility—is to protect the American people. That's our most important job. And this requires Congress to create a new department of homeland security so we can better do our job. I think this work can be done soon. The Congress is coming back for a brief period of time. And in that period of time, they can get the job done. If they put their mind to it, they can get a job done on behalf of the American people. And I urge them to do so. . . .

On September the 11th, 2001, our nation was confronted by a new kind of war. See, we're at war. This is a war. This isn't a single isolated incident. We are now in the first war of the 21st century. And it's a different kind of war than we're used to. I explained part of the difference is the fact that the battlefield is now here at home. It's also a war where the enemy doesn't show up with airplanes that they own, or tanks or ships. . . . These are cold-blooded killers. That's all they are. The new kind of war has now placed our police and firefighters and rescue workers on the front lines. You're already on the front lines. Now [you're on] another line. There's another front—to do our duty to the American people.

For the courageous individuals on September the 11th, it was a day of great loss. But it was also a day of great, great honor. It reminded the American people of the sacrifices that the people who wear the uniform go through on a daily basis, and the risks that you take every day.

We still weep and mourn for those who lost lives to save others. But we also recognize there's a renewal in America of appreciation for what you do. The entire nation appreciated the calm determination, the steady hand, the ability to respond under severe circumstances. And like our military, which is also on the front line of the war against terror, you deserve all the tools and resources to do your work. This country is going to support you, because we now understand the stakes.

Since September the 11th, every level of government has taken important steps to better prepare against terrorism. We've now been notified. We understand that history has called us into action. There should be no doubt in anybody's mind [about] the nature of the enemy. There should be no doubt in anybody's mind that we must do everything we can to protect the homeland.

For the first time ever, Customs agents are now at overseas ports inspecting containers before they come close to the United States. In other words, we're adjusting to the new world we're in. We've put more marshals now on airplanes. Everybody's aware of that. We've stepped up security at our power plants and our ports, and, as importantly, at our border crossings. We need to know who's coming into the country, what they're bringing into the country, and if they're leaving when they say they're going to leave. We need to know that for the sake of the homeland.

We've deployed detection equipment to look for weapons of mass destruction. Whoever would have thought that this country needed to use technologies to prevent people from smuggling in weapons of mass destruction? But we needed to have that technology in place, so we can better protect the American people. There's a real threat that somebody might smuggle in one of these weapons that would create incredible havoc here at home. So we're on alert. We're stockpiling enough smallpox vaccine for every man, woman, and child in America.

The U.S. Patriot Act has helped us detect and disrupt terrorist activity in this country. . . . [Any] time we get a hint that somebody is thinking about doing something to America, we're moving on it. Any time we get an inkling that somebody is planning to hurt the American people, to take innocent life, we're using every tool we can to disrupt and deny. And we're doing that at the local level and at the state level and at the federal level. That's what the American people expect, and that's what's going to happen.

We act decisively in the clearest areas of vulnerability. We're moving. And this is only the beginning of our effort to protect our country from a global threat. The threats to the homeland are growing threats. These people aren't going away any time soon. And so the need for action is important.

And one of my jobs is to make sure nobody gets complacent. One of my jobs is to remind people of the stark realities that we face. See, every morning I go into that great Oval Office and read threats to our country—every morning. . . . Some of them are blowhards, but we take every one of them seriously. It's the new reality.

The Congress is in session today, and the House and the Senate have pressing responsibilities to work with us for our security. And I'm confident they'll meet those responsibilities. And the single most important business before Congress is the creation of a department of homeland security. Certain members of the Senate and the House have got all kinds of agendas they'd like to discuss. The single most important one is to get this bill done.

The importance of the homeland security [bill is] that we'll be able to better coordinate and organize, and that there [will] be clear lines of authority. One reason this department works so well, and one reason the center we just saw works well is there's great coordination with clear lines of authority. And that's important. That's what you do here in Washington, and that's what we ought to do at the federal level, as well, in this new department.

The responsibility for protecting the homeland here in Washington, at least at the federal level, is spread out among more than 100 different organizations, and not one organization has the primary responsibility. Each agency operates separately, sometimes completely unaware of what others are doing. The result is duplication that we cannot afford, and inefficiencies which create problems.

So I set out to do something about it, for the good of the country. And that is to call for a single Cabinet-level department of government, staffed by dedicated professionals who wake up every single day with one overriding duty, to protect the American people. That's their duty. That's their most important responsibility.

The new department will work, of course, with our state and local authorities to avert attacks, to plan for emergencies, and to respond. That's the functions of the new department. We've got to make sure our first responders are well-equipped and trained and organized for their duties. You do a fine job here in Washington; there are some places that need help, and the new department will help first responders.

The new department will control our borders. I mentioned the border— we need to know who's coming in, we need—but there's three agencies on the border right now, and they're all full of fine people. They wear different uniforms, they have different strategies. Sometimes they talk, sometimes they don't. There is a better way to enforce our border here in America.

It will bring together scientists who develop technologies that detect biological, chemical, and nuclear weapons, and discover drugs and treatments to protect our citizens. So there will be a scientific component in this new department.

For the first time in our history information on the threats to America will be gathered and analyzed, together with information on our vulnerabilities, in one place. We've got a lot of good people working hard to collect intelligence. This new agency will analyze the intelligence to address vulnerabilities here in America.

Establishing the new department will require the largest reorganization of the federal government since 1940. In other words, it's not going to be easy. But I think Congress understands the need to do that. And I think Congress is [willing] to take the task. I want to thank very much the House of Representatives for passing a good bill, one that gives me the authority and the flexibility to work hard to defend America.

The Senate—it got stuck in the Senate. But it looks like it's going to come out of the Senate, I hope. And we're working hard to bring it forth in a way that will enable this President and future Presidents to meet the needs of the United States. To meet the threats, I must be able—and future Presidents must be able—to move people and resources where they're needed, and to do it quickly, without being forced to comply with a thick book of rules.

The enemy moves quickly and America must move quickly. We cannot have bureaucratic rules preventing this President and future Presidents from meeting the needs of the American people. To meet the threats to our country, a President must have the authority, as every President since John F. Kennedy has had, to waive certain rights for national-security purposes. It makes no sense in a time of war to diminish the capacity of the President to be able to put the right people at the right time at the right place.

This debate is often misunderstood. The rights of federal workers should be [fully] protected in the department of homeland security. Every employee will be treated fairly and protected from discrimination. The men and women who work in that department will need and want leadership that can act quickly and decisively, without getting bogged down in endless disputes. When the department is created, we've got to do it right. It is our chance to do it right. And I will not give up national-security authority at the price for creating a department we badly need to secure America.

Fortunately, I'm encouraged by the ongoing discussions. I believe we can get this done. I believe Congress can show the country that they can finish their work on a high note of achievement. That's what the people want. The people want us to come together and work together and do what's right. And I think Congress can show that's possible to do.

Securing our homeland means not only a new department of homeland security, it means hunting these killers down one at a time. It means staying on task. It means [making] sure that the doctrines still exist. And there's one out there that says, you're either with us or with the enemy. That was true right after September the 11th, and it's very true today. We're calling on all these nations that love freedom to join us in an international manhunt. There's no cave deep enough for these people to hide in, as far as I'm concerned. There's no shadow of the world dark enough for them to kind of slither around in. We're after them, and it's going to take a while. It can take a while.

We're after them one person at a time. We owe that to the American people. We owe that to our children.

I can't imagine what was going through their [minds] when they hit us. They must have thought we'd just file a lawsuit. They just don't understand America, do they? They don't understand our love for freedom. They don't understand that, when it comes to our freedoms, it doesn't matter how long it takes, nor the cost; we will do our duty.

The world's going to be more peaceful as a result of America being strong and resolved. Peace is going to happen. You see, the enemy hit us and, out of the evil done to this country, is going to come some incredible good—a more secure America, a more peaceful world.

People will look back—your kids and your grandkids will look back and say, you know, my dad or my mother was involved, actively involved in one of the most dramatic periods in our country's history. And I'm confident they'll look back and say, I'm proud of their service, because America became a better place as a result of their sacrifices.

I'm honored you had me here. May God bless you and your families. May God bless your work. And may God continue to bless America.


## Remarks by the President at Speech upon the Signing of the Homeland Security Act of 2002
### November 25, 2002

Today, we are taking historic action to defend the United States and protect our citizens against the dangers of a new era. With my signature, this act of Congress will create a new Department of Homeland Security, ensuring that our efforts to defend this country are comprehensive and united.

The new department will analyze threats, will guard our borders and airports, protect our critical infrastructure, and coordinate the response of our nation for future emergencies. The Department of Homeland Security will focus the full resources of the American government on the safety of the American people. This essential reform was carefully considered by Congress and enacted with strong bipartisan majorities. . . .

From the morning of September the 11th, 2001, to this hour, America has been engaged in an unprecedented effort to defend our freedom and our security. We're fighting a war against terror with all our resources, and we're determined to win.

With the help of many nations—with the help of ninety—nations, we're tracking terrorist activity, we're freezing terrorist finances, we're disrupting terrorist plots, we're shutting down terrorist camps, we're on the hunt [for] one person at a time. Many terrorists are now being interrogated. Many terrorists have been killed. We've liberated a country.

We recognize our greatest security is found in the relentless pursuit of these cold-blooded killers. Yet, because terrorists are targeting America, the front of the new war is here in America. Our life changed and changed in dramatic fashion on September the 11th, 2001.

In the last fourteen months, every level of our government has taken steps to be better prepared against a terrorist attack. We understand the nature of the enemy. We understand they hate us because of what we love. We're doing everything we can to enhance security at our airports and power plants and border crossings. We've deployed detection equipment to look for weapons of mass destruction. We've given law enforcement better tools to detect and disrupt terrorist cells which might be hiding in our own country.

And through separate legislation I signed earlier today, we will strengthen security at our nation's 361 seaports, adding port-security agents, requiring ships to provide more information about the cargo, crew, and passengers they carry. And I want to thank the members of Congress for working hard on this important piece of legislation as well.

The Homeland Security Act of 2002 takes the next critical steps in defending our country. The continuing threat of terrorism, the threat of mass murder on our own soil will be met with a unified, effective response.

Dozens of agencies charged with homeland security will now be located within one Cabinet department with the mandate and legal authority to protect our people. America will be better able to respond to any future attacks, to reduce our vulnerability, and, most important, prevent the terrorists from taking innocent American lives.

The Department of Homeland Security will have nearly 170,000 employees, dedicated professionals who will wake up each morning with the overriding duty of protecting their fellow citizens. As federal workers, they have rights, and those rights will be fully protected. And I'm grateful that the Congress listened to my concerns and retained the authority of the President to put the right people in the right place at the right time in the defense of our country. . . .

The Secretary-designate and his team have an immense task ahead of them. Setting up the Department of Homeland Security will involve the most extensive reorganization of the federal government since Harry Truman signed the National Security Act. To succeed in their mission, leaders of the new department must change the culture of many diverse agencies—directing all of them toward the principal objective of protecting the American people. The effort will take time, and focus, and steady resolve. It will also require full support from both the administration and the Congress. Adjustments will be needed along the way. Yet this is pressing business, and the hard work of building a new department, begins today.

When the Department of Homeland Security is fully operational, it will enhance the safety of our people in very practical ways.

First, this new department will analyze intelligence information on terror threats collected by the CIA, the FBI, the National Security Agency, and others. The department will match this intelligence against the nation's vulnerabilities—and work with other agencies, and the private sector, and state and local governments to harden America's defenses against terror.

Second, the department will gather and focus all our efforts to face the challenge of cyberterrorism, and the even worse danger of nuclear, chemical, and biological terrorism. This department will be charged with encouraging research on new technologies that can detect these threats in time to prevent an attack.

Third, state and local governments will be able to turn for help and information to one federal domestic-security agency, instead of more than twenty agencies that currently divide these responsibilities. This will help our local governments work in concert with the federal government for the sake of all the people of America.

Fourth, the new department will bring together the agencies responsible for border, coastline, and transportation security. There will be a coordinated effort to safeguard our transportation systems and to secure the border so that we're better able to protect our citizens and welcome our friends.

Fifth, the department will work with state and local officials to prepare our response to any future terrorist attack that may come. We have found that the first hours and even the first minutes after the attack can be crucial in saving lives, and our first responders need the carefully planned and drilled strategies that will make their work effective.

The Department of Homeland Security will also end a great deal of duplication and overlapping responsibilities. Our objective is to spend less on administrators in offices and more on working agents in the field—less on overhead and more on protecting our neighborhoods and borders and waters and skies from terrorists.

With a vast nation to defend, we can neither predict nor prevent every conceivable attack. And in a free and open society, no department of government can completely guarantee our safety against ruthless killers, who move and plot in shadows. Yet our government will take every possible measure to safeguard our country and our people.

We're fighting a new kind of war against determined enemies. And public servants long into the future will bear the responsibility to defend Americans against terror. This administration and this Congress have the duty of putting that system into place. We will fulfill that duty. With the Homeland Security Act, we're doing everything we can to protect America. We're showing the resolve of this great nation to defend our freedom, our security, and our way of life.

It's now my privilege to sign the Homeland Security Act of 2002.

# December 2002

**Radio Address by the President to the People of Iran on Radio Farda**
December 20, 2002

I'm pleased to send warm greetings to the people of Iran and to welcome you to the new Radio Farda broadcast.

For many years, the United States has helped bring news and cultural broadcasts for a few hours every day to the Iranian people via Radio Freedom. Yet the Iranian people tell us that more broadcasting is needed, because the unelected few who control the Iranian government continue to place severe restrictions on access to uncensored information. So we are now making our broadcast available to more Iranians by airing news and music and cultural programs nearly 24 hours a day, and we are pleased to continue Voice of America and VOA TV services to Iran.

The people of Iran want to build a freer, more prosperous country for their children, and live in a country that is a full partner in the international community. Iranians also deserve a free press to express themselves [and] help build an open, democratic, and free society.

My thoughts and prayers are with the Iranian people, particularly the families of the many Iranians who are in prison today for daring to express their hopes and dreams for a better future. We continue to stand with the people of Iran in your quest for freedom, prosperity, honest and effective government, judicial due process, and the rule of law. And we continue to call on the government of Iran to respect the will of its people and be accountable to them.

As I have said before, if Iran respects its international obligations and embraces freedom and tolerance, it will have no better friend than the United States of America.

# January 2003

**Excerpted Remarks from President's State of the Union Address**
January 28, 2003

Mr. Speaker, Vice President Cheney, members of Congress, distinguished citizens, and fellow citizens: Every year, by law and by custom, we meet here to consider the state of the union. This year, we gather in this chamber deeply aware of decisive days that lie ahead.

You and I serve our country in a time of great consequence. During this session of Congress, we have the duty to reform domestic programs vital to our country; we have the opportunity to save millions of lives abroad from a terrible disease. We will work for a prosperity that is broadly shared, and we will answer every danger and every enemy that threatens the American people.

In all these days of promise and days of reckoning, we can be confident. In a whirlwind of change and hope and peril, our faith is sure, our resolve is firm, and our union is strong.

This country has many challenges. We will not deny, we will not ignore, we will not pass along our problems to other Congresses, to other presidents, and other generations. We will confront them with focus and clarity and courage. . . .

This nation can lead the world in sparing innocent people from a plague of nature. And this nation is leading the world in confronting and defeating the man-made evil of international terrorism.

There are days when our fellow citizens do not hear news about the war on terror. There's never a day when I do not learn of another threat, or receive reports of operations in progress, or give an order in this global war against a scattered network of killers. The war goes on, and we are winning.

To date, we've arrested or otherwise dealt with many key commanders of al Qaeda. They include a man who directed logistics and funding for the

September the 11th attacks; the chief of al Qaeda operations in the Persian Gulf, who planned the bombings of our embassies in East Africa and the *USS Cole*; an al Qaeda operations chief from Southeast Asia; a former director of al Qaeda's training camps in Afghanistan; a key al Qaeda operative in Europe; a major al Qaeda leader in Yemen. All told, more than three thousand suspected terrorists have been arrested in many countries. Many others have met a different fate. Let's put it this way—they are no longer a problem to the United States and our friends and allies.

We are working closely with other nations to prevent further attacks. America and coalition countries have uncovered and stopped terrorist conspiracies targeting the American embassy in Yemen, the American embassy in Singapore, a Saudi military base, ships in the Straits of Hormuz and the Straits of Gibraltar. We've broken al Qaeda cells in Hamburg, Milan, Madrid, London, Paris, as well as Buffalo, New York.

We have the terrorists on the run. We're keeping them on the run. One by one, the terrorists are learning the meaning of American justice.

As we fight this war, we will remember where it began—here, in our own country. This government is taking unprecedented measures to protect our people and defend our homeland. We've intensified security at the borders and ports of entry, posted more than fifty thousand newly trained federal screeners in airports, begun inoculating troops and first responders against smallpox, and are deploying the nation's first early warning network of sensors to detect biological attack. And this year, for the first time, we are beginning to field a defense to protect this nation against ballistic missiles.

I thank the Congress for supporting these measures. I ask you tonight to add to our future security with a major research and production effort to guard our people against bioterrorism, called Project Bioshield. The budget I send you will propose almost $6 billion to quickly make available effective vaccines and treatments against agents like anthrax, botulinum toxin, Ebola, and plague. We must assume that our enemies would use these diseases as weapons, and we must act before the dangers are upon us.

Since September the 11th, our intelligence and law-enforcement agencies have worked more closely than ever to track and disrupt the terrorists. The FBI is improving its ability to analyze intelligence, and is transforming itself to meet new threats. Tonight, I am instructing the leaders of the FBI, the CIA, the Homeland Security, and the Department of Defense to develop a Terrorist Threat Integration Center, to merge and analyze all threat information in a single location. Our government must have the very best information possible, and we will use it to make sure the right people are in the right places to protect all our citizens.

Our war against terror is a contest of will in which perseverance is power. In the ruins of two towers, at the western wall of the Pentagon, on a field in Pennsylvania, this nation made a pledge, and we renew that pledge tonight: Whatever the duration of this struggle, and whatever the difficulties, we will not permit the triumph of violence in the affairs of men—free people will set the course of history.

Today, the gravest danger in the war on terror, the gravest danger facing America and the world, is outlaw regimes that seek and possess nuclear, chemical, and biological weapons. These regimes could use such weapons for blackmail, terror, and mass murder. They could also give or sell those weapons to terrorist allies, who would use them without the least hesitation.

This threat is new; America's duty is familiar. Throughout the 20th century, small groups of men seized control of great nations, built armies and arsenals, and set out to dominate the weak and intimidate the world. In each case, their ambitions of cruelty and murder had no limit. In each case, the ambitions of Hitlerism, militarism, and Communism were defeated by the will of free peoples, by the strength of great alliances, and by the might of the United States of America.

Now, in this century, the ideology of power and domination has appeared again, and seeks to gain the ultimate weapons of terror. Once again, this nation and all our friends are all that stand between a world at peace, and a world of chaos and constant alarm. Once again, we are called to defend the safety of our people, and the hopes of all mankind. And we accept this responsibility.

America is making a broad and determined effort to confront these dangers. We have called on the United Nations to fulfill its charter and stand by its demand that Iraq disarm. We're strongly supporting the International Atomic Energy Agency in its mission to track and control nuclear materials around the world. We're working with other governments to secure nuclear materials in the former Soviet Union, and to strengthen global treaties banning the production and shipment of missile technologies and weapons of mass destruction.

In all these efforts, however, America's purpose is more than to follow a process—it is to achieve a result: The end of terrible threats to the civilized world. All free nations have a stake in preventing sudden and catastrophic attacks. And we're asking them to join us, and many are doing so. Yet the course of this nation does not depend on the decisions of others. Whatever action is required, whenever action is necessary, I will defend the freedom and security of the American people.

Different threats require different strategies. In Iran, we continue to see a government that represses its people, pursues weapons of mass destruction, and supports terror. We also see Iranian citizens risking intimidation and death as they speak out for liberty and human rights and democracy. Iranians, like all people, have a right to choose their own government and determine their own destiny—and the United States supports their aspirations to live in freedom.

On the Korean Peninsula, an oppressive regime rules a people living in fear and starvation. Throughout the 1990s, the United States relied on a negotiated framework to keep North Korea from gaining nuclear weapons. We now know that that regime was deceiving the world, and developing those weapons all along. And today the North Korean regime is using its nuclear program to incite fear and seek concessions. America and the world will not be blackmailed.

America is working with the countries of the region—South Korea, Japan, China, and Russia—to find a peaceful solution, and to show the North Korean government that nuclear weapons will bring only isolation, economic stagnation, and continued hardship. The North Korean regime will find respect in the world and revival for its people only when it turns away from its nuclear ambitions.

Our nation and the world must learn the lessons of the Korean Peninsula and not allow an even greater threat to rise up in Iraq. A brutal dictator, with a history of reckless aggression, with ties to terrorism, with great potential wealth, will not be permitted to dominate a vital region and threaten the United States.

Twelve years ago, Saddam Hussein faced the prospect of being the last casualty in a war he had started and lost. To spare himself, he agreed to disarm of all weapons of mass destruction. For the next twelve years, he systematically violated that agreement. He pursued chemical, biological, and nuclear weapons, even while inspectors were in his country. Nothing to date has restrained him from his pursuit of these weapons—not economic sanctions, not isolation from the civilized world, not even cruise-missile strikes on his military facilities.

Almost three months ago, the United Nations Security Council gave Saddam Hussein his final chance to disarm. He has shown instead utter contempt for the United Nations, and for the opinion of the world. The 108 UN inspectors were not sent to conduct a scavenger hunt for hidden materials across a country the size of California. The job of the inspectors is to verify that Iraq's regime is disarming. It is up to Iraq to show exactly where it is hiding its banned weapons, lay those weapons out for the world to see, and destroy them as directed. Nothing like this has happened.

The United Nations concluded in 1999 that Saddam Hussein had biological weapons sufficient to produce over 25,000 liters of anthrax—enough doses to kill several million people. He hasn't accounted for that material. He's given no evidence that he has destroyed it.

The United Nations concluded that Saddam Hussein had materials sufficient to produce more than 38,000 liters of botulinum toxin—enough to subject millions of people to death by respiratory failure. He hadn't accounted for that material. He's given no evidence that he has destroyed it.

Our intelligence officials estimate that Saddam Hussein had the materials to produce as much as 500 tons of sarin, mustard, and VX nerve agent. In such quantities, these chemical agents could also kill untold thousands. He's not accounted for these materials. He has given no evidence that he has destroyed them.

U.S. intelligence indicates that Saddam Hussein had upwards of thirty thousand munitions capable of delivering chemical agents. Inspectors recently turned up sixteen of them—despite Iraq's recent declaration denying their existence. Saddam Hussein has not accounted for the remaining 29,984 of these prohibited munitions. He's given no evidence that he has destroyed them.

From three Iraqi defectors we know that Iraq, in the late 1990s, had several mobile biological-weapons labs. These are designed to produce germ-warfare agents, and can be moved from place to a place to evade inspectors. Saddam Hussein has not disclosed these facilities. He's given no evidence that he has destroyed them.

The International Atomic Energy Agency confirmed in the 1990s that Saddam Hussein had an advanced nuclear-weapons development program, had a design for a nuclear weapon, and was working on five different methods of enriching uranium for a bomb. The British government has learned that Saddam Hussein recently sought significant quantities of uranium from Africa. Our intelligence sources tell us that he has attempted to purchase high-strength aluminum tubes suitable for nuclear-weapons production. Saddam Hussein has not credibly explained these activities. He clearly has much to hide.

The dictator of Iraq is not disarming. To the contrary, he is deceiving. From intelligence sources we know, for instance, that thousands of Iraqi security personnel are at work hiding documents and materials from the UN inspectors, sanitizing inspection sites, and monitoring the inspectors themselves. Iraqi officials accompany the inspectors in order to intimidate witnesses.

Iraq is blocking U-2 surveillance flights requested by the United Nations. Iraqi intelligence officers are posing as the scientists inspectors are supposed to interview. Real scientists have been coached by Iraqi officials on what to say. Intelligence sources indicate that Saddam Hussein has ordered that scientists who cooperate with U.N. inspectors in disarming Iraq will be killed, along with their families.

Year after year, Saddam Hussein has gone to elaborate lengths, spent enormous sums, taken great risks to build and keep weapons of mass destruction. But why? The only possible explanation, the only possible use he could have for those weapons, is to dominate, intimidate, or attack.

With nuclear arms or a full arsenal of chemical and biological weapons, Saddam Hussein could resume his ambitions of conquest in the Middle East and create deadly havoc in that region. And this Congress and the America n people must recognize another threat. Evidence from intelligence sources, secret communications, and statements by people now in custody reveal that Saddam Hussein aids and protects terrorists, including members of al Qaeda. Secretly, and without fingerprints, he could provide one of his hidden weapons to terrorists, or help them develop their own.

Before September the 11th, many in the world believed that Saddam Hussein could be contained. But chemical agents, lethal viruses, and shadowy terrorist networks are not easily contained. Imagine those 19 hijackers with other weapons and other plans—this time armed by Saddam Hussein. It would take one vial, one canister, one crate slipped into this country to bring a day of horror like none we have ever known. We will do everything in our power to make sure that that day never comes.

Some have said we must not act until the threat is imminent. Since when have terrorists and tyrants announced their intentions, politely putting us on notice before they strike? If this threat is permitted to fully and suddenly emerge, all actions, all words, and all recriminations would come too late. Trusting in the sanity and restraint of Saddam Hussein is not a strategy, and it is not an option.

The dictator who is assembling the world's most dangerous weapons has already used them on whole villages—leaving thousands of his own citizens dead, blind, or disfigured. Iraqi refugees tell us how forced confessions are obtained—by torturing children while their parents are made to watch. International human-rights groups have catalogued other methods used in the torture chambers of Iraq: Electric shock, burning with hot irons, dripping acid on the skin, mutilation with electric drills, cutting out tongues, and rape. If this is not evil, then evil has no meaning.

And tonight I have a message for the brave and oppressed people of Iraq: Your enemy is not surrounding your country—your enemy is ruling your country. And the day he and his regime are removed from power will be the day of your liberation.

The world has waited twelve years for Iraq to disarm. America will not accept a serious and mounting threat to our country, and our friends and our allies. The United States will ask the U.N. Security Council to convene on February the 5th to consider the facts of Iraq's ongoing defiance of the world. Secretary of State Powell will present information and intelligence about Iraq's illegal-weapons programs, its attempt to hide those weapons from inspectors, and its links to terrorist groups.

We will consult. But let there be no misunderstanding: If Saddam Hussein does not fully disarm, for the safety of our people and for the peace of the world, we will lead a coalition to disarm him.

Tonight I have a message for the men and women who will keep the peace, members of the American Armed Forces: Many of you are assembling in or near the Middle East, and some crucial hours may lay ahead. In those hours, the success of our cause will depend on you. Your training has prepared you. Your honor will guide you. You believe in America, and America believes in you.

Sending Americans into battle is the most profound decision a President can make. The technologies of war have changed; the risks and suffering of war have not. For the brave Americans who bear the risk, no victory is free from sorrow. This nation fights reluctantly, because we know the cost and we dread the days of mourning that always come.

We seek peace. We strive for peace. And sometimes peace must be defended. A future lived at the mercy of terrible threats is no peace at all. If war is forced upon us, we will fight in a just cause and by just means—sparing, in every way we can, the innocent. And if war is forced upon us, we will fight with the full force and might of the United States military—and we will prevail.

And as we and our coalition partners are doing in Afghanistan, we will bring to the Iraqi people food and medicines and supplies—and freedom.

Many challenges, abroad and at home, have arrived in a single season. In two years, America has gone from a sense of invulnerability to an awareness of peril; from bitter division in small matters to calm unity in great causes. And we go forward with confidence, because this call of history has come to the right country.

Americans are a resolute people who have risen to every test of our time. Adversity has revealed the character of our country, to the world and to ourselves. America is a strong nation, and honorable in the use of our strength. We exercise power without conquest, and we sacrifice for the liberty of strangers.

Americans are a free people, who know that freedom is the right of every person and the future of every nation. The liberty we prize is not America's gift to the world, it is God's gift to humanity.

We Americans have faith in ourselves, but not in ourselves alone. We do not know—we do not claim to know—all the ways of Providence, yet we can trust in them, placing our confidence in the loving God behind all of life, and all of history.

May He guide us now. And may God continue to bless the United States of America.

# February 2003

### Statement by the President Regarding the
### United Nations Security Council and Iraq
February 6, 2003

The Secretary of State has now briefed the United Nations Security Council on Iraq's illegal-weapons programs, its attempts to hide those weapons, and its links to terrorist groups. I want to thank Secretary Powell for his careful and powerful presentation of the facts.

The information in the Secretary's briefing and other information in our possession was obtained through great skill, and often at personal risk. Uncovering secret information in a totalitarian society is one of the most difficult intelligence challenges. Those who accept that challenge, both in our intelligence services and in those of our friends and allies, perform a great service to all free nations. And I'm grateful for their good work.

The Iraqi regime's violations of Security Council resolutions are evident, and they continue to this hour. The regime has never accounted for a vast arsenal of deadly biological and chemical weapons. To the contrary, the regime is pursuing an elaborate campaign to conceal its weapons materiels, and to hide or intimidate key experts and scientists, all in direct defiance of Security Council 1441.

This deception is directed from the highest levels of the Iraqi regime, including Saddam Hussein, his son, the vice president, and the very official responsible for cooperating with inspectors. In intercepted conversations, we have heard orders to conceal materiel from the UN inspectors. And we have seen through satellite images concealment activity at close to 30 sites, including movement of equipment before inspectors arrive.

The Iraqi regime has actively and secretly attempted to obtain equipment needed to produce chemical, biological, and nuclear weapons. Firsthand witnesses have informed us that Iraq has at least seven mobile factories for the production of biological agents, equipment mounted on trucks and rails to evade discovery. Using these factories, Iraq could produce within just months hundreds of pounds of biological poisons.

The Iraqi regime has acquired and tested the means to deliver weapons of mass destruction. All the world has now seen the footage of an Iraqi Mirage aircraft with a fuel tank modified to spray biological agents over wide areas. Iraq has developed spray devices that could be used on unmanned aerial vehicles with ranges far beyond what is permitted by the Security Council. A UAV launched from a vessel off the American coast could reach hundreds of miles inland.

Iraq has never accounted for thousands of bombs and shells capable of delivering chemical weapons. The regime is actively pursuing components for prohibited ballistic missiles. And we have sources that tell us that Saddam Hussein recently authorized Iraqi field commanders to use chemical weapons—the very weapons the dictator tells the world he does not have.

One of the greatest dangers we face is that weapons of mass destruction might be passed to terrorists, who would not hesitate to use those weapons. Saddam Hussein has longstanding, direct, and continuing ties to terrorist networks. Senior members of Iraqi intelligence and al Qaeda have met at least eight times since the early 1990s. Iraq has sent bomb-making and document-forgery experts to work with al Qaeda. Iraq has also provided al Qaeda with chemical and biological weapons training.

We also know that Iraq is harboring a terrorist network, headed by a senior al Qaeda terrorist planner. The network runs a poison and explosive training center in northeast Iraq, and many of its leaders are known to be in Baghdad. The head of this network traveled to Baghdad for medical treatment and stayed for months. Nearly two dozen associates joined him there and have been operating in Baghdad for more than eight months.

The same terrorist network operating out of Iraq is responsible for the murder, the recent murder, of an American citizen, an American diplomat, Laurence Foley. The same network has plotted terrorism against France, Spain, Italy, Germany, the Republic of Georgia, and Russia, and was caught producing poisons in London. The danger Saddam Hussein poses reaches across the world.

This is the situation as we find it. Twelve years after Saddam Hussein agreed to disarm, and ninety days after the Security Council passed Resolution 1441 by a unanimous vote, Saddam Hussein was required to make a full declaration of his weapons programs. He has not done so. Saddam Hussein was required to fully cooperate in the disarmament of his regime; he has not done so. Saddam Hussein was given a final chance; he is throwing that chance away.

The dictator of Iraq is making his choice. Now the nations of the Security Council must make their own. On November 8th, by demanding the immediate disarmament of Iraq, the United Nations Security Council spoke with clarity and authority. Now the Security Council will show whether its words have any meaning. Having made its demands, the Security Council must not back down, when those demands are defied and mocked by a dictator.

The United States would welcome and support a new resolution which makes clear that the Security Council stands behind its previous demands. Yet resolutions mean little without resolve. And the United States, along with a growing coalition of nations, is resolved to take whatever action is necessary to defend ourselves and disarm the Iraqi regime.

On September the 11th, 2001, the American people saw what terrorists could do, by turning four airplanes into weapons. We will not wait to see what terrorists or terrorist states could do with chemical, biological, radiological or nuclear weapons. Saddam Hussein can now be expected to begin another round of empty concessions, transparently false denials. No doubt, he will play a last-minute game of deception. The game is over.

All the world can rise to this moment. The community of free nations can show that it is strong and confident and determined to keep the peace. The United Nations can renew its purpose and be a source of stability and security in the world. The Security Council can affirm that it is able and prepared to meet future challenges and other dangers. And we can give the Iraqi people their chance to live in freedom and choose their own government.

Saddam Hussein has made Iraq into a prison, a poison factory, and a torture chamber for patriots and dissidents. Saddam Hussein has the motive and the means and the recklessness and the hatred to threaten the American people. Saddam Hussein will be stopped.

## Excerpted Remarks from of President's Speech to the American Enterprise Institute
Washington, D.C.
February 26, 2003

We meet here during a crucial period in the history of our nation, and of the civilized world. Part of that history was written by others; the rest will be written by us. On a September morning, threats that had gathered for years, in secret and far away, led to murder in our country on a massive scale. As a result, we must look at security in a new way, because our country is a battlefield in the first war of the 21st century.

We learned a lesson: The dangers of our time must be confronted actively and forcefully, before we see them again in our skies and in our cities. And we set a goal: We will not allow the triumph of hatred and violence in the affairs of men.

Our coalition of more than 90 countries is pursuing the networks of terror with every tool of law enforcement and with military power. We have arrested, or otherwise dealt with, many key commanders of al Qaeda. Across the world, we are hunting down the killers one by one. We are winning. And we're showing them the definition of American justice. And we are opposing the greatest danger in the war on terror: Outlaw regimes arming with weapons of mass destruction.

In Iraq, a dictator is building and hiding weapons that could enable him to dominate the Middle East and intimidate the civilized world—and we will not allow it. This same tyrant has close ties to terrorist organizations, and could supply them with the terrible means to strike this country—and America will not permit it. The danger posed by Saddam Hussein and his weapons cannot be ignored or wished away. The danger must be confronted. We hope that the Iraqi regime will meet the demands of the United Nations and disarm, fully and peacefully. If it does not, we are prepared to disarm Iraq by force. Either way, this danger will be removed.

The safety of the American people depends on ending this direct and growing threat. Acting against the danger will also contribute greatly to the long-term safety and stability of our world. The current Iraqi regime has shown the power of tyranny to spread discord and violence in the Middle East. A liberated Iraq can show the power of freedom to transform that vital region, by bringing hope and progress into the lives of millions. America's interests in security, and America's belief in liberty, both lead in the same direction: To a free and peaceful Iraq.

The first to benefit from a free Iraq would be the Iraqi people themselves. Today they live in scarcity and fear, under a dictator who has brought them nothing but war, and misery, and torture. Their lives and their freedom matter little to Saddam Hussein—but Iraqi lives and freedom matter greatly to us.

Bringing stability and unity to a free Iraq will not be easy. Yet that is no excuse to leave the Iraqi regime's torture chambers and poison labs in operation. Any future the Iraqi people choose for themselves will be better than the nightmare world that Saddam Hussein has chosen for them.

If we must use force, the United States and our coalition stand ready to help the citizens of a liberated Iraq. We will deliver medicine to the sick, and we are now moving into place nearly three million emergency rations to feed the hungry.

We'll make sure that Iraq's fifty-five thousand food distribution sites, operating under the Oil for Food program, are stocked and open as soon as possible. The United States and Great Britain are providing tens of millions of dollars to the U.N. High Commission on Refugees, and to such groups as the World Food Program and UNICEF, to provide emergency aid to the Iraqi people.

We will also lead in carrying out the urgent and dangerous work of destroying chemical and biological weapons. We will provide security against those who try to spread chaos, or settle scores, or threaten the territorial integrity of Iraq. We will seek to protect Iraq's natural resources from sabotage by a dying regime, and ensure those resources are used for the benefit of the owners—the Iraqi people.

The United States has no intention of determining the precise form of Iraq's new government. That choice belongs to the Iraqi people. Yet we will ensure that one brutal dictator is not replaced by another. All Iraqis must have a voice in the new government, and all citizens must have their rights protected.

Rebuilding Iraq will require a sustained commitment from many nations, including our own: We will remain in Iraq as long as necessary, and not a day more. America has made and kept this kind of commitment before—in the peace that followed a world war. After defeating enemies, we did not leave behind occupying armies, we left constitutions and parliaments. We established an atmosphere of safety, in which responsible, reform-minded local leaders could build lasting institutions of freedom. In societies that once bred fascism and militarism, liberty found a permanent home.

There was a time when many said that the cultures of Japan and Germany were incapable of sustaining democratic values. Well, they were wrong. Some say the same of Iraq today. They are mistaken. The nation of Iraq—

with its proud heritage, abundant resources, and skilled and educated people—is fully capable of moving toward democracy and living in freedom.

The world has a clear interest in the spread of democratic values, because stable and free nations do not breed the ideologies of murder. They encourage the peaceful pursuit of a better life. And there are hopeful signs of a desire for freedom in the Middle East. Arab intellectuals have called on Arab governments to address the "freedom gap" so their peoples can fully share in the progress of our times. Leaders in the region speak of a new Arab charter that champions internal reform, greater [political] participation, economic openness, and free trade. And from Morocco to Bahrain and beyond, nations are taking genuine steps toward [political] reform. A new regime in Iraq would serve as a dramatic and inspiring example of freedom for other nations in the region.

It is presumptuous and insulting to suggest that a whole region of the world—or the one-fifth of humanity that is Muslim—is somehow untouched by the most basic aspirations of life. Human cultures can be vastly different. Yet the human heart desires the same good things, everywhere on Earth. In our desire to be safe from brutal and bullying oppression, human beings are the same. In our desire to care for our children and give them a better life, we are the same. For these fundamental reasons, freedom and democracy will always and everywhere have greater appeal than the slogans of hatred and the tactics of terror.

Success in Iraq could also begin a new stage for Middle Eastern peace, and set in motion progress towards a truly democratic Palestinian state. The passing of Saddam Hussein's regime will deprive terrorist networks of a wealthy patron that pays for terrorist training, and offers rewards to families of suicide bombers. And other regimes will be given a clear warning that support for terror will not be tolerated.

Without this outside support for terrorism, Palestinians who are working for reform and long for democracy will be in a better position to choose new leaders: True leaders who strive for peace; true leaders who faithfully serve the people. A Palestinian state must be a reformed and peaceful state that abandons forever the use of terror.

For its part, the new government of Israel—as the terror threat is removed and security improves—will be expected to support the creation of a viable Palestinian state, and to work as quickly as possible toward a final status agreement. As progress is made toward peace, settlement activity in the occupied territories must end. And the Arab states will be expected to meet their responsibilities to oppose terrorism, to support the emergence of a peaceful and democratic Palestine, and state clearly they will live in peace with Israel.

The United States and other nations are working on a road map for peace. We are setting out the necessary conditions for progress toward the goal of two states, Israel and Palestine, living side by side in peace and security. It is the commitment of our government—and my personal commitment—to implement the road map and to reach that goal. Old patterns of conflict in the Middle East can be broken, if all concerned will let go of bitterness, hatred, and violence, and get on with the serious work of economic development and political reform, and reconciliation. America will seize every opportunity in pursuit of peace. And the end of the present regime in Iraq would create such an opportunity.

In confronting Iraq, the United States is also showing our commitment to effective international institutions. We are a permanent member of the United Nations Security Council. We helped to create the Security Council. We believe in the Security Council—so much that we want its words to have meaning.

The global threat of proliferation of weapons of mass destruction cannot be confronted by one nation alone. The world needs today and will need tomorrow international bodies with the authority and the will to stop the spread of terror and chemical and biological and nuclear weapons. A threat to all must be answered by all. High-minded pronouncements against prolif-eration mean little unless the strongest nations are willing to stand behind them—and use force if necessary. After all, the United Nations was created, as Winston Churchill said, to "make sure that the force of right will, in the ultimate issue, be protected by the right of force."

Another resolution is now before the Security Council. If the council responds to Iraq's defiance with more excuses and delays, if all its authority proves to be empty, the United Nations will be severely weakened as a source of stability and order. If the members rise to this moment, then the Council will fulfill its founding purpose.

I've listened carefully, as people and leaders around the world have made known their desire for peace. All of us want peace. The threat to peace does not come from those who seek to enforce the just demands of the civilized world; the threat to peace comes from those who flout those demands. If we have to act, we will act to restrain the violent, and defend the cause of peace. And by acting, we will signal to outlaw regimes that in this new century, the boundaries of civilized behavior will be respected.

Protecting those boundaries carries a cost. If war is forced upon us by Iraq's refusal to disarm, we will meet an enemy who hides his military forces behind civilians, who has terrible weapons, who is capable of any crime. The dangers are real, as our soldiers and sailors, airmen, and Marines fully understand. Yet, no military has ever been better prepared to meet these challenges.

Members of our Armed Forces also understand why they may be called to fight. They know that retreat before a dictator guarantees even greater sacrifices in the future. They know that America's cause is right and just: Liberty for an oppressed people, and security for the American people. And I know something about these men and women who wear our uniform: They will complete every mission they are given with skill, and honor, and courage.

Much is asked of America in this year 2003. The work ahead is demanding. It will be difficult to help freedom take hold in a country that has known three decades of dictatorship, secret police, internal divisions, and war. It will be difficult to cultivate liberty and peace in the Middle East, after so many generations of strife. Yet the security of our nation and the hope of millions depend on us, and Americans do not turn away from duties because they are hard. We have met great tests in other times, and we will meet the tests of our time.

We go forward with confidence, because we trust in the power of human freedom to change lives and nations. By the resolve and purpose of America, and of our friends and allies, we will make this an age of progress and liberty. Free people will set the course of history, and free people will keep the peace of the world.

# March 2003

## Presidential Radio Address to the Nation
March 8, 2003

Good morning. This has been an important week on two fronts of our war against terror. First, American and Pakistani authorities captured the mastermind of the September the 11th attacks against our country, Khalid Sheik Mohammed. This is a landmark achievement in disrupting the al Qaeda network, and we believe it will help us prevent future acts of terror. We are currently working with over 90 countries and have dealt with over 3,000 terrorists, who have been detained, arrested, or otherwise will not be a problem for the United States.

Second, the Chief United Nations Weapons Inspector reported yesterday to the Security Council on his efforts to verify Saddam Hussein's compliance with Resolution 1441. This resolution requires Iraq to fully and unconditionally disarm itself of nuclear, chemical, and biological weapons materials, as well as the prohibited missiles that could be used to deliver them. Unfortunately, it is clear that Saddam Hussein is still violating the demands of the United Nations by refusing to disarm.

Iraqi's dictator has made a public show of producing and destroying a few prohibited missiles. Yet our intelligence shows that even as he is destroying these few missiles, he has ordered the continued production of the very same type of missiles. Iraqi operatives continue to play a shell game with inspectors, moving suspected prohibited materials to different locations every twelve to twenty-four hours. And Iraqi weapons scientists continue to be threatened with harm should they cooperate in interviews with UN inspectors.

These are not the actions of a regime that is disarming. These are the actions of a regime engaged in a willful charade. If the Iraqi regime were disarming, we would know it—because we would see it; Iraq's weapons would be presented to inspectors and destroyed. Inspection teams do not need more time, or more personnel—all they need is what they have never received, the full cooperation of the Iraqi regime. The only acceptable outcome is the outcome already demanded by a unanimous vote of the Security Council: Total disarmament.

Saddam Hussein has a long history of reckless aggression and terrible crimes. He possesses weapons of terror. He provides funding and training and safe haven to terrorists who would willingly deliver weapons of mass destruction against America and other peace-loving countries.

The attacks of September the 11, 2001, showed what the enemies of America did with four airplanes. We will not wait to see what terrorists or terror states could do with weapons of mass destruction. We are determined to confront threats wherever they arise. And, as a last resort, we must be willing to use military force. We are doing everything we can to avoid war in Iraq. But if Saddam Hussein does not disarm peacefully, he will be disarmed by force.

Across the world, and in every part of America, people of goodwill are hoping and praying for peace. Our goal is peace—for our own nation, for our friends, for our allies, and for all the peoples of the Middle East. People of goodwill must also recognize that allowing a dangerous dictator to defy the world and build an arsenal for conquest and mass murder is not peace at all; it is pretense. The cause of peace will be advanced only when the terrorists lose a wealthy patron and protector, and when the dictator is fully and finally disarmed.

### Presidential Address to the Nation
March 17, 2003

My fellow citizens, events in Iraq have now reached the final days of decision. For more than a decade, the United States and other nations have pursued patient and honorable efforts to disarm the Iraqi regime without war. That regime pledged to reveal and destroy all its weapons of mass destruction as a condition for ending the Persian Gulf War in 1991.

Since then, the world has engaged in twelve years of diplomacy. We have passed more than a dozen resolutions in the United Nations Security Council. We have sent hundreds of weapons inspectors to oversee the disarmament of Iraq. Our good faith has not been returned.

The Iraqi regime has used diplomacy as a ploy to gain time and advantage. It has uniformly defied Security Council resolutions demanding full disarmament. Over the years, UN weapons inspectors have been threatened by Iraqi officials, electronically bugged, and systematically deceived. Peaceful efforts to disarm the Iraqi regime have failed again and again—because we are not dealing with peaceful men.

Intelligence gathered by this and other governments leaves no doubt that the Iraq regime continues to possess and conceal some of the most lethal weapons ever devised. This regime has already used weapons of mass destruction against Iraq's neighbors and against Iraq's people.

The regime has a history of reckless aggression in the Middle East. It has a deep hatred of America and our friends. And it has aided, trained, and harbored terrorists, including operatives of al Qaeda.

The danger is clear: Using chemical, biological, or, one day, nuclear weapons, obtained with the help of Iraq, the terrorists could fulfill their stated ambitions and kill thousands or hundreds of thousands of innocent people in our country, or any other.

The United States and other nations did nothing to deserve or invite this threat. But we will do everything to defeat it. Instead of drifting along toward tragedy, we will set a course toward safety. Before the day of horror can come, before it is too late to act, this danger will be removed.

The United States of America has the sovereign authority to use force in assuring its own national security. That duty falls to me, as Commander-in-Chief, by the oath I have sworn, by the oath I will keep.

Recognizing the threat to our country, the United States Congress voted overwhelmingly last year to support the use of force against Iraq. America tried to work with the United Nations to address this threat because we wanted to resolve the issue peacefully. We believe in the mission of the United Nations. One reason the UN was founded after the Second World War was to confront aggressive dictators, actively and early, before they can attack the innocent and destroy the peace.

In the case of Iraq, the Security Council did act, in the early 1990s. Under Resolutions 678 and 687—both still in effect—the United States and our allies are authorized to use force in ridding Iraq of weapons of mass destruction. This is not a question of authority, it is a question of will.

Last September, I went to the UN General Assembly and urged the nations of the world to unite and bring an end to this danger. On November 8th, the Security Council unanimously passed Resolution 1441, finding Iraq in material breach of its obligations, and vowing serious consequences if Iraq did not fully and immediately disarm.

Today, no nation can possibly claim that Iraq has disarmed. And it will not disarm so long as Saddam Hussein holds power. For the last four-and-a-half months, the United States and our allies have worked within the Security Council to enforce that Council's long-standing demands. Yet, some permanent members of the Security Council have publicly announced they will veto any resolution that compels the disarmament of Iraq. These governments share our assessment of the danger, but not our resolve to meet it. Many nations, however, do have the resolve and fortitude to act against this threat to peace, and a broad coalition is now gathering to enforce the just demands of the world. The United Nations Security Council has not lived up to its responsibilities, so we will rise to ours.

In recent days, some governments in the Middle East have been doing their part. They have delivered public and private messages urging the dictator to leave Iraq, so that disarmament can proceed peacefully. He has thus far refused. All the decades of deceit and cruelty have now reached an end. Saddam Hussein and his sons must leave Iraq within 48 hours. Their refusal to do so will result in military conflict, commenced at a time of our choosing. For their own safety, all foreign nationals—including journalists and inspectors—should leave Iraq immediately.

Many Iraqis can hear me tonight in a translated radio broadcast, and I have a message for them. If we must begin a military campaign, it will be directed against the lawless men who rule your country and not against you. As our coalition takes away their power, we will deliver the food and medicine you need. We will tear down the apparatus of terror and we will help you to build a new Iraq that is prosperous and free. In a free Iraq, there will be no more wars of aggression against your neighbors, no more poison factories, no more executions of dissidents, no more torture chambers and rape rooms. The tyrant will soon be gone. The day of your liberation is near.

It is too late for Saddam Hussein to remain in power. It is not too late for the Iraqi military to act with honor and protect your country by permitting the peaceful entry of coalition forces to eliminate weapons of mass destruction. Our forces will give Iraqi military units clear instructions on actions they can take to avoid being attacked and destroyed. I urge every member of the Iraqi military and intelligence services, if war comes, do not fight for a dying regime that is not worth your own life.

And all Iraqi military and civilian personnel should listen carefully to this warning. In any conflict, your fate will depend on your action. Do not destroy oil wells, a source of wealth that belongs to the Iraqi people. Do not obey any command to use weapons of mass destruction against anyone, including the

Iraqi people. War crimes will be prosecuted. War criminals will be punished. And it will be no defense to say, "I was just following orders."

Should Saddam Hussein choose confrontation, the American people can know that every measure has been taken to avoid war, and every measure will be taken to win it. Americans understand the costs of conflict because we have paid them in the past. War has no certainty, except the certainty of sacrifice.

Yet the only way to reduce the harm and duration of war is to apply the full force and might of our military, and we are prepared to do so. If Saddam Hussein attempts to cling to power, he will remain a deadly foe until the end. In desperation, he and terrorist groups might try to conduct terrorist operations against the American people and our friends. These attacks are not inevitable. They are, however, possible. And this very fact underscores the reason we cannot live under the threat of blackmail. The terrorist threat to America and the world will be diminished the moment that Saddam Hussein is disarmed.

Our government is on heightened watch against these dangers. Just as we are preparing to ensure victory in Iraq, we are taking further actions to protect our homeland. In recent days, American authorities have expelled from the country certain individuals with ties to Iraqi intelligence services. Among other measures, I have directed additional security of our airports, and increased Coast Guard patrols of major seaports. The Department of Homeland Security is working closely with the nation's governors to increase armed security at critical facilities across America.

Should enemies strike our country, they would be attempting to shift our attention with panic and weaken our morale with fear. In this, they would fail. No act of theirs can alter the course or shake the resolve of this country. We are a peaceful people—yet we're not a fragile people, and we will not be intimidated by thugs and killers. If our enemies dare to strike us, they and all who have aided them will face fearful consequences.

We are now acting because the risks of inaction would be far greater. In one year, or five years, the power of Iraq to inflict harm on all free nations would be multiplied many times over. With these capabilities, Saddam Hussein and his terrorist allies could choose the moment of deadly conflict when they are strongest. We choose to meet that threat now, where it arises, before it can appear suddenly in our skies and cities.

The cause of peace requires all free nations to recognize new and undeniable realities. In the 20th century, some chose to appease murderous dictators, whose threats were allowed to grow into genocide and global war. In this century, when evil men plot chemical, biological, and nuclear terror, a policy of appeasement could bring destruction of a kind never before seen on this earth.

Terrorists and terror states do not reveal these threats with fair notice, in formal declarations—and responding to such enemies only after they have struck first is not self-defense, it is suicide. The security of the world requires disarming Saddam Hussein now.

As we enforce the just demands of the world, we will also honor the deepest commitments of our country. Unlike Saddam Hussein, we believe the Iraqi people are deserving and capable of human liberty. And when the dictator has departed, they can set an example to all the Middle East of a vital and peaceful and self-governing nation.

The United States, with other countries, will work to advance liberty and peace in that region. Our goal will not be achieved overnight, but it can come over time. The power and appeal of human liberty is felt in every life and every land. And the greatest power of freedom is to overcome hatred and violence, and turn the creative gifts of men and women to the pursuits of peace.

That is the future we choose. Free nations have a duty to defend our people by uniting against the violent. And tonight, as we have done before, America and our allies accept that responsibility.

Good night, and may God continue to bless America.

## Presidential Address to the Nation on the Commencement of Military Operations Against Iraq
### March 19, 2003

My fellow citizens, at this hour, American and coalition forces are in the early stages of military operations to disarm Iraq, to free its people, and to defend the world from grave danger.

On my orders, coalition forces have begun striking selected targets of military importance to undermine Saddam Hussein's ability to wage war. These are opening stages of what will be a broad and concerted campaign. More than 35 countries are giving crucial support—from the use of naval and air bases, to help with intelligence and logistics, to the deployment of combat units. Every nation in this coalition has chosen to bear the duty and share the honor of serving in our common defense.

To all the men and women of the United States Armed Forces now in the Middle East, the peace of a troubled world and the hopes of an oppressed people now depend on you. That trust is well placed.

The enemies you confront will come to know your skill and bravery. The people you liberate will witness the honorable and decent spirit of the American military. In this conflict, America faces an enemy who has no regard for conventions of war or rules of morality. Saddam Hussein has placed Iraqi troops and equipment in civilian areas, attempting to use innocent men, women, and children as shields for his own military—a final atrocity against his people.

I want Americans and all the world to know that coalition forces will make every effort to spare innocent civilians from harm. A campaign on the harsh terrain of a nation as large as California could be longer and more difficult than some predict. And helping Iraqis achieve a united, stable, and free country will require our sustained commitment.

We come to Iraq with respect for its citizens, for their great civilization, and for the religious faiths they practice. We have no ambition in Iraq, except to remove a threat and restore control of that country to its own people.

I know that the families of our military are praying that all those who serve will return safely and soon. Millions of Americans are praying with you for the safety of your loved ones and for the protection of the innocent. For your sacrifice, you have the gratitude and respect of the American people. And you can know that our forces will be coming home as soon as their work is done.

Our nation enters this conflict reluctantly—yet our purpose is sure. The people of the United States and our friends and allies will not live at the mercy of an outlaw regime that threatens the peace with weapons of mass murder. We will meet that threat now, with our Army, Air Force, Navy, Coast Guard, and Marines, so that we do not have to meet it later with armies of fire-fighters and police and doctors on the streets of our cities.

Now that conflict has come, the only way to limit its duration is to apply decisive force. And I assure you, this will not be a campaign of half measures, and we will accept no outcome but victory.

My fellow citizens, the dangers to our country and the world will be overcome. We will pass through this time of peril and carry on the work of peace. We will defend our freedom. We will bring freedom to others and we will prevail.

May God bless our country and all who defend her.

## Presidential Radio Address to the Nation
March 22, 2003

Good morning. American and coalition forces have begun a concerted campaign against the regime of Saddam Hussein. In this war, our coalition is broad, more than forty countries from across the globe. Our cause is just, the security of the nations we serve and the peace of the world. And our mission is clear, to disarm Iraq of weapons of mass destruction, to end Saddam Hussein's support for terrorism, and to free the Iraqi people.

The future of peace and the hopes of the Iraqi people now depend on our fighting forces in the Middle East. They are conducting themselves in the highest traditions of the American military. They are doing their job with skill and bravery, and with the finest of allies beside them. At every stage of this conflict the world will see both the power of our military, and the honorable and decent spirit of the men and women who serve.

In this conflict, American and coalition forces face enemies who have no regard for the conventions of war or rules of morality. Iraqi officials have placed troops and equipment in civilian areas, attempting to use innocent men, women, and children as shields for the dictator's army. I want Americans and all the world to know that coalition forces will make every effort to spare innocent civilians from harm.

A campaign on harsh terrain in a vast country could be longer and more difficult than some have predicted. And helping Iraqis achieve a united, stable, and free country will require our sustained commitment. Yet, whatever is required of us, we will carry out all the duties we have accepted.

Across America this weekend, the families of our military are praying that our men and women will return safely and soon. Millions of Americans are praying with them for the safety of their loved ones and for the protection of all the innocent. Our entire nation appreciates the sacrifices made by military families, and many citizens who live near military families are showing their support in practical ways, such as by helping with child care, or home repairs. All families with loved ones serving in this war can know this: Our forces will be coming home as soon as their work is done.

Our nation entered this conflict reluctantly, yet with a clear and firm purpose. The people of the United States and our friends and allies will not live at the mercy of an outlaw regime that threatens the peace with weapons of mass murder. Now that conflict has come, the only way to limit its duration is to apply decisive force. This will not be a campaign of half-measures. It is a fight for the security of our nation and the peace of the world, and we will accept no outcome but victory.

### Excerpts of Remarks by the President in Speech to SOCOM and CENTCOM Community
Tampa, Florida
March 26, 2003

We are pleased to see so many family members who are here. We want to thank you for coming. And I want you to know your nation appreciates your commitment and your sacrifice in the cause of peace and freedom.

We're also proud to be here today with our friends and allies, representative of the forty-eight nations across the world who have joined America in Operation Iraqi Freedom. Over the last week the world has witnessed the skill and honor and resolve of our military in the course of battle. We have seen the character of this new generation of American Armed Forces. We've seen their daring against ruthless enemies and their decency to an oppressed people. Millions of Americans are proud of our military, and so am I. I am honored to be the Commander-in-Chief. . . .

People across this country are praying. They are praying that . . . those families and loved ones will find comfort and grace in their sorrow. We pray that God will bless and receive each of the fallen, and we thank God that liberty found such brave defenders.

At MacDill Air Force Base, I know you're proud of a certain Army general who couldn't—(applause)—who couldn't be with us today on account of some pressing business. (Laughter and applause) Tommy Franks has my respect, the respect of our military, and the thanks of the United States of America.

MacDill is the Command Center of our Special Operations Forces—the silent warriors who were first on the ground . . . in Iraq. And here at CENTCOM, you coordinate the work of a grand coalition that is disarming a dangerous enemy and freeing a proud people.

Every nation in our coalition understands the terrible threat we face from weapons of mass destruction. Every nation represented here refuses to live in a future of fear, at the mercy of terrorists and tyrants. And every nation here today shares the same resolve: We will be relentless in our pursuit of victory.

Our military is making good progress in Iraq; yet this war is far from over. As they approach Baghdad, our fighting units are facing the most desperate elements of a doomed regime. We cannot know the duration of this war, but we are prepared for the battle ahead. We cannot predict the final day of the Iraqi regime, but I can assure you, and I assure the long-suffering people of Iraq, there will be a day of reckoning for the Iraqi regime, and that day is drawing near.

Many of you here today were also involved in the liberation of Afghanistan. The military demands are very different in Iraq. Yet our coalition is showing the same spirit, the same resolve—that spirit and resolve that destroyed the al Qaeda terror camps, that routed the Taliban, and freed the people of Afghanistan.

In Iraq today, our military is focused and unwavering. We have an effective plan of battle and the flexibility to meet every challenge. Nothing—nothing—will divert us from our clear mission. We will press on through every hardship. We will overcome every danger. And we will prevail.

It has been six days since the major ground war began. It's been five days since the major air war began. And every day has brought us closer to our objective. At the opening of Operation Iraqi Freedom, Special Forces helped to secure air fields and bridges and oil fields, to clear the way for our forces and to prevent sabotage and environmental catastrophe. Our pilots and cruise missiles have struck vital military targets with lethal precision.

We've destroyed the base of a terrorist group in northern Iraq that sought to attack America and Europe with deadly poisons. We have moved over two hundred miles to the north, toward Iraq's capital, in the last three days. And the dictator's major Republican Guard units are now under direct and intense attack. Day by day, Saddam Hussein is losing his grip on Iraq; day by day, the Iraqi people are closer to freedom.

We are also taking every action we can to prevent the Iraqi regime from using its hidden weapons of mass destruction. We are attacking the command structure that could order the use of those weapons. Coalition troops have taken control of hundreds of square miles of territory to prevent the launch of missiles, and chemical or biological weapons.

Every victory in this campaign, and every sacrifice, serves the purpose of defending innocent lives, in America and across the world, from the weapons of terror. We will not wait to meet this danger, with firefighters and police and doctors on the streets of our own cities. Instead, we are meeting the danger today with our Army, Navy, Air Force, Coast Guard, and Marines.

All the nations in our coalition are contributing to our steady progress. British ground forces have seized strategic towns and ports. The Royal Air Force is striking targets throughout Iraq. The Royal Navy is taking command of coastal waters. The Australian military is providing naval gunfire support, and Special Forces, and fighter aircraft on missions deep in Iraq. Polish military forces have secured an Iraqi oil platform in the Persian Gulf. A Danish submarine is monitoring Iraqi intelligence providing early warning. Czech, Slovak, Polish, and Romanian forces, soon to be joined by Ukrainian and Bulgarian forces, are forward deployed in the region, prepared to respond in the event of an attack of weapons of mass destruction anywhere in the region. Spain is providing important logistical and humanitarian support. Coalition forces are skilled and courageous, and we are honored to have them by our side.

In the early stages of this war, the world is getting a clearer view of the Iraqi regime and the evil at its heart. In the ranks of that regime are men whose idea of courage is to brutalize unarmed prisoners. They wage attacks while posing as civilians. They use real civilians as human shields. They pretend to surrender, then fire upon those who show them mercy. This band of war criminals has been put on notice: The day of Iraq's liberation will also be a day of justice.

And in the early stages of this war, we have also seen the honor of the American military and our coalition. Protecting innocent civilians is a central commitment of our war plan. Our enemy in this war is the Iraqi regime, not the people who have suffered under it. As we bring justice to a dictator, today we started bringing humanitarian aid in large amounts to an oppressed land.

We are treating Iraqi prisoners of war according to the highest standards of law and decency. Coalition doctors are working to save the lives of the wounded, including Iraqi soldiers. One of our servicemen said this about the injured Iraqis he treated: "We can't blame them for the mistreatment their government is doing to our soldiers. I'm all for treating them. That's what we do. That's our job."

Our entire coalition has a job to do, and it will not end with the liberation of Iraq. We will help the Iraqi people to find the benefits and assume the duties of self-government. The form of those institutions will arise from Iraq's own culture and its own choices. Yet this much is certain: The twenty-four million people of Iraq have lived too long under a violent criminal gang calling itself a government.

Iraqis are a good and gifted people. They deserve better than a life spent bowing before a dictator. The people of Iraq deserve to stand on their feet as free men and women—the citizens of a free country.

This goal of a free and peaceful Iraq unites our coalition. And this goal comes from the deepest convictions of America. The freedom you defend is the right of every person and the future of every nation. The liberty we prize is not American's gift to the world; it is God's gift to humanity.

The Army Special Forces define their mission in a motto, "To liberate the oppressed." Generations of men and women in uniform have served and sacrificed in this cause. Now the call of history has come once again to all in our military and to all in our coalition. We are answering that call. We have no ambition in Iraq except the liberation of its people. We ask no reward except a durable peace. And we will accept no outcome short of complete and final success.

The path we are taking is not easy, and it may be long. Yet we know our destination. We will stay on the path—mile by mile—all the way to Baghdad, and all the way to victory.

Thank you, all. And may God bless America.


## Remarks by President Bush and Prime Minister Blair on Iraq War
Camp David, Maryland
March 27, 2003


THE PRESIDENT: Thank you all. It's my honor to welcome my friend and Prime Minister of Great Britain, Tony Blair, back to Camp David. America has learned a lot about Tony Blair over the last weeks. We've learned that he's a man of his word. We've learned that he's a man of courage, that he's a man of vision. And we're proud to have him as a friend.

The United States and United Kingdom are acting together in a noble purpose. We're working together to make the world more peaceful; we're working together to make our respective nations and all the free nations of the world more secure; and we're working to free the Iraqi people.

British, American, Australian, Polish, and other coalition troops are sharing the duties of this war, and we're sharing the sacrifices of this war. Together, coalition forces are advancing day by day, in steady progress, against the enemy. Slowly, but surely, the grip of terror around the throats of the Iraqi people is being loosened.

We appreciate the bravery, the professionalism of the British troops, and all coalition troops. Together we have lost people, and the American people offer their prayers to the loved ones of the British fallen, just as we offer our prayers to the loved ones of our own troops who have fallen.

We're now engaging the dictator's most hardened and most desperate units. The campaign ahead will demand further courage and require further sacrifice. Yet we know the outcome: Iraq will be disarmed; the Iraqi regime will be ended; and the long-suffering Iraqi people will be free.

In decades of oppression, the Iraqi regime has sought to instill the habits of fear in the daily lives of millions; yet, soon, the Iraqis will have the confidence of a free people. Our coalition will stand with the citizens of Iraq in the challenges ahead. We are prepared to deliver humanitarian aid on a large scale—and as a matter of fact, are beginning to do so as we speak.

Today the Prime Minister and I also urge the United Nations to immediately resume the Oil-for-Food program. More than half the Iraqi people depend on this program as their sole source of food. This urgent humanitarian issue must not be politicized, and the Security Council should give Secretary General Annan the authority to start getting food supplies to those most in need of assistance.

As we address the immediate suffering of the Iraqi people, we're also committed to helping them over the long-term. Iraq's greatest long-term need is a representative government that protects the rights of all Iraqis. The form of this government will be chosen by the Iraqi people, not imposed by outsiders. And the Prime Minister and I are confident that a free Iraq will be a successful nation.

History requires more of our coalition than a defeat of a terrible danger. I see an opportunity, as does Prime Minister Blair, to bring renewed hope and progress to the entire Middle East. Last June 24th, I outlined a vision of two states, Israel and Palestine, living side-by-side in peace and security. Soon, we'll release the road map that is designed to help turn that vision into reality. And both America and Great Britain are strongly committed to implementing that road map.

For nearly a century, the United States and Great Britain have been allies in the defense of liberty. We've opposed all the great threats to peace and security in the world. We shared in the costly and heroic struggle against Nazism. We shared the resolve and moral purpose of the Cold War. In every challenge, we've applied the combined power of our nations to the cause of justice, and we're doing the same today. Our alliance is strong, our resolve is firm, and our mission will be achieved.

Mr. Prime Minister.

PRIME MINISTER BLAIR: Thank you, Mr. President, and thank you for your welcome. Thank you for your strength and for your leadership at this time.

And I believe the alliance between the United States and Great Britain has never been in better or stronger shape.

Can I also offer the American people, on behalf of the British people, our condolences, our sympathy, our prayers for the lives of those who have fallen in this conflict, just as we have offered the condolences, the sympathy, and the prayers to the families of our own British servicemen.

Just under a week into this conflict, let me restate our complete and total resolve. Saddam Hussein and his hateful regime will be removed from power. Iraq will be disarmed of weapons of mass destruction, and the Iraqi people will be free. That is our commitment, that is our determination, and we will see it done.

We had this morning a presentation of the latest military situation, which shows already the progress that has been made. It's worth just recapping it, I think, for a moment. In less than a week, we have secured the southern oil fields and facilities, and so protected that resource and wealth for the Iraqi people and avoided ecological disaster. We've disabled Iraq's ability to launch external aggression from the west.

Our forces are now within 50 miles of Baghdad. They've surrounded Basra. They've secured the key port of Umm Qasr. They've paved the way for humanitarian aid to flow into the country. And they brought real damage on Iraq's command and control. So we can be confident that the goals that we have set ourselves will be met.

I would like to pay tribute to the professionalism and integrity of our forces and those of the United States of America [and] our other coalition allies, and to say how their professionalism, as well as their skill and their bravery, stand in sharp contrast to the brutality of Saddam's regime.

Day by day, we have seen the reality of Saddam's regime—his thugs prepared to kill their own people; the parading of prisoners of war; and now, the release of those pictures of executed British soldiers. If anyone needed any further evidence of the depravity of Saddam's regime, this atrocity provides it. It is yet one more flagrant breach of all the proper conventions of war. More than that, to the families of the soldiers involved, it is an act of cruelty beyond comprehension. Indeed, it is beyond the comprehension of anyone with an ounce of humanity in their souls.

On behalf of the British government, I would like to offer my condolences particularly to the family and the friends of those two brave young men who died in the service of their country, and to the ordinary Iraqi people, to whom we are determined to bring a better future.

The future of the Iraqi people is one reason why much of our discussion has focused on humanitarian issues. Again, here we have the ship, the *Sir Galahad*, loaded with tons of supplies destined for the people of Iraq. The other immediate humanitarian priority is to restart the UN Oil-for-Food program, which the President and I discussed, and which I will be discussing with Kofi Annan later this evening. And this is urgent.

We also discussed the post-conflict issues. Contrary to a lot of the comment on this, the position is exactly as the President and I set out in the Azores—namely, that we will work with the UN, our allies and partners and bilateral donors. We will seek new UN Security Council resolutions to affirm Iraq's territorial integrity, to ensure rapid delivery of humanitarian relief, and endorse an appropriate post-conflict administration for Iraq.

But let me emphasize once again that our primary focus now is, and must be, the military victory, which we will prosecute with the utmost vigor. And the immediate priority for the United Nations is, as the President was indicating a moment or two ago, the Oil-for-Food program.

In addition, as has just been said to you, we had an excellent discussion of the Middle East, and we both share a complete determination to move this forward. It is, indeed, often overlooked that President Bush is the first U.S. President publicly to commit himself to a two-state solution, an Israel confident of its security and a viable Palestinian state. And I welcome the decision announced recently to publish the road map as soon as the confirmation of the new Palestinian prime minister is properly administered.

Finally, I would just like to say this: I think it is important that we recognize at this time that the goals that we are fighting for are just goals. Whatever the difficulty of war, let us just remember this is a regime that has brutalized its people for well over two decades. Of course, there will be people fiercely loyal to that regime who will fight all the way; they have no option. But I have no doubt at all that the vast majority of ordinary Iraqi people are desperate for a better and different future, for Iraq to be free, for its government to be representative of its people, for the human rights of the people to be cared for.

And that is why, though of course our aim is to rid Iraq of weapons of mass destruction and make our world more secure, the justice of our cause lies in the liberation of the Iraqi people. And to them we say, we will liberate you. The day of your freedom draws near.

## Excerpts from President's Speech on Operations
## Liberty Shield and Iraqi Freedom
Philadelphia, Pennsylvania
March 31, 2003

Thank you very much for that warm welcome. It is an honor to be here at one of our nation's busiest ports and one of our country's greatest cities.

Philadelphia and its port [show] the hardworking spirit of this country. It speaks to our economic might. Most importantly, Philadelphia talks about a proud history. After all, it was in this place that we first declared our dedication to liberty. We still believe that all men are created equal and have the right to be free. And that is true for Americans, and that is true for men and women in Iraq.

We know that liberty must be defended by every generation. Today in the Middle East, and on other fronts in the war on terror, this generation of Americans is fighting bravely in the cause of freedom. . . .

This is a time of great consequence for our country. Right now men and women from every part of America, supported by a strong coalition, are fighting to disarm a dangerous regime and to liberate an oppressed people.

It has been eleven days since the major ground war began. In this short time, our troops have preformed brilliantly, with skill and with bravery. They make us proud. In eleven days, coalition forces have taken control of most of western and southern Iraq. In eleven days, we've seized key bridges, opened a northern front, nearly achieved complete air superiority, and are delivering tons of humanitarian aid. By quick and decisive action, our troops are preventing Saddam Hussein from destroying the Iraqi people's oil fields. Our forces moved into Iraqi missile-launch areas that threatened neighboring countries. Many dangers lie ahead, but day by day, we are moving closer to Baghdad. Day by day, we are moving closer to victory.

Our victory will mean the end of a tyrant who rules by fear and torture. Our victory will remove a sponsor of terror, armed with weapons of terror. Our victory will uphold the just demands of the United Nations and the civilized world. And when victory comes, it will be shared by the long-suffering people of Iraq, who deserve freedom and dignity.

The dictator's regime has ruled by fear and continues to use fear as a tool of domination to the end. Many Iraqis have been ordered to fight or die by Saddam's death squads. Others are pressed into service by threats against their children. Iraqi civilians attempting to flee to liberated areas have been shot and shelled from behind by Saddam's thugs. Schools and hospitals have been used to store military equipment. They serve as bases for military operations. Iraqis who show friendship toward coalition troops are murdered in cold blood by the regime's enforcers.

The people of Iraq have lived in this nightmare world for more than two decades. It is understandable that fear and distrust run deep. Yet, here in the city where America itself gained freedom, I give this pledge to the citizens of Iraq: We're coming with a mighty force to end the reign of your oppressors. We are coming to bring you food and medicine and a better life. And we are coming, and we will not stop, we will not relent until your country is free. . . .

All Americans understand that we face a continuing threat of terrorism. We know that our enemies are desperate; we know that they're dangerous. The dying regime in Iraq may try to bring terror to our shores. Other parts of the global terror network may view this as a moment to strike, thinking that we're distracted. They're wrong.

We are meeting threats and acting to prevent dangers. The United States and allied troops are shattering the al Qaeda network. We're hunting them down, one at a time. We're finding them, we're interrogating them, and we're bringing them to justice.

We will end the Iraqi regime, an ally of terrorist groups and a producer of weapons of mass destruction. And here at home, we're acting. Shortly before we begin the liberation of Iraq, we launched Operation Liberty Shield, to implement additional measures to defend the American homeland against terrorist attacks.

This nationwide effort is focused on five specific areas. First, we are taking even greater security measures at our borders and ports. We have relocated hundreds of security personnel on our borders. We've added additional reconnaissance aircraft patrols at our borders. And the Coast Guard is monitoring ports for suspicious activity. This nation is determined. Friends and immigrants will always be welcome in this land. Yet we will use all our power to keep out the terrorists and the criminals so they can't hurt our citizens.

Second, we are strengthening protections throughout our national transportation system. We're enforcing temporary flight restrictions over some of our major cities. We've stepped up surveillance of hazardous material shipments within our country and taken measures to keep them away from places where large numbers of people gather. This nation is determined. We will do all in our power to make sure our skies and rails and roads are safe from terror.

Third, we've increased surveillance of suspected terrorists. Certain individuals with ties to Iraqi intelligence services have been ordered out of this country. We're interviewing Iraqi-born individuals on a voluntary basis for two reasons: To gain information on possible terrorist plans, and to make sure they've not experienced discrimination or hate crimes. This nation is determined. Iraqi Americans will be protected, and enemy agents will be stopped.

Fourth, under Operation Liberty Shield, we are guarding our nation's important infrastructure with greater vigilance. Under the direction of our governors, thousands of National Guardsmen and state police officers are protecting chemical facilities and nuclear power sites, key electrical grids and other potential targets. This country is determined. We will keep up our guard and do all we can to protect our fellow citizens.

And, finally, we're strengthening the preparedness of our public-health system. The Departments of Agriculture and Health and Human Services have increased field inspections of livestock and crops. Public-health officials have increased medical surveillance in major cities. This nation is determined. We will stand watch against the dangers of the new era.

After our nation was attacked on September the 11th, 2001, America made a decision: We will not wait for our enemies to strike before we act against them. We're not going to permit terrorists and terror states to plot and plan and grow in strength while we do nothing.

The actions we're taking in Operation Liberty Shield are making this nation more secure. And the actions we're taking abroad against a terror network and against the regime in Iraq are removing a grave danger to all free nations. In every case, by acting today, we are saving countless lives in the future.

America has many advantages in this war on terror. We have resolute citizens. We're vigilant, and know that freedom must be defended. We have a just cause to guide us. And we have the strength and character of the men and women who serve our country.

You in the Coast Guard take rightful pride in the uniform you wear and the mission you have accepted. You, and all who serve in our military, are ready for any challenge. And by your skill, and by your courage, we will prevail.

May God bless you, and may God bless America.

# April 2003

## Excerpted Remarks by the President in Speech to Military Personnel and their Families
Camp Lejeune, North Carolina
April 3, 2003

We really appreciate your welcome and we're proud to be with the Marines and sailors and families of Camp Lejeune. There's no finer sight, no finer sight, than to see twelve hundred United States Marines and Corpsmen—unless you happen to be a member of the Iraqi Republican Guard.

For more than sixty years, Marines have gone forth from Camp Lejeune to fight our country's battles. Now America has entered a fierce struggle to protect the world from a grave danger and to bring freedom to an oppressed people. As the forces of our coalition advance, we learn more about the atrocities of the Iraqi regime and the deep fear that Saddam Hussein has instilled in the Iraqi people. Yet no scheme of this enemy, no crime of a dying regime will divert us from our mission. We will not stop until Iraq is free.

When freedom needs defending, America turns to our military. And as they do their job, our men and women in uniform count on their families—like you all here today. This is a time of hardship for many military families. Some of you have been separated from your loved ones for quite a while because of long deployments. All of America is grateful for your sacrifice. And Laura and I are here to thank each one of you.

We're here to thank the Marines. I also want to thank the men and women of the Marine Forces Reserve who are serving here and abroad. Hundreds of reserve units across America have been activated in this time of war, and our country thanks these fine citizens and their employers for putting duty first. . . .

All around Camp Lejeune are monuments to the heroic achievements of the United States Marines. In the 14 days since the major ground war began, the Marine Corps has added new achievements to its great story.

On the first day of the campaign, Marine units were ordered to secure six hundred Iraqi oil wells and prevent environmental disaster. And that mission was accomplished. U.S. Marines and our Royal Marine allies were sent in to take the Al Faw Peninsula and clear a path for humanitarian aid, and that job was done.

In the tough fighting at Al Nasiriyah, Marines continue to push back the enemy, and are showing the unrelenting courage worthy of the name Task Force Tarawa. Two nights ago, Marines and Special Operations forces set out on a daring rescue mission—and thanks to their skill and courage, a brave young soldier is now free.

These missions are difficult and they are dangerous, but no one becomes a Marine because it's easy. Now our coalition moves forward. Marines are in the thick of the battle. And what we have begun, we will finish.

The United States and our allies pledged to act if the dictator did not disarm. The regime in Iraq is now learning that we keep our word. By our actions, we serve a great and just cause: We will remove weapons of mass destruction from the hands of mass murderers. Free nations will not sit and wait, leaving enemies free to plot another September the 11th, this time, perhaps with chemical or biological or nuclear terror. And by defending our own security, we are freeing the people of Iraq from one of the cruelest regimes on earth.

At this hour, coalition forces are clearing southern cities and towns of the dictator's death squads and enforcers. Our Special Forces and Army paratroopers, working with Kurdish militia, have opened a northern front against the enemy. Army and Marine divisions are engaging the enemy and advancing to the outskirts of Baghdad.

From the skies above, coalition aircraft and cruise missiles are removing hundreds of military targets from Iraq. A vice is closing, and the days of a brutal regime are coming to an end.

Some servants of the regime have chosen to fill their final days with acts of cowardice and murder. In combat, Saddam's thugs shield themselves with women and children. They have killed Iraqi citizens who welcome coalition troops. They force other Iraqis into battle, by threatening to torture or kill their families. They've executed prisoners of war. They've waged attacks under the white flag of truce. They concealed combat forces in civilian neighborhoods and schools and hospitals and mosques.

In this war, the Iraqi regime is terrorizing its own citizens, doing everything possible to maximize Iraqi civilian casualties, and then to exploit the deaths they've caused for propaganda. These are war criminals and they will be treated like war criminals.

In stark contrast, the citizens of Iraq are coming to know what kind of people we have sent to liberate them. American forces and our allies are treating innocent civilians with kindness, and showing proper respect to soldiers who surrender. Many Americans have seen the picture of Marine Lance Corporal Marcco Ware carrying a wounded Iraqi soldier on his shoulders to safety, for medical treatment. That's the picture of the strength and goodness of the U.S. Marines. That is a picture of America. People in the United States are proud of the honorable conduct of our military, and I'm proud to lead such brave and decent Americans.

I'm also proud that coalition victories are bringing food and water and medicine to the Iraqi people. Our coalition partners have constructed a pipeline to bring clean water to Umm Qasr. We're delivering emergency rations to the hungry. Right now, ships carrying enough American grain to feed millions are bound for Iraq. We're bringing aid, and we're bringing something more—we're bringing hope.

A man in one Iraqi village said this to one of our soldiers: "I want my freedom. I don't want food or water. I just want my freedom." America hears that man. We hear all Iraqis who yearn for liberty. And the people of Iraq have my pledge: Our fighting forces will press on until your entire country is free.

The Iraqi people deserve to live in peace under leaders they have chosen. They deserve a government that respects the rights of every citizen and ethnic group. They deserve a country that is united, that's independent, and that is released from years of sanctions and sorrow. Our coalition has one goal for the future of Iraq—to return that great country to its own people.

Building a free and prosperous Iraq after the regime is gone will be the work of the Iraqi people for years to come. And they will have our help. Today the goal is to remove the Iraqi regime and to rid Iraq of weapons of mass destruction. And that is the task of the United States military and our coalition.

All who serve in this mission can know this: Your fellow citizens are behind you and our government will give you every tool you need for victory.

People of this country take pride in your victories, and we share in your losses. Camp Lejeune has lost some good Marines. Every person who dies in the line of duty leaves a family that lives in grief. Every Marine who dies in the line of duty leaves comrades who mourn their loss.

There is a tradition in the Corps that no one who falls will be left behind on the battlefield. Our country has a tradition, as well. No one who falls will be forgotten by this grateful nation. We honor their service to America and we pray their families will receive God's comfort and God's grace.

These are sacrifices in a high calling—the defense of our nation and the peace of the world. Overcoming evil is the noblest cause and the hardest work. And the liberation of millions is the fulfillment of America's founding promise. The objectives we've set in this war are worthy of America, worthy of all the acts of heroism and generosity that have come before.

Once again, we are applying the power of our country to ensure our security and to serve the cause of justice. And we will prevail.

Our Armed Services have performed brilliantly in Operation Iraqi Freedom. Moving a massive force over 200 miles of enemy territory in a matter of days is a superb achievement. Yet there is work ahead for our coalition, for the American Armed Forces, and for the United States Marines. Having traveled hundreds of miles, we will now go the last 200 yards. The course is set. We're on the advance. Our destination is Baghdad, and we will accept nothing less than complete and final victory.

May God bless our country and all who defend her. *Semper fi.*

## Presidential Message to the Iraqi People
April 10, 2003

This is George W. Bush, the President of the United States. At this moment, the regime of Saddam Hussein is being removed from power, and a long era of fear and cruelty is ending. American and coalition forces are now operating inside Baghdad—and we will not stop until Saddam's corrupt gang is gone. The government of Iraq, and the future of your country, will soon belong to you.

The goals of our coalition are clear and limited. We will end a brutal regime, whose aggression and weapons of mass destruction make it a unique threat to the world. Coalition forces will help maintain law and order, so that Iraqis can live in security. We will respect your great religious traditions, whose principles of equality and compassion are essential to Iraq's future. We will help you build a peaceful and representative government that protects the rights of all citizens. And then our military forces will leave. Iraq will go forward as a unified, independent, and sovereign nation that has regained a respected place in the world.

The United States and its coalition partners respect the people of Iraq. We are taking unprecedented measures to spare the lives of innocent Iraqi citizens, and are beginning to deliver food, water, and medicine to those in need. Our only enemy is Saddam's brutal regime—and that regime is your enemy as well.

In the new era that is coming to Iraq, your country will no longer be held captive to the will of a cruel dictator. You will be free to build a better life, instead of building more palaces for Saddam and his sons, free to pursue economic prosperity without the hardship of economic sanctions, free to travel and speak your mind, free to join in the political affairs of Iraq. And all the people who make up your country—Kurds, Shi'a, Turkomans, Sunnis, and others—will be free of the terrible persecution that so many have endured.

The nightmare that Saddam Hussein has brought to your nation will soon be over. You are a good and gifted people—the heirs of a great civilisation that contributes to all humanity. You deserve better than tyranny and corruption and torture chambers. You deserve to live as free people. And I assure every citizen of Iraq: Your nation will soon be free. Thank you.

## Presidential Radio Address to the Nation
### April 12, 2003

Good morning. Over the last several days, the world has watched as the regime of Saddam Hussein began passing into history. We will always remember the first images of a nation released from decades of tyranny and fear. The conflict continues in Iraq, and our military may still face hard fighting. Yet the statues of the dictator and all the works of his terror regime are falling away.

From the beginning and to this very hour, members of the American and coalition forces have conducted themselves with all the skill and honor we expect of them. Our enemies have seen their valor. The people of Iraq are seeing their compassion as our military provides food, water, and medical treatment to all in need, including captured Iraqi soldiers. As Army Master Sergeant Howard Kutcher, of Delaware, said of his service in the Middle East, "I am not here to conquer. I am here to help."

In one city, American soldiers encountered a crowd of Iraqi citizens who thought our troops were about to storm a nearby mosque. Just then, Lt. Colonel Chris Hughes ordered his men to get down on one knee and point their weapons to the ground. This gesture of respect helped defuse a dangerous situation and made our peaceful intentions clear.

Coalition forces have also come upon scenes that explain why fear runs so deep among the Iraqi people. In Baghdad on Tuesday, U.S. Marines helped to free more than one hundred children who, according to one report, had been jailed for refusing to join the dictator's Baath Party Youth Organization. Malnourished and wearing rags, the children were overjoyed to see their parents and our liberating forces. In the words of Lt. Colonel Fred Padilla, Commander of the 1st Battalion 5th Marines, "The children just streamed out of the gates and their parents just started to embrace us."

"Hundreds of kids," he said, "were swarming us and kissing us."

As Saddam's regime of fear is brought to an end, the people of Iraq are revealing the true hopes they have always held. It should surprise no one that Iraqis, like all people, resent oppression and welcome their own freedom. It should surprise no one that in every nation and every culture, the human heart desires the same good things: Dignity, liberty, and a chance to build a better life.

As people throughout Iraq celebrate the arrival of freedom, America celebrates with them. We know that freedom is the gift of God to all mankind, and we rejoice when others can share it.

On Wednesday in central Baghdad, one of the Iraqi men who took a sledgehammer to the pedestal of the giant statue of Saddam had this to say, "I'm 49, but I never lived a single day. Only now will I start living."

Millions of Iraqis feel the same as their country is finally returned to them. The nightmare of Saddam Hussein's rule in Iraq is ending. Soon, the good and gifted people of Iraq will be free to choose their leaders who respect their rights and reflect their character. In all that is to come, they will have the goodwill of the entire world. And they will have the friendship of the people of the United States.


## Excerpted Remarks by the President from Speech at the Ford Community and Performing Arts Center
Dearborn, Michigan
April 28, 2003


Many Iraqi Americans know the horrors of Saddam Hussein's regime first-hand. You also know the joys of freedom you have found here in America. You are living proof the Iraqi people love freedom and living proof the Iraqi people can flourish in democracy. People who live in Iraq deserve the same freedom that you and I enjoy here in America. And after years of tyranny and torture, that freedom has finally arrived.

I have confidence in the future of a free Iraq. The Iraqi people are fully capable of self-government. Every day Iraqis are moving toward democracy and embracing the responsibilities of active citizenship. Every day life in Iraq improves as coalition troops work to secure unsafe areas and bring food and medical care to those in need.

America pledged to rid Iraq of an oppressive regime, and we kept our word. America now pledges to help Iraqis build a prosperous and peaceful nation, and we will keep our word again. . . .

Right before I came in here I had the opportunity to meet with some extraordinary men and women, our fellow Americans who knew the cruelties of the old Iraq. And like me, they believed deeply in the promise of a new Iraq.

I spoke with Najda Egaily, a Sunni Muslim from Basra who moved to the United States five years ago. Najda learned the price of dissent in Iraq in 1988, when her brother-in-law was killed after laughing at a joke about Saddam Hussein in a house that was bugged.

In Iraq, Najda says, we could never speak to anyone about Saddam Hussein—we had to make sure the windows were closed. The windows are now open in Iraq. Najda and her friends will never forget seeing the images of liberation in Baghdad. Here's what she said: We called each other and we were shouting; we never believed that Saddam Hussein would be gone.

AUDIENCE MEMBER: He's gone. (Applause)

THE PRESIDENT: Like Najda, a lot of Iraqis—a lot of Iraqis—feared the dictator, the tyrant would never go away. You're right—he's gone. (Applause.) . . .

I talked to Tarik Daoud, a Catholic from Basra who now lives in Bloomfield Hills. When the dictator's regime fell, here's what Tariq said: I am more hopeful today than I've been since 1958. We need to take the little children in Iraq and hold their hands and really teach them what freedom is all about. He says: The new generation could really make democracy work.

He's right to be optimistic. From the beginning of this conflict we have seen brave Iraqi citizens taking part in their own liberation. Iraqis have warned our troops about land mines and enemy hideouts and military arsenals.

Earlier this month, Iraqis helped Marines locate the seven American prisoners of war, who were then rescued in northern Iraq. One courageous Iraqi man gave Marines detailed layouts of a hospital in An Nasiriyah, which led to the rescue of American soldier Jessica Lynch.

Iraqi citizens are now working closely with our troops to restore order to their cities, and improve the life of their nation. In Basra, hundreds of police volunteers have joined with coalition forces to patrol the streets. In Baghdad, more than a thousand citizens are doing joint patrols with coalition troops.

And residents are also working with coalition troops to collect unexploded munitions from neighborhoods, and repair the telephone system. People are working to improve the lives of the average citizens in Iraq.

I want you to listen to what an Iraqi engineer said who was working with U.S. Army engineers to restore power to Baghdad. He said: We are very glad to work with the Americans to have power for the facilities. The Americans are working to help us. Iraqi Americans, including some from Michigan, are building bridges between our troops and Iraqi civilians. Members of the free Iraqi forces are serving as translators for our troops, and are delivering humanitarian aid to the citizens.

One of these volunteers, an Iraqi American who fled Saddam Hussein's regime in 1991, recently returned to his homeland with the 101st Airborne Division. A few weeks ago, when he first saw the cheering crowds of Iraqis welcome coalition troops in Hillah he wept. He said people could hardly believe what was happening, and he told them: Believe it—liberation is coming.

Yes, there were some in our country who doubted the Iraqi people wanted freedom, or they just couldn't imagine they would be welcoming to a liberating force. They were mistaken, and we know why. The desire for freedom is not the property of one culture, it is the universal hope of human beings in every culture.

Whether you're Sunni or Shia or Kurd or Chaldean or Assyrian or Turkoman or Christian or Jew or Muslim—no matter what your faith, freedom is God's gift to every person in every nation. As freedom takes hold in Iraq, the Iraqi people will choose their own leaders and their own government. America has no intention of imposing our form of government or our culture. Yet we will ensure that all Iraqis have a voice in the new government and all citizens have their rights protected.

In the city of An Nasiriyah, where free Iraqis met recently to discuss the political future of their country, they issued a statement beginning with these words: Iraq must be democratic.

That historic declaration expresses the commitment of the Iraqi people and their friends, the American people. The days of repression from any source are over. Iraq will be democratic.

The work of building a new Iraq will take time. That nation is recovering not just from weeks of conflict, but from decades of totalitarian rule.

In a nation where the dictator treated himself to palaces with gold faucets and grand fountains, four out of ten citizens did not even have clean water to drink. While a former regime exported milk, and dates, and corn, and grain for its own profit, more than half a million Iraqi children were malnourished. As Saddam Hussein let more than $200 million worth of medicine and medical supplies sit in warehouses, one in eight Iraqi children were dying before the age of five. And while the dictator spent billions on weapons, including gold-covered AK-47s, nearly a quarter of Iraqi children were born underweight. Saddam Hussein's regime impoverished the Iraqi people in every way.

Today, Iraq has only about half as many hospitals as it had in 1990. Seventy percent of its schools are run-down and over-crowded. A quarter of the Iraqi children are not in a school at all. Under Saddam's regime, the Iraqi people did not have a power system they could depend on. These problems plagued Iraq long before the recent conflict. We're helping the Iraqi people to address these challenges, and we will stand with them as they defeat the dictator's legacy.

Right now, engineers are on the ground working with Iraqi experts to restore power, and fix broken water pipes in Baghdad and other cities. We're working with the International Red Cross, the Red Crescent Societies, the International Medical Corps, and other aid agencies to help Iraqi hospitals get safe water and medical supplies and reliable electricity. Our coalition is cooperating with the United Nations to help restart the ration-distribution system that provides food at thousands of sites in Iraq. And coalition medical facilities have treated Iraqis for everything from fractures and burns to symptoms of stroke.

One Iraqi man who was given medical help with his wife and sister aboard the U.S. Navy ship *Comfort*, said: They treat us like family. There are babies in Iraq who are not cared for by their mothers as well as the nurses have cared for us.

Already, we are seeing important progress in Iraq. It wasn't all that long ago that the statue fell, and now we're seeing progress.

Rail lines are reopening, and fire stations are responding to calls. Oil—Iraqi oil, owned by the Iraqi people—is flowing again to fuel Iraq's power plants. In Hillah, more than eighty percent of the city now has running water. City residents can buy meats and grains and fruits and vegetables at local shops. The mayor's office, the city council have been reestablished.

In Basra, where more than half of the water-treatment facilities were not working before the conflict—more than half weren't functioning—water supplies are now reaching ninety percent of the city. The opulent presidential palace in Basra will now serve a new and noble purpose. We've established a water-purification unit there, to make hundreds of thousands of liters of clean water available to the residents of the city of Basra.

Day by day, hour by hour, life in Iraq is getting better for the citizens. Yet much work remains to be done. I have directed Jay Garner and his team to help Iraq achieve specific long-term goals. And they're doing a superb job. Congress recently allocated nearly $2.5 billion for Iraq's relief and reconstruction. With that money, we are renewing Iraq with the help of experts from inside our government, from private industry, from the international community, and, most importantly, from within Iraq.

We are dispatching teams across Iraq to assess the critical needs of the Iraqi people. We're clearing land mines. We're working with Iraqis to recover artifacts, to find the hoodlums who ravished the National Museum of Antiquities in Baghdad. Like many of you here, we deplore the actions of the citizens who ravished that museum. And we will work with the Iraqi citizens to find out who they were and to bring them to justice.

We're working toward an Iraq where, for the first time ever, electrical power is reliable and widely available. One of our goals is to make sure everybody in Iraq has electricity. Already, seventeen major power plants in Iraq are functioning. Our engineers are meeting with Iraqi engineers. We're visiting power plants throughout the country, and determining which ones need repair, which ones need to be modernized, and which ones are obsolete, power plant by power plant. More Iraqis are getting the electricity they need.

We're working to make Iraq's drinking water clean and dependable. American and Iraqi water-sanitation engineers are inspecting treatment plants across the country to make sure they have enough purification chemicals and power to produce safe water.

We're working to give every Iraqi access to immunizations and emergency treatment, and to give sick children and pregnant women the health care they need. Iraqi doctors and nurses and other medical personnel are now going back to work. Throughout the country, medical specialists from many countries are identifying the needs of Iraqi hospitals, for everything from equipment and repairs to water [and] medicines.

We're working to improve Iraqi schools by funding a back-to-school campaign that will help train and recruit Iraqi teachers, provide supplies and equipment, and bring children across Iraq back into clean and safe schools.

And as we do that, we will make sure that the schools are no longer used as military arsenals and bunkers, and that teachers promote reading, rather than regime propaganda. And because Iraq is now free, economic sanctions are pointless. It is time for the United Nations to lift the sanctions so the Iraqis could use some resources to build their own prosperity.

Like so many generations of immigrants, Iraqi Americans have embraced and enriched this great country, without ever forgetting the land of your birth. Liberation for Iraq has been a long time coming, but you never lost faith. You knew the great sorrow of Iraq. You also knew the great promise of Iraq, and you shared the hope of the Iraqi people.

You and I both know that Iraq can realize those hopes. Iraq can be an example of peace and prosperity and freedom to the entire Middle East. It'll be a hard journey, but at every step of the way, Iraq will have a steady friend in the American people.

May God continue to bless the United States of America, and long live a free Iraq.

# May 2003

**Remarks by the President from Speech on the *USS Abraham Lincoln***
**on the Cessation of Combat Operations in Iraq**
At Sea Off the Coast of San Diego, California
May 1, 2003

Thank you all very much. Admiral Kelly, Captain Card, officers, and sailors of the *USS Abraham Lincoln*, my fellow Americans: Major combat operations in Iraq have ended. In the battle of Iraq, the United States and our allies have prevailed. And now our coalition is engaged in securing and reconstructing that country.

In this battle, we have fought for the cause of liberty, and for the peace of the world. Our nation and our coalition are proud of this accomplishment— yet, it is you, the members of the United States military, who achieved it. Your courage, your willingness to face danger for your country and for each other, made this day possible. Because of you, our nation is more secure. Because of you, the tyrant has fallen, and Iraq is free.

Operation Iraqi Freedom was carried out with a combination of precision and speed and boldness the enemy did not expect, and the world had not seen before. From distant bases or ships at sea, we sent planes and missiles that could destroy an enemy division, or strike a single bunker. Marines and soldiers charged to Baghdad across 350 miles of hostile ground, in one of the swiftest advances of heavy arms in history. You have shown the world the skill and the might of the American Armed Forces.

This nation thanks all the members of our coalition who joined in a noble cause. We thank the Armed Forces of the United Kingdom, Australia, and Poland, who shared in the hardships of war. We thank all the citizens of Iraq who welcomed our troops and joined in the liberation of their own country. And tonight, I have a special word for Secretary Rumsfeld, for General Franks, and for all the men and women who wear the uniform of the United States: America is grateful for a job well done.

The character of our military through history—the daring of Normandy, the fierce courage of Iwo Jima, the decency and idealism that turned enemies into allies—is fully present in this generation. When Iraqi civilians looked into the faces of our servicemen and women, they saw strength and kindness and goodwill. When I look at the members of the United States military, I see the best of our country, and I'm honored to be your Commander-in-Chief.

In the images of falling statues, we have witnessed the arrival of a new era. For a hundred of years of war, culminating in the nuclear age, military technology was designed and deployed to inflict casualties on an ever-growing scale. In defeating Nazi Germany and Imperial Japan, Allied forces destroyed entire cities, while enemy leaders who started the conflict were safe until the final days. Military power was used to end a regime by breaking a nation.

Today, we have the greater power to free a nation by breaking a danger-ous and aggressive regime. With new tactics and precision weapons, we can achieve military objectives without directing violence against civilians. No device of man can remove the tragedy from war; yet it is a great moral advance when the guilty have far more to fear from war than the innocent.

In the images of celebrating Iraqis, we have also seen the ageless appeal of human freedom. Decades of lies and intimidation could not make the Iraqi people love their oppressors or desire their own enslavement. Men and women in every culture need liberty like they need food and water and air. Everywhere that freedom arrives, humanity rejoices; and everywhere that freedom stirs, let tyrants fear.

We have difficult work to do in Iraq. We're bringing order to parts of that country that remain dangerous. We're pursuing and finding leaders of the old regime, who will be held to account for their crimes. We've begun the search for hidden chemical and biological weapons and already know of hundreds of sites that will be investigated. We're helping to rebuild Iraq, where the dic-tator built palaces for himself, instead of hospitals and schools. And we will stand with the new leaders of Iraq as they establish a government of, by, and for the Iraqi people.

The transition from dictatorship to democracy will take time, but it is worth every effort. Our coalition will stay until our work is done. Then we will leave, and we will leave behind a free Iraq.

The battle of Iraq is one victory in a war on terror that began on September the 11, 2001—and still goes on. That terrible morning, 19 evil men—the shock troops of a hateful ideology—gave America and the civilized world a glimpse of their ambitions. They imagined, in the words of one terrorist, that September the 11th would be the "beginning of the end of America." By seeking to turn our cities into killing fields, terrorists and their allies believed that they could destroy this nation's resolve, and force our retreat from the world. They have failed.

In the battle of Afghanistan, we destroyed the Taliban, many terrorists, and the camps where they trained. We continue to help the Afghan people lay roads, restore hospitals, and educate all of their children. Yet we also have dangerous work to complete. As I speak, a Special Operations task force, led by the 82nd Airborne, is on the trail of the terrorists and those who seek to undermine the free government of Afghanistan. America and our coalition will finish what we have begun.

From Pakistan to the Philippines to the Horn of Africa, we are hunting down al Qaeda killers. Nineteen months ago, I pledged that the terrorists would not escape the patient justice of the United States. And as of tonight, nearly one-half of al Qaeda's senior operatives have been captured or killed.

The liberation of Iraq is a crucial advance in the campaign against terror. We've removed an ally of al Qaeda, and cut off a source of terrorist funding. And this much is certain: No terrorist network will gain weapons of mass destruction from the Iraqi regime, because the regime is no more.

In these nineteen months that changed the world, our actions have been focused and deliberate and proportionate to the offense. We have not forgotten the victims of September the 11th—the last phone calls, the cold murder of children, the searches in the rubble. With those attacks, the terrorists and their supporters declared war on the United States. And war is what they got.

Our war against terror is proceeding according to principles that I have made clear to all: Any person involved in committing or planning terrorist attacks against the American people becomes an enemy of this country, and a target of American justice.

Any person, organization, or government that supports, protects, or harbors terrorists is complicit in the murder of the innocent, and equally guilty of terrorist crimes.

Any outlaw regime that has ties to terrorist groups and seeks or possesses weapons of mass destruction is a grave danger to the civilized world—and will be confronted. (Applause)

And anyone in the world, including the Arab world, who works and sacrifices for freedom has a loyal friend in the United States of America.

Our commitment to liberty is America's tradition—declared at our founding; affirmed in Franklin Roosevelt's Four Freedoms; asserted in the Truman Doctrine and in Ronald Reagan's challenge to an evil empire. We are committed to freedom in Afghanistan, in Iraq, and in a peaceful Palestine. The advance of freedom is the surest strategy to undermine the appeal of terror in the world. Where freedom takes hold, hatred gives way to hope. When freedom takes hold, men and women turn to the peaceful pursuit of a better life. American values and American interests lead in the same direction: We stand for human liberty.

The United States upholds these principles of security and freedom in many ways—with all the tools of diplomacy, law enforcement, intelligence, and finance. We're working with a broad coalition of nations that understand the threat and our shared responsibility to meet it. The use of force has been—and remains—our last resort. Yet all can know, friend and foe alike, that our nation has a mission: We will answer threats to our security, and we will defend the peace.

Our mission continues. Al Qaeda is wounded, not destroyed. The scattered cells of the terrorist network still operate in many nations, and we know from daily intelligence that they continue to plot against free people. The proliferation of deadly weapons remains a serious danger. The enemies of freedom are not idle, and neither are we. Our government has taken unprecedented measures to defend the homeland. And we will continue to hunt down the enemy before he can strike.

The war on terror is not over; yet it is not endless. We do not know the day of final victory, but we have seen the turning of the tide. No act of the terrorists will change our purpose, or weaken our resolve, or alter their fate. Their cause is lost. Free nations will press on to victory.

Other nations in history have fought in foreign lands and remained to occupy and exploit. Americans, following a battle, want nothing more than to return home. And that is your direction tonight. After service in the Afghan and Iraqi theaters of war—after 100,000 miles, on the longest carrier deployment in recent history, you are homeward bound. Some of you will see new family members for the first time—150 babies were born while their fathers were on the *Lincoln*. Your families are proud of you, and your nation will welcome you.

We are mindful, as well, that some good men and women are not making the journey home. One of those who fell, Corporal Jason Mileo, spoke to his parents five days before his death. Jason's father said, "He called us from the center of Baghdad, not to brag, but to tell us he loved us. Our son was a soldier."

Every name, every life is a loss to our military, to our nation, and to the loved ones who grieve. There's no homecoming for these families. Yet we pray, in God's time, their reunion will come.

Those we lost were last seen on duty. Their final act on this earth was to fight a great evil and bring liberty to others. All of you—all in this generation of our military—have taken up the highest calling of history. You're defending your country, and protecting the innocent from harm. And wherever you go, you carry a message of hope—a message that is ancient and ever new. In the words of the prophet Isaiah, "To the captives, 'come out,' and to those in darkness, 'be free.'"

Thank you for serving our country and our cause. May God bless you all, and may God continue to bless America.


### Excerpted Remarks by the President from Speech at Memorial Day Service at Arlington National Cemetery
Arlington, Virginia
May 26, 2003

Veterans, honored guests, and my fellow Americans, we come to this Memorial Day with deep awareness of recent loss and recent courage.

Beyond the Tomb of the Unknowns, in Section 60 of Arlington Cemetery, we have laid to rest Americans who fell in the battle of Iraq. One of the funerals was for Marine Second Lieutenant Frederick Pokorney Jr., of Jacksonville, North Carolina. His wife, Carolyn, received a folded flag. His two-year-old daughter, Taylor, knelt beside her mother at the casket to say a final good-bye.

An uncle later said of this fine lieutenant, "He was proud of what he was doing and proud of his family, a hard-working guy—the best guy you can ever know. I hope the American people don't forget." This nation does not forget.

Last month, in Section 60, First Lieutenant Rob Jenkins was buried, along with five other members of a bomber crew. They were lost when their plane was shot down over North Africa in 1942. Rob Jenkins had joined the Army Air Corps after Pearl Harbor, and he was twenty years old on his final mission.

Six decades later, his plane was found and the remains of the crew were carefully identified, returned home, and buried with military honors. Rob's sister, Helen, said, "We were very proud that the government would care that much. After all, it was such a long time ago." This nation does not forget.

On Memorial Day, Americans place flags on military graves, walk past a wall of black granite in Washington, D.C., and many families think of a face and voice they miss so much. Today, we honor the men and women who have worn the nation's uniform and were last seen on duty. From the battles of Iraq and Afghanistan, to the conflicts in Korea and Vietnam, to the trials of World Wars, to the struggles that made us a nation, today we recall that liberty is always the achievement of courage.

And today we remember all who have died, all who are still missing, and all who mourn. And on this day, especially, our nation is grateful to the brave and fallen defenders of freedom. In every generation of Americans we have found courage equal to the tasks of our country. The farms and small towns and city streets of this land have always produced free citizens who assume the discipline and duty of military life. And time after time, they have proven that the moral force of democracy is mightier than the will and cunning of any tyrant.

The widow of one of our Marines in Iraq made this point very simply. "There is good and evil in the world." she said, "That's what's going on. And he was the good." All the good people we honor today were willing to die in the service of our country and our cause. Yet all of them wanted to live. And the images they carried with them at the end were the people they loved and the familiar sights of home.

Not long before his death last month, Army Captain James Adamouski of Springfield, Virginia, wrote this to his wife Meighan. "I do my job 110 percent and don't get distracted or discouraged when I'm out flying on missions. However, when I have some down time and get to really thinking, I realize that for all the good times—all the good things we're doing here, I just plain miss you."

In his last letter home from the Middle East, Staff Sergeant Lincoln Hollin, of Malden. Illinois, said how much he appreciated getting mail from his family. He added, "I wish my truck and boat knew how to write." (Laughter) "I sure do miss them." He went on, "Today would be a beautiful fishing day. I can see it now: Drop my electronic anchors, kick my feet up, three poles out with hooks in search for that elusive, yet lovable, catfish."

Americans like these did not fight for glory, but to fulfill a duty. They did not yearn to be heroes, they yearned to see Mom and Dad again, and to hold their sweethearts, and to watch their sons and daughters grow. They wanted the daily miracle of freedom in America, yet they gave all that up and gave life itself for the sake of others.

Their sacrifice was great, but not in vain. All Americans and every free nation on earth can trace their liberty to the white markers of places like Arlington National Cemetery. And may God keep us ever grateful.

Almost seven weeks ago, an Army Ranger, Captain Russell Rippetoe, was laid to rest in Section 60. Captain Rippetoe's father, Joe, a retired Lieutenant Colonel, gave a farewell salute at the grave of his only son. Russell Rippetoe served with distinction in Operation Iraqi Freedom, earning both the Bronze Star and the Purple Heart.

On the back of his dog tag were engraved these words, from the Book of Joshua, "Have not I commanded thee? Be strong and of good courage. Be not afraid, neither be thou dismayed, for the Lord thy God is with thee." This faithful Army captain has joined a noble company of service and sacrifice gathered row by row. These men and women were strong and courageous, and not dismayed. And we pray they have found their peace in the arms of God.

May God bless America.